COCKROACHES IN HEAD

From Legendary Insanity to Absolute Truth

AODH MACKY

Published 2019 by Avonova - Rotorua, New Zealand.
A catalogue record for this book is available from the National Library of New Zealand.
ISBN 978-0-47-345961-1

CONTENTS

Author's Preface

It's been many years since I left the Legion. Sometimes I become disgusted at myself when I get that intruding sentiment of missing it. How is it, when I once hated the place so much, I now sometimes long to be back there again, away from the maze of civilian possibilities? Once more, I firmly remind myself that it's just part of the long process of reintegrating back into civilian life.

But on one particular day that sentiment is absent. I'm not thinking about the Legion. I'm just attempting to enjoy the liberty of doing as I please. I'm standing at a farmers market. It doesn't matter where, but it's a beautiful, still and sunny day.

For some reason I find myself stopping at a specific stall where there are many bags of spices on display. Some spices are whole. Others are ground to a fine powder. Once permission is granted in the form of a friendly gesture, I take a small inviting metal scoop. I scoop and I smell, giving an unconscious half bow each time as a sign of respect to the earths produce.

On any other day I would have just pointed and asked "What's that spice called, and this one and that one?" My mind would be in a hurry to comprehend the depth of each smell with a name. But this time is different. This day is unusual. I don't want to know names. I just want to smell. On this calm day, I don't want words to corrupt and blind me. I don't want to hold any prejudice against a specific spice. I just want to smell their wordless essence. I'm walking gently in the otherworld, that realm between this world and the spirit world.

What about this book then? Is it nothing but words, nothing but corruptions and prejudices? If that is true, then what's the point in writing a collection of words? Well, there is no point. That's the paradox which offers a glimpse at universal truth, like a bolt of lightning, a falling apple, a flicker of oneness.

Sometimes it takes a million words to realise that.

Don't get me wrong, of course we need words. They are practical and can even be magical. But they are like raindrops on a still ocean. Their limits limit us, yet they point to a deeper truth, a wordless one. My name is Kevin James just as much as a scoop full of ground cloves. But my name was also once Gregory Sims; Legionnaire Gregory Sims.

This Autobiography mainly describes my stubbornness and struggle to finish a five year contract in the French Foreign Legion. Both my experiences there and in my childhood lay the foundation for what is to come. My story continues after the Legion, providing an in depth account of the confusing experience of what has been understood in our western society as psychosis or schizophrenia. But I take a different view of what that really is. My view is not merely just my opinion either. It is direct experience. It comes from a deep wisdom that existed before I was even born.

Psychosis is an overwhelming mystical experience of our true divine nature. It only becomes an illness when we identify with our fear based conditioned mind. It doesn't help to be in an environment which has no tolerance of the spiritual nature of psychosis. If we are strong enough to break through our mind or the "Optical delusion" as Albert Einstein called it, the sacredness of psychosis offers us a life changing realisation of connectedness with all that is. In doing so, we are left with no choice but to feel pure love. Fear is the product of denial. It is not an easy path to arrive at pure love. God knows, many have suffered immensely on their journeys.

We also need to be to be strong enough to stand up to all those who don't support this view. But it is not so easy to separate ourselves from our mind. Our mind is the ultimate trickster. Often it is only ourselves that needs convincing, regardless of others.

I acknowledge that not everyone is ready for the revelation that lies beyond our mind. I wasn't when it first happened to me. When I had my first psychosis, I still listened to the lies of the trickster. These lies only led to fear, paranoia and ego inflation. Another one of his lies was that I was mentally ill.

I never had a mentor to help guide me through my experiences. Without peer support, I was stigmatised and labelled as "schizophrenic" by the environment in which I found myself. This environment included professionals with great power, authority and influence. It also included friends and family members. I know that sounds sad. On the contrary, it was the best thing that ever happened to me! Why?

I achieved the impossible; I turned schizophrenia, what most people think of as a terribly serious and chronic disease of the brain, an awful infliction, into the spiritual gold that every single human being is searching for, consciously or unconsciously; union with God, self-transcendence.

Slowly, I began to comprehend that the sickness was not in my schizophrenia but in the rising global materialistic and schizophrenic way of living. It is this same way of living responsible for colonial conquests and genocide across the world, for the witch-hunts, for the two world wars and more recently; the sickening institutional child abuse in Ireland. It is this same dividing ideology that has led us to cut down most of the trees across the world. It has hijacked world religions, leading billions astray. But in a more subtle and acceptable form, this sickness is the root of our everyday individual and selfish existence. This sickness is the "Optical delusion" Einstein was pointing to. Strangely though, it is a necessary sickness as we are not all ready for the alternative.

The Emerald Isle of *Eire* was once an island forest. It was where I was born. Cut off from my Celtic roots, native language and connectedness with the traditional way of life, I grew up in a shallow society. I learnt to become an individual and look out at the world of other individuals with scepticism and mistrust.

The real mental illness is this globally accepted logical "reality" in which peace is always fleeting and we are never satisfied. My story opens up a dialogue on our true nature and our true reality, while questioning the idea of absolute authority.

Before we begin, I want to help you by revealing that there is a deeper intention that motivates the writing of this book, which forces pen to paper. I cannot name this intention. I cannot know this intention. But let us just say that it is this same intention which is responsible for anything even existing.

Bear with me for a moment while we try something. For the sake of it, let us create in our imagination a new spice. Ok? This is a spice which has never been discovered on earth. It smells of everything and of nothing, of all goodness and pleasure but also of all suffering and pain. Its aroma is both boring and exciting at the same time. This is a spice that reveals truth in a lie. You may name it if you please. This is your creation. Now, let us ask this new spice a question. "What's the greatest force on Earth; Love, Hate, Gravity or Life itself?"

The spices deep aroma answers "What exists without a name?"

Cockroaches In Head is a waste of time for those who possess time. I am a waster for those who believe time is money. But just in case I've lost you already, let us get practical again. The following is deadly serious. I will make three brave statements from the beginning. I could sit on the fence on such topics but I've decided not to. This is where I stand and it may help you decide if you want to read on.

First of all, I believe that people who have had psychotic experiences and have been diagnosed as having a mental illness such as schizophrenia or bipolar disorder were actually scratching on the surface of ultimate truth, a truth that shatters all of society's restraints. Our socially conditioned mind is terrified of this truth. Our mind dismisses the psychosis as pure rubbish.

I agree that sometimes these people do not have the mental and physical strength to integrate their experiences into our mainstream way of living. But it's more likely that they do not have the moral support and guidance of a peer to realise that they have actually been offered grace, the gift of God. When this precious gift is denied, it becomes a mental illness. Sadly, that is so often the case.

When the potential of the psychotic experience to liberate the individual is denied, this same potential energy then transforms itself into a burden under the label of mental illness. This burden becomes a lifelong cross which the person must carry. Unfortunately, many (an estimated one per cent of the global population has schizophrenia; that is 70 million people!) are expected to deteriorate for the rest of their limited lives under heavy medication, believing their illness, their burden and their lie. They often become surrounded by people who feel sorry for them and treat them as inferior, robing their independence. Mass industries of professionals are employed to care for, contain and control these people. Of course, in order to justify elevated medical salaries across the globe, and in the interests of pharmaceutical companies, it is always easier to see these people as sick rather than gifted, as a patient rather than a potential mystic or shaman.

Secondly, I believe that Jesus of Nazareth, the Christian son of God was one of these people. He ended up suffering greatly by crucifixion. Like many others who are touched by grace, he could not control his psychosis. He struggled to comprehend and integrate his divinity into his humanity. He abandoned his normal, perhaps even boring life as a carpenter. Going AWOL and neglecting his physical care, he became homeless just like many people in today's world. His grandiose and manic behaviour were part of his charisma and ability to charm others. Believing in the foretold prophecy of a future messiah according to Judaism, he succumbed to grandiose religious delusions by attempting to fulfil that prophecy. He desperately needed guidance from a peer. The Kingdom of Heaven he was pointing to was nothing more than his own psychosis. Alive today, he would most likely be viewed as a complete maniac or schizophrenic. He would surely spend time as a patient in a mental hospital.

Having said that, I also feel that Jesus could, if he was alive today, potentially become a guru, just like others who accept their psychotic experience and allow it to liberate them. As a spiritual leader he could help others realise their own divinity. It is possible to be both. Yes, he was God incarnate, and yes, he was mentally ill. You see, this in its essence, is the central point that I am making in this book. It has been the biggest and most important realisation of my life. But it is also an eternal one. Only in the mind-blowing experience of psychosis could I truly understand Jesus Christ. Mental illness is the struggle to integrate our divinity into our man-made identities.

But did Jesus Christ die in vain on the cross? Yes and no. Yes, because he could have shown us that we don't have to suffer so much. And no, because he showed us that we can be equally divine as he was. That is what he wanted, for us to become like him. That was his only real message.

In the third place and finally, I believe that there are people in this world who know they are God but who keep their mouth shut about it, as people will likely think they are crazy. They were once overwhelmed by such a realisation. They played with the idea for a long time before fully accepting it. They have come to realise that their psychotic experience was in fact a mystical one. Now, for them, it doesn't seem like such a big deal but at the same time, it is all that really matters in this life. And life goes on after all.

Attempts to deny it were futile and only led to continuous bouts of ill health, mental and physical. I am one of those people and I live with this paradox; I don't know what God is and therefore I don't know what I am. But I know that God's energy can go both ways, it takes any form. It equally fills our worst nightmares and our most benevolent intentions. God knows nothing. God is not our projection. But let me ask you this;

Can we bring children into this world without telling them who they are? I mean who they really are beyond their name and gender, beyond their nationality and race. Yes, of course we can. We have been using religion and science to do so for a long time. What would happen however, if we told every child born that there was no ultimate authority beyond themselves? What if we told them that they were God, but we don't know what God is, we just know that we love them?

Aodh Macky

Adieu Vieille Europe

Nous les damnés de la terre entière,
Nous les blessés de toutes les guerres,
Nous ne pouvons pas oublier
Un malheur, une honte, une femme qu'on adorait.
Nous qu'avons l'sang chaud dans les veines,
Cafard en tête au coeur les peines
Pour recevoir, donner des gnons, crénom de nom,
Sans peur, en route pour la Légion.

Adieu vieille Europe,
Que le diable t'emporte.
Adieu vieux pays,
Pour le ciel si brûlant de l'Algérie.
Adieu souvenir, notre vie va finir.
Il nous faut du soleil, de l'espace,
Pour redorer nos carcasses.

Salut camarades,
Donnons-nous l'accolade,
Nous allons sac au dos, flingue en main,
Faire ensemble le même chemin.
A nous le désert,
Comme au marin la mer.
Il nous faut du soleil, de l'espace,
Pour redorer nos carcasses.

Chant de la Legion Etranger

Farewell Old Europe

We the damned of the entire world,
We the casualties of all wars,
We cannot forget
An evil, a shame, a woman once cherished.
We who have hot blood in our veins,
Cockroaches in our heads and hate in our hearts
To receive, to give penance, for our disgraced names,
Without fear, we join the Legion.

Farewell old Europe,
May the Devil take you.
Goodbye old country,
For the burning heaven of Algeria.
Goodbye memories, our lives will end.
We need the sun and freedom,
To restore our carcasses.

Salut camarades,
Let us embrace,
We will be backpacking, gun in hand,
Together along the same path.
We own the desert,
Like a sailor the sea,
We need the sun, and freedom,
To restore our carcasses.

Foreign Legion Song

NORTH

BEFORE THE LEGION

"A human being is a part of the whole called by us 'Universe',
A part limited in time and space.
He experiences himself, his thoughts and feelings as something
Separated from the rest, a kind of optical delusion of his
consciousness.
This delusion is a kind of prison for us,
Restricting us to our personal desires and
To affection for a few persons nearest to us.
Our task must be to free ourselves from this prison by widening
our Circle of compassion to embrace all living creatures
And the whole of nature in its beauty."

Albert Einstein (1879-1955)

KILLESTER

I grew up on the north side of Ireland's capital city, Dublin, in a suburb called Killester. Looking back on my teenage years, I realise that I was very unhappy. I didn't always understand some of the reasons for this discontentment growing up. Ok, my childhood was not the worst of all time. I know there are terror stories out there that make mine seem irrelevant. But it was my childhood and this is my story.

With hindsight I could later see more reasons for why I joined the Legion. I grew up in a house where there was a constant unease or discomfort. My father was constantly on edge, angry and not nice to be around despite his many skills and enthusiasms. To be fair, we were exposed to all sorts of adventure. This would seem to be great for kids. We went camping, fishing and exploring. Dad was constantly using his creativity and making things in his workshop. Once, he made a radio from scratch using wood and copper wire. This was very impressive to me. But sadly, I wasn't able to get enough positive affirmation from him and I ran to my mother.

My father had his own unresolved issues. It was too painful for him to show love. He was quick to criticise and as a child I felt that he was often very cynical, angry and mean. I felt that my mother was usually kinder but this was of no avail because she was absent minded and passive. She was always distracted or preoccupied when I would try to get her attention. I was a sad and angry child because I felt that she never had the courage to stand up to my father who was a bully. I felt I would get a better response talking to our dog. Our dogs name was

Snap. Even Snap could feel the tension in the house. It was an appropriate name for a dog that lived in such an unpredictable, unstable and uncomfortable environment.

I was a sensitive child. This sensitivity has remained with me until this day. Sensitivity is a trait which can be both good and bad. It is a trait that I have come to learn to accept as part of me. We often hear people say "Stop being so fussy" or "He is so sensitive." But sensitiveness is a broad term. People are sensitive to different things and have different degrees of sensitivity. There is a danger in being hypersensitive. When we are prone to feeling too much, our psyche not being able to handle strong feelings can reject them. Our emotional side can shut down or lock up. We become emotionally numb. Like a soldier, the world for us highly sensitive people can become very black and white because of this. Then we actually end up feeling nothing despite our predisposition to sensitivity.

Some of us with stronger senses can also become more at risk of developing a psychosis. But on the plus side we also have a strong intuition and sense of the magic and wonder that is concealed and blurred out by the rat race. Something deep inside us recognises the façade of this logical and shallow existence.

It would be obvious to guess that sensitivity involves only the five senses. This is true to some degree but it is only when we allow these five senses to provide us with a complete interpretation of the external that over sensitiveness has begun. We become lost in a world of forms. We believe the lie of our separate lives. We then feel uncomfortable and irritable, as our senses are bombarded. If we examine this unease, we can realise that it is a calling. Our soul is calling us home.

It is difficult to put my early childhood from two years old through to eight years of age in any particular order. There are scatterings of memories from that period. Here are some of them.

When I was very small, I believed that my family; my older brother and my parents weren't my real family. I felt isolated and alone in a family of four. In our bathroom there stood only three toothbrushes together in a glass, I would keep mine in a separate place. When I had to sit on the toilet seat, I would use a lot of paper to clean all the edges. Then I would line every part of the seat with paper. I didn't want their dirt on me.

I always had the sense of discomfort in situations where I believed others were comfortable. One evening, I was eating out with my family at a restaurant. I remember being squeezed tight and not having enough room to eat my food. My father's elbows would intrude and invade my space. He would look down in disapproval and say to me that it was I who was taking up to much room with my elbows. This annoyed me very much. Eating slowly became a time of discomfort when it should be a sacred time.

I hated my father, although I obviously wanted to love him and I needed his love. One image that stayed with me was when I wanted to go for a pee in the toilet one day. My dad came into the bathroom, invading my space and started peeing into the toilet next to me. We both peed together. I didn't like it. I felt small and uncomfortable. That image stuck in my head.

Like many people who grow up as the younger brother, I was teased and bullied. I was the younger brother by three years. However, I still felt as though my situation was worse than the average. At five years old, I enjoyed playing with the girl next door, Gráinne, in the sanctuary of her house. But every time I came home from next-door, my brother would jeer and laugh at me. He teased me, saying that I was a sissy and played "Footsie with Grainne." I began to believe that I was a sissy and I hated that.

He would never grow tired of teasing me. He was constantly

on my back with insults. I was born with my left leg slightly in-toed. He would make fun of this and he acted out my walk, exaggerating how I walked inwardly. I made a constant effort to walk straight to avoid his teasing.

I had always felt a weakness in my left hip and groin area. I never got medical advice as a child for this. Years later during my service with the Legion, I got an inguinal hernia on the left side of my groin that required surgery. This only made the discomfort worse. Ever since, I have had chronic pain and problems with my left leg and hip along with Sciatica and pain up into my left shoulder and neck. Physical pain is a huge trigger for developing psychosis and for addictions, which is often overlooked.

On one particular day in my scrabble of memories, when I was about six years old, I was playing in my brother's bedroom. He had drawn with a black marker, a set of eyes onto my chin, while I lay on the floor. This made an upside down face on my chin. He thought that this was hilarious. Then all of a sudden, he attempted to kiss me on my lips. I saw what he was about to do and it felt wrong. I moved away. I was shocked and confused. One day he was causing me emotional agony with his teasing and bullying and now he was trying to kiss me causing confusion, disgust and resentment. But he too was a confused child and victim of a disturbing home environment.

When I was eight years old, my brother developed a story that he was running away from home. He would come and tell me this story in a sad voice. I believed him. I was actually happy with this news, a break from the torment he caused me. He would continue to say in the same sad voice that I could keep all his toys when he would run away. He would then walk off and leave me for a while. Then when he saw that he had me fooled, he would come back and start laughing loudly at me, saying it was a big lie. The more he performed this little act of his, the more I grew to hate him.

I needed to cover up my shame about my feminine side. There was no room for softness in that house. Softness was weakness and love could not shine. No more softness, no more playing with girls. All that stuff was sissy stuff. I had to be strong too because my father and my brother were bullies and I couldn't bear to hug my mother either. My heart grew cold. I became more and more sad.

Wait! What about those old feelings? Those feelings of love and warmth I once had when I played with Gráinne next door or when I could embrace my mum as a toddler. What happened to those soft feelings, those girly ones? No! I have to lock them up forever. Those feelings are not for boys, not for soldiers.

But I did have my feminine side and my desperate need for love. And it was frightening, more frightening than bullies, soldiers, guns and God the father who art in Heaven.

When I was eight years old, I would hide in my bedroom and read comics; The Beano and The Dandy. I would read them on my own while indulging in a little secret. In one of the cartoon stories, there was Dennis the Menace and Walter the Softy. I was torn between the two of them. Dennis caused mischief but seemed strong and cool. Walter was a Sissy and played with girls and liked flowers. Walter was kind and loving. Sometimes I wanted to be there with Walter, his gentleness, his flowers and perfume, and all that love. I felt ashamed and confused. Dennis was the brave courageous soldier type, the ruler, the strong one, the one I needed to be like. So I pushed Walter away, away with his softness, girlyness and love.

I also tried to forget earlier memories of my friendship with Gráinne. We had been close friends. But I couldn't bear to hear my brother's words anymore which still echoed in my soul "footsie footsie, Kevin plays footsie with Gráinne." I became sad and bitter. The warmth of that soft friendship with Gráinne ended. I no longer played with girls and I began to hate Walter the Softy. I buried my need and desire for femininity and love. I buried Walter in his patch of flowers, in his Garden of Eden. Snap died and we buried her too.

An embarrassing moment when I was eight years old made me feel that my world had ended. My brother and I were both altar boys in the local church. During a mass service while we were both kneeling at the altar, I farted accidently. I was mortified. I felt that the whole church had heard it. I felt sick with embarrassment and shame. I knew my brother was smiling to himself, fuelled with new ammo to torment me afterwards. As I cried on the walk home feeling my life was ruined, he indulged in satisfaction. He danced around me making farting noises and jeering me "The farter from Killester, Kevin is the farter from Killester, hahaha." He was getting his kicks. I was very sad. The anger was growing inside me too.

The years nervously ticked by and I became a teenager in the image of Dennis the Menace. But by then, we were five people living in that old bungalow in Abbeyfield, Killester. Abbeyfield was an estate of houses originally built for Irishmen returning from the Great War almost a century before. God knows what tragedies they experienced at the battle front during "The War to end all wars."

My family of five consisted of the Bastard, the Coward, the Bully, me the Sissy disguised as Dennis the Menace, and my little brother who I loved dearly. With the Coward distracted by the Bastard, the Bully made a Soldier out of the Sissy, who tried to protect the only one of my family I cared about. My younger brother was named after a great Italian footballer with long curly hair who was my idol; Roberto Baggio.

Then when I was fourteen years old, I found out that I had an older sister, a dark secret hidden unfairly from my life but not anymore. I discovered that she came from a different mother.

She grew up in a different part of Ireland. Thanks to her, I started to remember Gráinne. I dug Walter the Softy back up many years later, allowing him his righteous place on earth. I integrated my feminine side into my masculinity. I became a happier better person, a man even. But that would take a long time. First, I would have to go to war, a war against myself and the prison of my mind. That for me was the real "War to end all wars."

As a teenager, I was growing up fast. It was only a matter of time when this jeering and mean treatment from my brother and father would have to be challenged. For my survival, I knew I had to take a stance. I knew as I was growing, I would one day be able to stand up to these two bullies.

My mam was a coward. She never stood up to my dad. God bless her. A bully needs a victim. God bless him too. She off loaded her anger onto us. Once, she boxed me in the head when I was twelve years old. I needed her love but I couldn't bear to touch her or smell her. If I had of been a little older and stronger there would have been a very different outcome to that punch. How can a child grow to find himself when surrounded with a father and older brother who were bullies, and a mother who was only a plastic dummy?

NEWBRIDGE

When I was about nine years old, I witnessed something which confirmed to me that I had lost all faith in my family. I was left powerless and terrified. Those adults who were around me on that day were, as far as I was concerned, heartless cowards. It was a Sunday Spring Afternoon and my family and extended family were on a day out in Newbridge house Park, in north county Dublin. There was my mother and father, two of my aunts and their husbands and children. There was my uncle who was my godfather, and his wife. There was a bunch of my cousins who were around my age too. And there was my older brother. My younger brother was not yet born.

Everybody was strolling along and we, the children, were playing. My brother was in his usual bullying mood but at least I could escape to the company of my cousins to avoid him. Then all of a sudden everyone stopped. We heard my brother shriek and cry for help in a terrified voice "Mam Mam Mam Help me Help me!"

At twenty metres away from the path in the rough grass, my father had him held tightly with one hand. My brother looked like an animal trying to escape. I could see my father's mean red face as he searched desperately with his other hand for a stick. It felt like time had frozen because all the cowards before me certainly had. I looked towards them, the other adults, for an answer. I was sure they would intervene and stop my father before he found that branch. But they didn't move. They just looked at each other like jelly babies.

My brother went silent when the strong branch stunned his

legs. The beating seemed to last forever. My father released all his pitiful tension and anger into those lashes across my brother's legs arms and back. My mother was crying and my aunt comforted her with an undeserving hug. This looked so crap. These grown men and women who I respected as those who had all the worldly answers, were suddenly reduced to cowardly scum. I stood there alone waiting for somebody to stop him. No one did. I felt violated and in a family I never chose. I didn't know who I hated more, my bastard father or all those cowards who done nothing.

Don't get me wrong, I did feel that I wanted to love my family and I did love them in some twisted confused way. But my blueprint for love was distorted. I couldn't bear to hug my mother or father. I didn't like any closeness with them. I wanted to love them and be loved but they disgusted me at the same time.

ABBEYFIELD

When I was twelve years old I had an original PlayStation games console. I loved it and I played it for hours. It was an enjoyable escape from my family. My favourite game was called Command and Conquer. In the game, you could choose a location on any type of landscape to build up your base and grow your army. The enemy would be doing the same on another area of the map. Then, when you were sufficiently strong you could attempt to eliminate the enemy.

I may have felt that I had little control over my life, but here in this game, I had an opportunity to have control over a whole army. From this world of fantasy, my interest in the Army continued to grow. It was related to a longing for security which came from a sense of insecurity. I imagined that as a soldier, I would be respected and idealised by others outside of the army. As a soldier, I would be honest and upright. But there were no soldiers in my family, only cowardly scum. Could I really become one?

Long before my time, men had joined armies. Many Irishmen had enlisted and were sent to the Great War for various reasons. One being, that there were not many other options in terms of work available to them. But why would somebody voluntarily go and join the army and put themselves through pain, discomfort and the possibility of death? I wondered. A common answer to this question which I held for myself was "I really want to challenge myself." Later I would begin to question that answer. Who is the I that is challenging the self? Maybe a better answer would be "I joined the army because I really want to find myself." Then an even better answer which I would discover later would be "I joined the Legion because I really was lost in my little world."

Potentially, I was ideal material for a life in the Legion; a lost soul. But it was not in the Legion that I would ever find myself. Rather, I would become even more lost. But the Legion was certainly the catalyst for change.

Before I joined the Legion I had been in the Irish Reserve Army in Dublin, known then as An Fórsa Cósanta Áitiúil. From the age of seventeen, I enjoyed being a soldier in the FCA. This status gave me a great boost of confidence. I enjoyed holding the belief that those strong commanding men above me were honourable and trustworthy. They wouldn't stand by like statues while a small fat man abused his young son, by viciously beating him with a hard wooden stick in broad daylight in a public park. Surely they would have stopped him.

The army provided me the chance, I suppose, to gain approval and recognition, something I craved from my father but did not receive. Bu the army was just another form of strict discipline, an authoritarian regime. Everywhere I looked, there were father figures. They must be the ones who had the answers, I expected. My father was strict in his ways. Army officers were strict in their ways. And God the Father, the ultimate, was strict in his ways too. Or so I believed.

The unconscious search for worldly answers continued without me knowing it. Was it my way of testing the accepted truth that you must seek before finding? Is it true that the father rules over his son? The same truth that claims God sent his son Jesus to earth, and that Army officers rule over their troops with the strongest bonds of father and son, one King over another. Where does it start and where does it end? For a soldier, it ends on the battlefield, in death. But in who's name?

In my teenage years I began doubting my own father early

on. This is normal adolescent development to a certain extent. I grew increasingly resentful and annoyed at his moods. They created anxiety and fear in the house. One night like many others, he could be heard arguing in the kitchen with my mother. Loud aggressive voices echoed upstairs to our bedrooms.

I now had a six year old younger brother. He was afraid when they argued loudly and rightly so. My sixteen years of fear had being transforming through my adolescent body into anger. I would no longer sit in my room, lie in my bed and allow this unease to disturb me. I ran to the kitchen amongst those thieves, thieves of parental love, and thieves of childhood comforts. I pushed him hard to announce my presence.

Like spears, his violent threats flew towards me. Even she told me to get lost. I ignored them both. To the cupboard armoury I went, grabbing a heavy black iron pan. A pan he had used to cook for us, to feed us. But food alone was never enough. With the pan held high above my head, I roared at him eye to eye, face to face. I could have smashed his skull but I couldn't do it. I felt weak again. He was still my father, my dictator, my ruler, my God.

We all dispersed in separate ways, but not the adrenaline. I lay awake in my room, angry, upset, sad and hopeless. She was a Coward and he was a Drunk Bully. So what the hell am I? My confused mind argued with itself. They are still my parents. I must love them. The Supreme Father has ordered it! I heard it in School, in Church. How could it be any other way? I don't have the answer. But wait, what's the question here? Sleep, come quickly, please.

THE CURRAGH

I was in the 11th Corps of Engineers of the FCA, based in McKee barracks in Dublin. My dad had worked with one of the army officers in the Irish Electrical Company (ESB). He had convinced me that the Engineers do a lot more things than the Infantry. While the Infantry focused solely on field skills, the Engineers along with basic field skills, spent more time on areas such as bridge building, demining and explosives. It sounded exciting and probably would for most seventeen year old boys.

My section in the FCA paraded for two hours every Thursday night. I was really delighted on receiving my uniform. I would spend a long time at home polishing up a nice shine on my boots. I looked forward to every Thursday evening. I would get an injection of self-esteem from cycling across the city from our home in Killester, to McKee Barracks in Cabra, every Thursday evening, dressed in my full combats and beret. I felt special. I felt grown up. I belonged to a group. I needed this sense of identity. But the two hours on a Thursday night was not enough. I wanted to be a soldier fully, not just half a soldier. I wanted my identity to be completed, without cracks or gaps, a soldier one hundred percent.

As soon as I had made up my mind that I wanted to be an Officer in the Permanent Irish Defence Forces, there was no convincing me otherwise. I was self-motivated and determined to fulfil this dream. I worked hard in the final years of secondary school to get a good Leaving Certificate, in order to increase my chances of being accepted as a Cadet. I gave my best effort in service with the FCA and during training exercises. I showed enthusiasm.

During an orienteering exercise at the Curragh camp, I finished in first position with a Corporal. We had set off running at a strong pace from the go. I had a good sense of direction. I understood quickly how to read maps. I also had a good level of fitness from playing Gaelic football with my local club, Raheny GAA. We were both exhausted on reaching the finish, having found all the hidden markers. It was a really good feeling when they announced us as the winning pair. I was being recognised as a quick learner by the NCOs and I was determined to uphold this positive image.

I was always punctual, respectable and serious about what I was asked to do during my service in the FCA. On the firing range, I was careful to follow the correct rules and procedures. During one training exercise in explosives, we were each required to clamp a detonator to a fuse line one by one. Then we had to light the end of this meter long fuse with a special match. It required precision to correctly clamp the detonator onto the fuse and to light the other end of the fuse with a special matchstick. I was so careful to do all the things correctly and well. I wanted to show the NCO in charge that I was competent. I wanted my ability and potential recognised. At the end of that annual summer camp, myself and two other recruits were given our Private two star badges during a presentation on the barracks square. It was a good feeling to celebrate this. We all went for pints of beer that night at the mess bar.

I had enjoyed my time in the FCA and I was committed to the tasks I had to perform. However, I started to notice that despite my enthusiasm, I felt distant and unable to join in the conversations during periods when we were hanging around together waiting. Some doubt began to creep in. I never expected on joining the army, that there would be so much time spent hanging around, waiting for something to happen. These times I disliked the most.

As I didn't smoke, I would just stand there as the others chatted, smoked and joked. I always felt left out of their silly conversations. I felt it was too hard to join in, so I decided that they were only talking rubbish most of the time. But I also felt a strong desire to be just like them. The apparent ease by which they told stories and jokes was something that I craved. But I had a stammer since early childhood, and I was terrified for it to come out. I hid it well. I was embarrassed of my stammer. I had so much to say but remained silent.

There was one soldier in my section who I admired. He was an older Three Star Private who had been in the Section for longer than I had. His uniform was always the most impressive. It was ironed and kept immaculate, as were his boots. He was very knowledgeable. He always gave me some friendly advice and tips about gun handling and maintaining my gear. I no longer had to cycle as he gave me a lift across the city every Thursday evening. He lived close by my home on the north side of Dublin. Martin and I became good friends.

When I remember a story he told me years later, it left me with a grin. It was a regular Thursday night on parade. I had been missing for some time. The section had been assembled as usual at the beginning of the night. The Officer in charge addressed the troops. "Irish Army Intelligence has informed us that Private Stefanazzi has joined the Foreign Legion. Does anyone know anything about this?" he said. Everyone turned and looked over towards Martin my friend, to see if he had any information. But he was just as surprised as the rest of them. He shrugged his shoulders, expressing his disbelief. I had left without telling anybody. I felt that anyone I did tell would have tried to talk me out of it. But it was also because the decision to go was a quick one and it was made over a disappointing

August afternoon.

I had completed my Fitness tests for the Cadetship competition in the Irish army. I had sat a formal interview during the summer months, hoping to start my future as an Army Cadet in September. I was just waiting for the response from the Army in the form of a letter. I felt confident after having given what 1 believed was a good interview. During the fitness tests, I gave it everything I had. I noticed on the day that I was in the top bracket of candidates in those fitness tests.

I had also taken an optional proficiency test as Gaeilge, demonstrating my good command of the Irish language. On top of all this, I had the experience of being in the FCA for over a year and I played both Gaelic football and hurling. I had achieved better than I expected in the Leaving Cert Exam by getting two A1 grades in both Technical Drawing and Biology. I felt that I had a great chance of being offered a Cadetship. I needed desperately to become an Officer in the Army. That was the dream; Officers and soldiers, fathers and sons, loyalty, brotherhood and tough Love. There was no other way. Or was there?

RAHENY

Not long after I had got my Leaving Cert results, my Mam told me that a letter for me had arrived from the Army. She could tell from the envelope. I went to a quiet place in the house to open it, in anticipation of the outcome. I said a little prayer to Our Father God. Either I was going to be a Cadet in the Irish Army or nothing. I wanted nothing more. There was no plan B or a desire to go to University.

I opened the envelope and read the short letter a few times over in case I had misread it. But it clearly pointed out my failure as a son. "Thank you for your interest and application, however we regret to inform you that you were unsuccessful in this campaign." No reasons, no feedback.

I was initially surprised and in a state of disbelief. Soon though, I was both upset and angry. This country didn't want me. I felt lost and I really didn't know what to do with myself. I did have different choices down on my application to university but my heart wasn't in that option. I had applied for both Architecture and Sport Science. I was sure to get a place in university. But I had no desire whatsoever to go. Then I had an idea, a radical one.

I'm going to show them, my so called family, my so called friends and the so called Irish Army! I'm going to show them what I am made of, show them of what I am capable. I deserve to be a worthy son. But why did I need to show anyone anything? What was it that I needed to prove or find? I was lost without knowing it. But I couldn't stand still. I felt betrayed by Ireland and betrayed by my family, whatever that meant. I'm going to join the French Foreign Legion. That's it, that's the answer. The decision was made, either by me or that heavenly fool in the clouds, but it was done.

Like many ex-Legionnaires, I have no regrets about joining. However I sometimes imagine going there again to join and I think "No way would I go through it all again." There is also a part of me that wonders why I have no regrets. Could it be that it is too painful to regret? How can I say that it was a waste of five years and that I hated everything about it, without that making me a hypocrite for not deserting? We were always told that nobody came knocking on our home doors asking us to join. That is very true. We came knocking. If you don't like it, you know where the gate is.

I often wonder what I would be like as a person if I had not gone there. Did it make me? Did it break me? Would my sense of self be different? Such questions don't allow for any answers so I allow myself to sometimes regret it too. It doesn't have to be one or the other. Regrets or not, what's done is done.

I knew very little about the French Foreign Legion except that it accepted men from any country in the world. I was determined not to tell anyone. But I needed to find out how could I actually join. I phoned my local library in Raheny and I booked a computer for an hour, that same afternoon. It was just before the dawn of smartphones. I knew I could find some answers thanks to the internet. After checking a few sources and scanning through forums, it seemed clear that there were recruitment centres around France in the major cities. The Legion's Fort de Nogent in Paris was the obvious choice for me. I could fly from Dublin to Paris with Aerlingus. I didn't want to hang around either, just get there and do it.

I finished my research online. I booked a flight for early the next morning. I also booked a taxi to collect me down the road from my house at four a.m. two hours before the flight departure time. According to information online I needed nothing except myself, my cock, two balls and a passport. I would probably get away with one bollocks.

The recruitment process unlike that for the Irish Cadetship was old-style, no telephoning, no application forms or CVs. I just had to get myself to one of the recruitment centres in a good enough physical state. There was no time for me to overthink it now that the flight was booked. I think that is what attracts so many men from countries like Ireland, the ability to join on a whim. I was eighteen years old. I was already addicted to the adrenaline of compulsive decisions.

That last night at home, I went along to the Raheny GAA club for a few beers. In the weeks leading up to that point, I had been helping out with coaching kids at the summer camp. All the coaches who were around my age were going for a few drinks in the club bar that night. I had developed a crush on one of the girl coaches who I worked with that last week. I was hoping to talk with her and ask her out. But at this point, even a kiss goodbye would do it for me.

As she was surrounded by her friends and seemed to be having a good time, it made the approach difficult. What's the point? My doubting mind held me back, as I was going to the Foreign Legion the next morning anyway. But what the hell, I guessed. I started chatting her up with whatever nonsense that came into my head. I tried to get her to leave with me to a different bar in Raheny village, just the two of us. But she was having none of it and was happy there with her friends. "Fuck it and Fuck her" I said to myself. I finished my pint and I headed home without saying goodbye to anyone. I'm outa here.

I woke up in a black silence. I left the house in the middle of the night. I felt calm and even good on my way to the airport in the taxi. At Dublin airport, I was enjoying a full Irish breakfast at a café before going through the departure gates. Then next thing I saw my mam and dad walk up and sit down at my table.

How on earth did they know and how did they find me here? But I kept eating and ignored them. I didn't care how they found out because no matter what they would say, or do, I'm going to France on that flight. I would take the both of them to the ground if they tried to stop me. I felt like an animal and I liked it. I was in control. The roles were reversed. Now, they were the kids.

I ignored their concerns and questions. I finished off my fry, licking my plate clean just as he had taught me. They were getting desperate and were pleading with me not to go. They sounded pathetic. I must have left something scribbled down on a piece of paper in the bin in my bedroom because they knew the Foreign Legion was my destination. The Legion was going to adopt me.

My mam started sobbing. They followed me like needy children as I headed towards the departure gates. My dad was getting angry towards me. I was filling up with adrenaline waiting for him to try and stop me. I think the Bully knew well that if he laid a hand on me, I would unleash all that backlog of hate and fear into him. His last pathetic attempt to stop me was "You are going to get raped in the Legion, Kevin." Such nice words of encouragement from him summed up my childhood experience in that line.

He was stopped by security. I walked straight through. I didn't look back at them. My new parents were waiting in France, about a thousand of them, and another seven thousand brothers.

SOUTH

IN THE LEGION

FRENCH FOREIGN LEGION ABBREVIATIONS

EV- Engagé Voluntaire (recruit)

LEG – Légionnaire (on receiving the Képi Blanc)

1CL – Légionnaire de première classe

CPL - Caporal

CCH – Caporal Chef

SGT – Sergent

SCH- Sergent Chef (Chef)

ADJ – Adjudant

ADC – Adjudant Chef

MAJ - Major

LTN – Lieutenant

CNE – Capitaine

CDT- Commandant

COL- Colonel

CDC – Chef de Corps (Colonel)

1RE- First Foreign Regiment (HQ)

4RE – Fourth Foreign Regiment (Training)

1REG – First Foreign Regiment of Engineers

2REI – Second Foreign Infantry Regiment

2REP – Second Foreign Regiment of Parachutists

1CIE – First Combat Company

2CIE – Second Combat Company

CCL – Company of Commandment and Logistics

PLD – Permission Long Durée (Leave)

AWOL – Absent Without Leave

VAB – Véhicule de l'Avant Blindé (Armored Personnel Carrier)

FORT DE NOGENT

It was a Monday morning when I arrived at the big archway and gates of Fort de Nogent. I had come straight from the Charles de Gaulle airport in a taxi. I had the address scribbled down on a little note of paper. I had just handed the slip of paper to the taxi man who had not one word of English. "La Légion?" he had said in a tone which meant - Do you really want to go there. It was a warm mid-morning in Paris with a hazy sunshine.

The person who opened the small hatch had dark ominous eyes that could reflect the blackness of any soul. "Passeport!" he demanded without any greeting. I reluctantly gave him my Irish passport, the first of many that would be replaced over the next five years. The hatch snapped shut and I was left standing outside for few minutes.

Suddenly the door creaked open and I was pointed to sit just inside the arch on a long wooden bench. The unease I felt during the first hour of waiting was lifted as another potential Engagé Voluntaire (EV) presented at those ominous gates. He soon joined me, sitting nervously on the other end of that tired bench. A distance between us left space for the next fool to sit. What felt like a second hour had passed without a word between us, when the Caporal Chef (CCH) arrived. "Debout!" he roared and we both jumped to our feet.

I didn't know what "Debout" meant but I didn't need a translation. Then he ordered us to open our mouths and stick out our tongue. I thought it was too soon to get a dental check-up. Five seconds is all he needed to have a quick glance at our back teeth. The other chap who looked Algerian was given his passport back and sent back out to the other side of the Gates. He was told to sort out his teeth at a dentist and then he could come back.

I was brought by the CCH to an old four story building further back. It looked like a soldiers billets. On the second floor, the CCH opened a door and about twelve other guys of different ages, different colours and hairstyles jumped up from a sitting position on the floor. I entered and found a spot on the floor where I could sit back against the wall. The door slammed shut. We all stared up at a tiny television in the corner of the room showing a french chat show. Lots of the participants on the show were joking and laughing and looking happy, while we all looked on in silence with an expressionless gaze.

Soon the door flung open again. A lean mean looking CCH pounced inside. The last guy who got to his feet was either snoozing or was sitting cross legged. "Pompe!" the CCH screamed at him. He fell to the floor, understanding the meaning of that word from the CCH's last visit. But his push-ups full range of motion was not to the CCH's liking. In order to help him improve form, the CCH stood with his boot firmly on the back of his head pushing down until the chap's forehead was flat on the floor. "Zéro" the CCH commenced. That was a free one. "Un, Deux, Trois" the CCH counted as the guy from Outer Mongolia or Timbuktu, I can't recall, pushed out his best push-ups with the added pressure of the CCH's boot resting on his head.

Another guy was called out to a nearby office. By now, two thirds of us wore faded blue tracksuits and whatever shoes or trainers we came with. The others including myself were still wearing our own civy clothes. I was called out next. It was the last time the name Stefanazzi would be used in the Legion for the next two years. I entered the office with the same CCH who wore those dark eyes.

An Adjudant (ADJ) was seated behind a wooden desk. The ADJ was a round man with a white complexion. He had a bald head and a Slavic accent. Czech, I guessed. My backpack and its contents were scattered on the table. There was my wallet with little cash, a Leatherman pocket tool, and my Irish passport. The ADJ threw a blue tracksuit on the floor in front of me and ordered me to put it on. I changed quickly. My civy clothes were packed into the backpack by the CCH. He then threw it onto the pile of other bags in the corner of the room. My Leatherman pocket tool was never to be seen again, a gift from my good friend Martin.

The ADJ showed me a name which he wrote on a brown envelope. "Sims Gregory, C'est ton nom" he ordered while pointing at the name and then back at me. Before returning back to the waiting room, the CCH showed me how to make Filter coffee in their office next door. He told me to check on it regularly and never let it go empty. A first chance to prove myself, I thought. He asked me if I spoke Italian after noticing my name on the passport but I replied that I had just a little French. I presumed that those dark menacing eyes were Italian and that he missed his former homeland. Underneath the darkness and anger in his eyes, lay sorrow and regret, the same deep longing that my great grandfather must have felt leaving Italy almost a century before. I returned to the other lost souls and took my place sitting on the floor, this time with my new name, an old blue tracksuit and a slight feeling of satisfaction.

That same day we were brought over to the canteen for lunch. While I was eating, the lad who I was sitting beside asked where I was from. I told him Ireland. He was Dutch. He then told me that there was another guy from Ireland there too. I was surprised. I found it hard to believe that there could be another Irish there at the same time among the twenty or so of us.

We were both delighted to meet each other. Brian was from Galway. He was a real character. He was about twice my age but it was great to have another Irish guy to chat with on the first day.

The second day, we were called, those with a new name and a blue tracksuit that is, to line up in the corridor. In French, we were told that we would be signing a contract for five years. One by one we arrived at a desk at the end of the corridor and signed a document with our Legion name on it. Judging by the speed at which it was done, nobody questioned or asked about the contract. We found out later that day that we were being sent to the south of France, to the Legion Headquarters in Aubagne. There, we would be put through a three week screening process.

After a couple more days in Fort de Nogent, spent sweeping up the first golden leaves to fall, the day came and we were put on a coach. We made the long way down to Aubagne.

AUBAGNE

During the few weeks at the 1RE in Aubagne waiting for the selection process to unfold, Brian and myself made a deal in the event that one of us did not make it through. Whoever did not make it and got sent away would contact the other's family in Ireland to inform them that one of us had been selected for the four months basic training in Castelnaudary. We managed to get hold of a pen somewhere. We both wrote down each other's family telephone numbers from Ireland on the insoles of our runners.

One of the questions during the selection process was if anyone had experience playing any musical instrument. It happened that Brian was a gifted guitarist, writing and playing his own songs back in Ireland. And I had been in the Artane Boys Band during my teenage years, not particularly because I liked it but because my mam had insisted on it. I played the clarinet. Brian and I both answered yes and we were both called to the Musical Section of the Legion there in Aubagne for an audition.

I played a song they put in front of me on the clarinet, demonstrating my ability to read music, while Brian impressed them with his talent using a guitar. However, as the guitar was not an orchestral instrument, his musical talent and potential was ignored. Where I had no interest in playing Music, Brian would have gladly taken up a position with Musique de la Légion étrangère. However it turned out that Brian was discharged after those initial three weeks in Aubagne. He did keep our promise. He called my family in Dublin when he got out.

There is a Building with a large backyard where the screening process takes place at the 1RE in Aubagne. We were approximately eighty or so EVs, divided into three groups, Blue, Green and Red. As we were the newbies, we joined the Blue group. The Green group had blue tracksuits like us but they stood out as they all had a skin-tight haircut. The Red group were, along with a skin tight haircut, dressed in brand new regular camouflage uniforms and boots. As EVs, they wore no beret to distinguish them from serving Legionnaires.

We had our first taste of what was to come in Legion training on our first day there in Aubagne. There was a Caporal (CPL) who was at the end of his contract. He had been drinking heavily in the club bar. He made us all line up out on the square of the recruiting yard as he staggered around us blabbering on about who knows what. The CCH on duty at the recruiting centre didn't seem to care and let the drunken CPL have his last little power trip. It might even help instil some fear and discipline into us.

The drunken CPL kept shouting "Lève la tête" repeatedly to anyone who did not have their head sufficiently pointing slightly up. Luckily, I understood some French. He grabbed the tall Dutch guys face hard by his cheeks and jerked it upwards, shouting again "Lève la tête" in his face. Not understanding French, he soon got the message.

As the CPL staggered around us sipping his bottle of Kronenbourg, he continued shouting about how we should be proud to be future Legionnaires. What I couldn't understand was that if he was so proud of his Legionnaire status, why was he leaving? It wouldn't be the first or last time I would have to question and deal with such rubbish. The fact that he was only about five foot tall pointed to a pitiful complex about his size. I was reminded about my father who at a similar size was a grumpy little man. I was glad to see the back of him but I quickly realised there would be even more of his type here.

One of the stages at the 1RE in Aubagne is to go in front of the "Gestapo" for questioning. They pretend that they know everything under the sun. Anyone who discloses to them any ongoing trial or trouble with the police is likely to be rejected at this stage. It is better to deny anything at this point because once you are accepted into the Legion, it's a lot more unlikely that you will be discharged because of former trouble in civy life. They have invested in you with training and supplies. But Brian disclosed something about a former conviction to the Gestapo at this early stage. I believe that was the reason for his rejection. The fact that he was in his late thirties and that he had attempted to join a few years before were other factors not in his favour.

FORMINGUERES

After those three weeks in Aubagne, we, the Red group were brought by train to the 4RE in Castelnaudary. There, we were assigned to the second Company (2CIE). One of the periods of basic training takes place at "Le Farm." For the three weeks spent at the Farm, we slept very little and ate very little. At the end of three weeks, we hiked fifty kilometres and then during a ceremony, we each put on our Kepi Blanc and rehearsed the Legionnaire's Code of Honour.

One day during a training manoeuvre at the Farm, a bunch of us were lying down and carrying out the routine safety checks before and after firing the FAMAS gun. I done something which the Sergent (SGT) didn't like. His booth came crashing down onto my head. We had helmets on but it was one of many bad tastes I had early on in the Legion which would slowly accumulate over the years, into complete disgust.

On another day at the Farm, a Chilean CPL held the barrel of his gun an inch from my mouth and threatened to smash my teeth in with it. It was hard not to take such things personal. But sometimes I noticed the same SGT and CPL arguing among one another. It reassured me in some way that their aggression wasn't personal towards me.

During meal times, we ate from a metal tray. The same evening after we completed the Kepi Blanc March, we were all exhausted but glad about completing it. While queuing up to be served tiny portions of food, I took an extra piece of bread. I didn't know that the exact amount of bread had been counted. We got only one piece of baguette each. There were exactly sixty two pieces. I was starving hungry and I didn't expect anyone would notice so I took two pieces while nobody was looking. The second piece I hid inside my vest and the other I placed on my tray.

We had only sat down to eat when the Chilean CPL shouted "Fermez vos gueules." We were chatting amongst ourselves which he didn't like. We were more talkative as usual at the table that evening having just got our Kepis. Some of us ignored him. The chatting continued. Then he announced "Everybody stand up, Outside, Now!"

Desperately, in a couple of seconds we pushed large last mouthfuls of food into our mouths leaving the half empty trays behind. Assembled outside, the Chilean CPL called two LEGs inside the canteen to help him throw all the food into black rubbish bags. We stood there disappointed and hungry. Earlier that day we had received our Kepi Blancs but now we were still been treated like shit.

After all the food was put in the bin he came outside. "If you can't eat in Silence, you won't eat at all" the little dark Chilean said with a mean laugh as we stood their assembled in the dark. Then the other CPL on duty from Tahiti said out load "Who stole an extra piece of bread. We counted the bread before dinner exactly. Now one piece is missing." Immediately, I grew worried as I remembered that extra piece of bread tucked inside my jacket. He continued "You all have two minutes to think about it. Then that person better own up."

I knew that nobody saw me taking it so I decided to stay quiet. But I was worried that if they carried out a search and found it on me, what might happen. Then there was a distraction. The SGT had arrived from the NCO's billets, to find out what was going on. He was not pleased at all when he discovered that all the food had been thrown in the rubbish. He pulled the Chilean CPL aside for another one of their arguments. It seemed as if they were close to having a brawl. I used this distraction as an opportunity. It was dark and I was in the back row which helped. In an instant I grabbed the piece of baguette from my vest and squeezing it together, I pushed it down into my left boot. I could have thrown it behind me into the darkness but I wanted to eat it later. Once the SGT had given the Chilean CPL a good telling off, he left. The two CPLs then got ready to search us for that missing bread.

They patted us down one by one but they didn't think of checking our boots. I was lucky to get away with it. I kind of liked my little success. There were times though during those three weeks at the Farm when I would get up in the middle of the night and creep out to the bins at the back of the kitchen. There, I would eat any scraps I could find. Despite my exhaustion every night, it was difficult to sleep with the hunger I felt.

One evening we were not allowed to sleep and we experienced our first "Nuit Blanche." They kept us up all night as collective punishment. The reason; a chap from Madagascar took a shit around the back of a shed and he was caught in the act. Either the toilets were full or he just liked to be in the outdoors while shitting, I was never quite sure why he done that. But three years on, that memory may have unconsciously influenced my own mischief but we will get to that story later.

As a result of the Malgache's dirty commando trick, instead of going to sleep that night, we stood in formation, all night long. And we stood in formation without any gaps, right up against each other, shoulder to shoulder and head to head. In that position, we sang Legion songs all night while the CPL's took turns sleeping. By three a.m. lads were getting irritated and almost fighting with each other. At four a.m. one guy fainted but he continued on. At seven a.m. we stopped singing and were allowed to shave and brush our teeth before breakfast and then a twelve kilometre run. We were beyond tired.

Back at the 4RE in Castelnaudary, our forming as Legionnaires continued. One evening, the Tahitian CPL locked the whole section into the toilets for a few hours and turned the lights off. Sixty two of us were crammed inside like sardines. Lads began panicking and fights broke out.

On another occasion, an English CPL was rightly pissed off when a Belgian LEG used his name to order a pizza to the base one night. The CPL's measures were a little extreme though. The CPL had us all lined up in the corridor and nobody confessed to it. He then went to his room and came back out with his helmet swinging around in his hand. In a rage, he ordered us to lie down on our backs side by side with our hands over our precious parts. One by one he swung his helmet from high above his head, slamming it down into the stomach of each LEG. There were sixty two of us and I was glad that I was not at the beginning of the line. But my turn would come. The waiting was terrible but then something happened.

After about twelve guys got their punishment, he hit one guy in the ribs who roared out in pain. There was a mass rebellion. Panic broke out and we all jumped to our feet. The CPL was rushed by about twenty lads. I thought that was the end for him. A SGT from the reception downstairs, on hearing the shouting, was up in a flash. We were all ordered to go to our bedrooms. I remember seeing the CPLs face as I walked off. He was white like a ghost and terrified. He looked pitiful. What kind of an army is this? I wondered.

Towards the end of the four months basic training at the 4RE in Castelnaudary, we completed a one hundred kilometre "Marche Raid" with full kit, over three days. On the last day, my left knee became very sore. When I expressed my concern, it fell on deaf ears and I was forced to march through the pain. I was given some anti-inflammatory gel by the SGT once we were back on base. But I felt some damage was done to my knee at the time. Years later, I still get stiffness and pain in the same knee.

Formiguères is a small village in the Pyrenees Mountains. Our whole section went there for a week towards the end of basic training. The Legion has a chalet there. That week was spent at a more relaxed pace. It was a well-earned break from the usual treatment back at the 4RE. We did some nice hikes in the mountains. The food was really good and the portions were big too. We did some all-terrain biking and orienteering in the beautiful surroundings. They put films on a big screen in a conference room in the evenings. The last day we had some free time in the afternoon to go into the nearby village and have a beer and look around in the shops. Then, that evening we all gathered as a section for drinks back at the chalet.

There were loads of drinks laid out with snacks. There were Bottles of Whisky, Ricard, Vodka, Beers and Soft drinks. I got extremely drunk that night and blacked out.

There had been a lot of singing. As with tradition, we each sang one of our own songs in groups according to our nationalities. The Russians sang a song, then the Romanians, the French, the Polish, the Argentinians, even the Chinese. As there were only two Anglophones in the whole section, myself and the English CPL, we were both asked to sing a song together. Being pissed drunk, I refused to sing a song with him. When it was my turn to sing, I gave an almighty "Gardez vous" to everyone's amusement. When I got their attention, I roared out the Irish National Anthem "Amhráin na Bhfiann." The hard drinking continued late into the night.

The next morning I awoke with a thumping headache and puzzled to my whereabouts. I was lying in my sleeping bag alone in the corridor away from my bedroom. I felt cold and wet all over. At breakfast I was the target of a lot of jokes and sneering. Apparently I had taken a piss on the NCOS bedroom door in the middle of the night, completely drunk. The SCH appeared with the sound of me pissing on their door, grabbed me and threw me straight into the shower with my clothes still on. Then I was sent to sleep in the corridor with my sleeping bag. I was embarrassed and ashamed but it seemed to amuse the whole section and even the NCOS. I was just another drunk Legionnaire after all or as they say in the Legion "Chiffon."

I never forgot my father's words back in Dublin Airport. He had said that I would get raped in the Legion. This was his best effort to stop me and it did have a profound effect. That morning on waking up in the corridor, not knowing what had happened, the possibility of it crossed my mind and terrified me. But it never did happen to me nor did I ever feel that it could.

Ironically however, there was a secret I kept to myself during my teenage years that I could never share with anyone. During my adolescence, growing up in Dublin, I did have some disturbing homosexual thoughts that I couldn't accept or come to terms with. I concealed them from my family. I buried them with Walter the Softy. When I was about twelve years old, I had a nightmare in which I told my parents that I might be gay because I was in love with my friend at school. The next morning I was humiliated. But then relief came when I realised that it was only a dream and I never told them. In secondary school, I continued to have attractions to some boys but mainly girls in school. Again I couldn't deal with the attractions to other boys and I bottled them up. I was sure I wasn't gay but I couldn't get my head around the possibility of bisexuality.

During my time in the Legion, these were also a deep secret of mine. They were never an issue. There were some rare times when I did fantasise about sexual acts with some fellow soldiers who were feminine in their appearance and to whom I was attracted. Not having a girlfriend and spending large amounts of time without seeing women didn't help the situation either. I was extremely uncomfortable and I buried these feelings only for them to resurface years later when I lost my mind. No way would I have ever considered acting on them. I was deeply ashamed that I could have such thoughts. I began feeling weak and unworthy of being a soldier. The war with my mind had started.

There was one LEG who didn't hide his blatant homosexuality. I felt sickened by the rumours of what had occurred one night at the 4RE in Castelnaudary, during basic training. It was a weekend night and the CPL on duty was very relaxed. He had allowed us the evening to ourselves. We could go across to the bar and the shop on the base and we could relax in our rooms that Saturday night. I used the opportunity to drink a few beers at the bar and grab a roast chicken with chips. I then went outside the billets and found a payphone. I made a phone call home to my family in Ireland for the first time since I left almost four months previously. I was met by the strange sound of my older brother crying on the phone when he realised it was me. I told him all was going well in the Legion. Maybe he did care about me after all but he certainly had a twisted way of showing it when we were growing up together.

The rumours had spread throughout the section the next day of what had happened the previous night. There was a Native American Indian chap. That night, he had allowed a bunch of Russians to perform anal sex on him one by one in his bedroom. I didn't directly witness it but I felt disgusted when I imagined that scene. I avoided that chap from then on. I didn't even want to look at him or shake his hand. I did have my own homosexual fantasies but they didn't include being sodomized by a bunch of fellow soldiers.

After our four months basic training in Castelnaudary, we all returned to Aubagne. We were assigned to our different

Regiments. Most guys were assigned to Regiments such as Infantry, Parachutists, Engineers and Cavalry. Few were also sent abroad to Regiments in the French Guyana and in Djibouti. When it was my turn, I was shocked when I was told that I would be staying right there at the 1RE headquarters in Aubagne. I would be assigned to the Legion's Music Section. I had almost forgotten when Brian and I were called for that audition four months previously. But I had absolutely no interest in joining the Music Section, while Brian would have done anything for that opportunity. I had to plead with the Officer until he gave in and I got an assignment to one of the two Engineer Regiments, the 1REG.

The next day, I left with about another eight LEGs for the 1REG accompanied by an instructor CPL from the 1REG. Years later and looking back, a career in the Music Section of the Legion wouldn't have been a bad thing. It would have been a lot more comfortable. But at eighteen years old, I wanted to be a soldier or become a soldier. Gradually though, I found out that taking on the role of a soldier wasn't what I expected it to be. It wasn't me. I grew to hate taking on the role. I slowly began to understand that it was an illusion I had created for myself to escape reality.

DJIBOUTI

During those five years in the Legion, I served overseas in the Ivory Coast, the Republic of Djibouti, and in Indonesia. There is not a whole lot to say about my time in those places, but some things do come to mind.

The Legion has a Regiment in Djibouti called the 13DBLE. Within the 13DBLE, there is one Company which rotates its troops every four months. The rotation is between Engineering and Infantry Companies from other Legion regiments. My Company, the 1CIE of the 1REG's turn had come to go there. During our four months in Djibouti, we spent an equal amount of time at the 13DBLE barracks in Djibouti town as we did out on the ground doing manoeuvres and training.

It was a very dry land. The local population were poor. While looking at that barren rocky land, one would struggle to see how any life could survive there. But as there were water sources and with that strong sun, they produced some amazing food. There was an abundance of fruit and vegetables at road-side stalls. Our food at the base was largely composed of local produce. Fresh fish from the sea and rice was often on our lunchtime menu. It was on the border of Ethiopia, the birthplace of mankind. The Ethiopians had to travel through Djibouti to access the sea.

Out on the ground, our training manoeuvres involved using a range of explosives. We also fired and trained with different weapons on designated firing ranges.

One day, our section was training on the use of the sniper rifle. Everyone got a turn to shoot. There were three rifles between us. Three of us were lying down and firing at long range targets. The SCH instructing us was kneeling close by. Using a set of binoculars to see the targets, he gave us our firing commands. The lad next to me was firing at the wrong target, but I got the blame for it. After we had finished firing that day and we were back assembled at the vehicles, the Lieutenant (LTN) called me over. He said "Sims, you messed up at the firing range because you weren't listening to the SCH's orders." I attempted to argue my point but he didn't let me talk. He just pointed to a large, heavy rock and said "Pick up that rock Sims, put it over your head, and run all the way up to the targets and back three times, Allez Allez Allez."

Again I tried to explain that there was a mix-up, but he wasn't interested. It was hot, and my head was even hotter inside. I had over a year of service and I was now a 1CL Legionnaire. I had been awarded my first stripe just before leaving for Djibouti. The first Section's tradition involved drinking a helmet full of beer with the 1CL badge inside. I had to stand on a stool while doing so. If you lowered the helmet or tried taking a break there would be lads standing nearby ready to top it up with more beer.

I thought that, at last when we were all trained soldiers, there would be less messing around like during basic training. But now I wondered if they would ever let up on this sort of thing. I had sucked it up during all the initial training, hoping that at some point, we would be treated like professional soldiers and allowed to get on with business. But it doesn't work like that in the Legion. They keep the pestering up.

Another thing on my mind that day was that I had recently spent two weeks in Hospital before going to Djibouti. I had surgery to repair an inguinal hernia, the size of a golf ball. My groin area was still sore and I was determined not to get another hernia. The procedure was a painful one, with a mesh placed inside. It was slow to heal. Now this idiot of a LTN in the desert heat, wanted to show off his authority.

I lifted up the heavy rock over my head, feeling the strain around my groin area where I had the surgery. I walked about five steps. Fuck that. I flung it down on the ground, and looking straight at the LTN. "Non, Je ne fais pas" I said. I reminded him that I had that operation for a hernia only a few months back. I didn't want another one popping out as a third ball in my scrotum. But he didn't care.

That evening while the section was relaxing, I would spend hours making a pyramid of rocks nearby to our Bivouac. It didn't stop there. Once that week of training was over and we were back at the base, I had my formal uniform on and was standing in the LTN's office. He officially assigned me ten periods of punishment - Dix tours de consignes. Each period was three hours long. While the others in my Section would finish work at five p.m. each day, I would spend every evening for ten days scrubbing the toilets and showers with a brush and detergent. This was the beginning of my remaining four years struggle to accept and conform to the Legion's strong tradition of complete unquestionable discipline and obedience.

One day not long after, we were preparing for an all-night march. It was a regimental exercise. The plan was that in the morning we would arrive at a Salt lake – Lac Assal. Other sections would arrive from different directions. There would be a regimental morning assembly of us all and our vehicles on the lake itself. We left the main base of the 13DBLE in the early evening of the night before. We drove for hours to our starting point.

Our section set off marching. We followed a dry river bed. It was a rocky trail through a small valley with dark cliffs surrounding us. We wore night vision goggles. I eventually took them off and put them in my bag. I preferred letting my eyes adjust to any residual light, however little, that there was. The night vision had a 2-D feel to it, and although vision was much better, it was hard to judge distances on a trail full of rocks.

We were going along at a good steady pace for a few hours when the near silence was broken. We heard the crashing sound of someone falling and the metallic noise of a FAMAS gun, banging off the rocks. We stopped marching while the LTN was helped up to his feet and he brushed himself off. We all continued on in the dark as if it never happened. Nobody spoke as we marched on but I had a smile on my face. I knew others too, along with their night vision goggles, had smiles on their faces.

At one point, the crumbling faint sound of our marching on dry ground broke again. But this time it was the screams of baboons, in caves all around us. It was an eerie feeling, and we longed for the first of the morning light.

With the morning light came the quick heat of the African sun. During that last stretch towards the salt lake, it saw us finish up any last water reserves we had. We arrived with sticky mouths, exhausted and thirsty, to the blinding white light of the salt lake. From night vision goggles to sun glasses, it was the brightest light that I've ever seen. I remember the utter frustration we all felt at the long time that was spent to get us perfectly assembled. All the vehicles were aligned as were the troops so that a helicopter could fly overhead taking photos, while the Colonel (CDC) of the 13DBLE addressed us all in a speech that I couldn't care less about. I wrote a poem about that night.

Horn of Africa

Heavy feet won't lighten load,
No loaves left.
A faller kneels,
Loosing hair before silent lions.

59

A lunar gaze shows no remorse,

Frozen but not yet solid.

Black honey sticks lips,

Baboon's laugh their sacred joke.

Some try hope,

That some holy bloke,

May offer up his golden yolk.

Pumping purple blood,

Limey eyes,

Samson stops.

Pulling peacefully,

Pupils welcome home an old friend.

Repos,

Wake, Rise and drink.

But no fish they say,

In this Salt lake.

One day in Djibouti that added to my growing doubt regarding my Legion Loyalty, I found myself on a hill with a small group. We were a group of five on that barren hillside in the middle of nowhere, tasked with monitoring an open plain close to the Somali border. We sat there with three sets of binoculars all day. We had nothing to make a shelter. The sun was directly above us like a grill. I noticed that myself and the two other 1CLs had very little water reserves. When I informed the Moldovan CPL of this, I knew by his response that I was dealing with a real gobshite.

He took out his water bottle to show me. He shook the little bit of warm water that was left inside. "Never drink the last bit," he said smartly, "that way you always have some left." An hour later, he was annoyed when I informed the SGT about the water issue. But it still took another couple of hours for them to act and only when one 1CL from the Czech Republic turned snow white. He said that he felt cold in the forty degrees heat and he started speaking gibberish. We called it in by radio. He was evacuated by helicopter and treated for heat stroke. "We need to get more water" the SGT said.

Several years after I left the Legion I read a sad case of a LEG in Djibouti who dropped dead from heat stroke. The newspaper article reported that when the LEG complained of exhaustion, they poured his water bottle over his head, gave him a beating and ordered that no more water be given to him. Soon after, he died. When the case went to trial in Paris, it was deemed that the Legion trains just like in a war situation and because of this, nobody was held accountable. I would say that the Legion get away with murder. Going back to the idea that the Legion was created "Not to spill French blood" I would like to ask what exactly "French blood" is or what is any blood for that matter?

Each time, after a long period out on the ground in Djibouti, we returned to the base, tired, hungry and dirty. It took us hours to clean all the equipment and vehicles. Then we would be allowed some time off. Despite the exhaustion, most of us would head into town. One night out on the town, a local man pushed around a small cart selling kebabs made from rat meat. LEGs with enough beer in them got stuck in.

Going out on the town usually involved going to a bar and drinking a rake of cold beers. It was easy to pick up a prostitute in the bars and go back to her place. It was the normal thing to do after having come back from a long period out on the ground. Djibouti was my first time to use a prostitute and it became an option I would choose several times since then. However, I found that the urge and excitement that proceeds paying for sex is usually followed by sadness and emptiness afterwards. It is a shallow pleasure lacking intimacy. It is a bit like being very hungry and munching into a poor kebab. It would be more nutritious and satisfying to have a nice slow cooked roast dinner. Similarly, it would be more spiritually nutritious, to take the time to get to know and build up a genuine attraction with a girl. The sex when it happens is then not based on money but a deeper attraction. The sex becomes love making. That is not to say that munching into the odd kebab is wrong, just as long as it is not made from rat meat!

INDONESIA

As we were approaching the end of our four months in Djibouti, a huge Earthquake created huge Tsunamis that spread across the Indian Ocean. It was Stevens's day, the day after Chistmas. Over 220,000 people were killed. As we were the only French Engineering Company already deployed in Djibouti, my section was chosen and tasked with going to Indonesia to assist. We embarked onto a French navy vessel called "Le Jean d'Arc." We crossed the Indian Ocean. Like good Legionnaires, we drank most of their wine reserves on the long voyage to Indonesia.

During that long trip across the Indian Ocean, we did some training up on deck each day to keep busy. We even did some target practice off the back of the ship using moving targets in the water. Lots of photos were taken as usual.

One afternoon we were all aligned up on deck with our black boots polished and our white Kepis on. All the other French troops were there too. Together we all made a formation in the shape of a fish and in the shape of the word "BERYX." A helicopter flew overhead taking photos. We were part of Operation Beryx, a humanitarian mission to assist the local population on the island of Sumatra.

That navy vessel, the helicopter carrier Joan of Arc, remained off the coast of Sumatra. We landed at the coastal town of Meulaboh by rubber dingy. We were on the west coast of the island of Sumatra. That region had been exposed to the full force of the tsunami. The first day ashore, we set up our camp along the water's edge. The Surrounding Sea looked dirty and there was much debris floating in it. We soon witnessed the scale of the devastation. Most buildings were levelled to the ground. There were masses of timber and debris everywhere.

As I was the only English speaking Legionnaire in our section, I accompanied the Capitaine (CNE) for much of the time. The CNE had little or no English. I acted as a translator when he met with international NGOs and local Government agencies. We made contact with the local task force and with the local control office. A plan was set up for how we could be of assistance there.

For those few weeks on land, we went to local schools that were affected. At the schools, we done repairs and repainted classrooms. Some days we helped clear roads. We cut up fallen trees using chainsaws. Supplies of food and water from the Joan of Arc were delivered by helicopter to the local population.

We didn't bring any weapons onshore. Many photos were taken. It seemed that we had to justify our presence there. The huge effort put in to getting some French troops to Indonesia seemed like a political move, a PR stunt. The place would take years to rebuild. Our efforts were minimal, a needle in a haystack.

One day, we were helping the local rescue services clear up some of the debris. Our LTN got an idea that we should stack up all the scrap wood from the most devastated areas, into large piles. His next idea was a very stupid one.

He ordered us set fire to these large mounds of timber. I still don't comprehend the logic behind it. There was the horrible stench of hidden, dead and bloated rotting bodies, all around the area among the mass of wood and debris. We wore masks, so bad was the smell. Now the LTN wanted to make bonfires all over the place. It was like bloody Halloween, a BBQ of dead bodies.

He definitely got proper bonfires because they got out of control. The fires began to engulf the whole area. Soon, we heard the sirens from pathetic mini fire engines arriving. They were small local vans carrying sea water. The LTN's face went red with the heat and embarrassment. He now looked more concerned and full of doubt regarding his innovative idea. Instead of fire-starting, he now ordered us to help the local firemen put out the fires.

For hours we helped tirelessly in the furious heat and horrendous smell, passing buckets to each other to help extinguish the fires. Again, photos were taken, seemingly showing our heroic efforts. Once back in France, we all received a letter of satisfaction from our COL, stating how we courageously extinguished a fire that risked destroying the area and its inhabitants. No one dared mention that it was a huge fire which we had started.

We spent about four weeks in Meulaboh before it was decided that we had completed our P.R. stunt and enough photos taken. I celebrated my twentieth birthday there with a 1.5 litre plastic bottle full of red wine. Every day we were given a ration of one cup of wine with our dinner. I had saved up a week's ration in the plastic bottle leading up to my birthday.

By chance, I had that day as a rest day off work. I went away from the camp to a quiet place by the ocean to be on my own. Watching the sunset, with the welcoming numbness of that plastic bottle of wine, the end of those five years seemed an awful long time away. But at least another chapter was over. The next day we were leaving.

By the end of the few weeks in Indonesia, we all had a pain in our bollocks as usual. We were glad to get back on the Joan of Arc, knowing that we were going back to France soon enough. The ship sailed around the Island of Sumatra towards Malaysia. We docked at a port close to Kuala Lumpur. We were each given three hundred US Dollars and told we had forty eight hours of time off - Quartier Libre. That was great news.

We showered and dressed into our civy clothes. We headed in to Kuala Lumpur on the local train. Then we broke up into little groups when we got there. The Soviets stuck together as did the Romanians. My Chilean friend Martinez and I made our own way around the city.

We booked ourselves a large two bedroom hotel suite. We found the Hard Rock café in Kuala Lumpur and got stuck into a meal of burger and chips, washing it down with a few large jugs of beer. Once our bellies were satisfied, our attention turned to getting laid.

We went around different bars drinking beer and eventually we picked up two prostitutes, which wasn't difficult. Back in our hotel suite, they were demanding more money than we had left. There was no bargaining with them and eventually we just kicked them out, not wanting to cause a scene.

The frustration built up from life in the Legion seemed to manifest into sexual compulsion. It was normal but at the same time, it was not. Along with alcohol, Sex became a way of calming or escaping my inner malaise. This inner malaise was difficult to put into words. For me, it was a sort of boredom but it was also a sad loneliness, a deep longing.

On leaving the Legion and as an ex-Legionnaire, this inability to experience simple everyday pleasures, along with a hyper sensitivity created a chronic irritability. Whether this itchy irritability was caused by alcohol and sexual compulsion or soothed by these two, is a hard question to answer. I feel that they are both sides of the same coin, a coin that must be melted down. This misalignment or distortion of myself, created an inner demon. A complete mental breakdown was required in order to heal. The result would be a re-forging of that coin into something beyond the material. The process that was left to complete would be to recover my displaced soul and allow myself to address my human need for true intimacy.

Dismantling an identity is a fearful process. Dismantling my Legionnaire's identity involved calming the noise in my head. I learned that boredom and irritability arouse out of an inability to relax. Fear and trauma were entangled into the whole bloody mess too.

LA JONQUERA

Back in France, I settled into routine life at the 1REG barracks. There was always some course or other to complete. I lived for the weekends. I counted down the days to every leave of absence - Permission long durée (PLD). I had made some friends in my Company by this stage. Sometimes we would go out on the weekends together.

My first visit to a real brothel was just over the border in Spain. There were five of us, an Australian, a Finish, An American, an Austrian and myself. It was a long weekend. It started with a Friday night out in Avignon, in a nightclub. The main thing I remember of that night was the Aussie chap. He was a real character. He was the joker in the group and even though he was wild and unpredictable, we all got a good laugh out of him. His party piece that night was "the seal" and he flapped around the dance floor on his belly. You couldn't hold a straight face at the sight it.

The next day, we all took a train down to Perpignan, drinking on the way of course. Arriving there, we paid a taxi to take us the thirty minute trip over the border with Spain, to the village of La Jonquera. There were a good few of Hotels and restaurants there as the area was known as a stop off place for truckers. We checked into our hotel and then went straight to a nearby restaurant. It was evening time by then. After a meal of Steak and chips and a few rounds of drinks, we ordered a large taxi to take us two kilometres up the highway to the renowned 'Lady Dallas' club.

The Finnish chap warned us not to bother too much with

drinking inside as the prices were really expensive. The whole idea of the place was to get in, get laid and get out. On arrival, it was a sight to behold. With all those neon lights, the lounge area was full with about forty women, the majority of which were in their twenty's and genuinely stunning. It seemed too good to be true. Many were from Eastern Europe. There were blonds, brunettes, and redheads and their bodies appeared smooth, toned and delicious. They wore skimpy clothing or bikinis of colours from pink to florescent green and orange. They were electric in the neon lighting.

We ordered one overpriced drink each and took in the sights from the bar. Leaning on the bar, I scanned the area and realised there was at least fifteen beautiful girls that already caught my eye. Before long, the way things were done became clear. By hanging out at the bar or sitting at a table, a girl would come up and ask you to buy her a drink. If she wasn't your type you could politely decline.

Soon enough, a young beauty approached. I guessed by her accent that she was from Romania. By now the five of us had all split up. We had agreed to meet up in an hours' time. I didn't need to think twice, there was an instant sexual attraction. We agreed the price. I took her hand and she led me off, as was the way things were done.

The place was run very smoothly. Towels, condoms and a room key were given at a little reception area before we made our way towards one of the many ensuite rooms. Any drinks were decanted into plastic cups. It was strange how effective and normal the whole process felt. And the feeling inside was definitely one that could become addictive.

After we were all satisfied, the plan was to head back to the village and continue drinking. Then maybe we would even return again later that night. But now the group had splintered. Me, the American and the Austrian decided to leave and go back to the village ourselves. The hour was passed and there was no sign of the other two lads.

The American was a new LEG but not a young man. He enlisted at thirty nine years old and he was now forty. His knees were bothering him with all the running in the Legion. His knees weren't any stronger now with all the drinking and shagging.

Just as the three of us were about to leave the club, he pulls out a small disposable camera. One of those throwaway plastic ones you get at a pharmacy. Immediately, I knew it was a stupid idea.

He starts snapping photos of the bar and around the place. In an instant, the two barmen hopped over the counter. In less than a few seconds, the American was lying on his back with his hands up defending himself as three huge security guards and the two barmen were pulling at him trying to get the camera off him. The Austrian and I felt guilty that we didn't do much to help him but it was a hopeless situation. After the rapid commotion, we helped him up to his feet and the three of us were thrown outside. It all happened so quickly. Somehow, he had managed to hold onto the camera but his shirt was torn and he had a few scuffs. That was my introduction to an organised brothel. Everything runs smoothly until you do something stupid.

But I still would end up going back there again, the following year, on my own. Even though I got a nice girl and was pleased temporarily, I realised how lonely and depressing it was without the group of lads. The trip down on the train together, the meal, the drinking, the craic, and the friendship, the comedown pints and banter afterwards were all part of the experience.

That night we all met up in a bar back near the Hotel. We found the other two lads. Listening all the boasting that went on afterwards; the Finnish giant had two girls, one was screaming in orgasm and the other wrapped around his head, never mind the Aussie guy's orgy, you would swear they were Pornstars!

CASTELNAUDARY

I was one of two selected from my company to undergo Radio and Signals training - Stage transmissions. I left for the 4RE in Castelnaudary not knowing that I would spend the next seven months or so there. As soon as I was finished my transmissions course of four months duration, my Chef de Section, an ADJ, informed me that I would be returning almost immediately to the 4RE to complete my Caporals course of ten weeks duration.

It seemed that I was being fast tracked into training and promotion. But I had already started to doubt if I wanted a career in the Legion. Returning to Castel after only one week of PLD, my motivation was minimal. I just about made it through my Caporals course.

In my five years of service, I spent almost one year at the 4RE. This included four months in basic training, four months in Radio and signals training, about three months on my Corporal's course and two weeks on a driving course getting my rigid truck licence. My time on my Caporals course was made worse by what had happened during my PLD after my Radio and signals course. It played on my mind.

I had arrived back in Dublin unofficially to surprise my family. I was supposed to stay in France during that short PLD but I went home. It was strange being back at my family home in Dublin where I had left over a year and a half before. I had forgotten how much I once wanted to get away from them all. But in truth, I did miss my little brother dearly. My parents and two brothers were still living there. I thought maybe things would change now that I was a Legionnaire. But I was only fooling myself. My childhood was long over and there was no second chance at childhood.

That afternoon when I arrived to the house I once called home without notice; there was a lot of stress in the household. I arrived at just the right time or wrong time depending on how you look at it. My father was in the middle of a nervous breakdown. He had been trying to build a second house in the back garden. While trying to take on this huge task, he had gone days without sleep. He was now in a hypomanic confused state in the back garden, talking to himself and he was very agitated. The sounds of him revving the chainsaw added to the anxiety in the house. He seemed possessed. My mother was still stuck in her cowardly approach. She was living there with my two brothers in a state of toxic fear. It was no situation for anyone to be in.

Instead of taking time to relax on my brief holiday, I was there to assist in breaking up a dysfunctional family. When I saw how bad the situation was, I ordered my mother and brothers out of the house. We all walked up the road away from that very uncomfortable environment.

That was the beginning of my mother separating from my father. The next few days he would spend some time in St. Patrick's Mental Hospital. He was very resistant to treatment. He denied that he was mentally ill. He could not admit it. It was too hard for him to let his whole life and the lie that held it together, crumble down in front of him. He was diagnosed with Bipolar disorder and had just experienced a hypomanic episode. But he likely had a glimpse of ultimate truth and it was too overwhelming for him to grasp. There was too much accumulated fear that denied Gods love to shine through his tormented mind. The buck would be passed on to me, the sins of our fathers; I would have the opportunity to break through the veil of God some years later.

All of his life he had never taken responsibility for his behaviour. As a result, our family home environment was always tense. It was a toxic environment of fear and anxiety. He had never accepted or looked for help for his issues and we all bore the brunt of it. Uncannily, this was all meant to be. I may have well inherited the genetic basis for a mental disorder from my parents, but I was willing to take responsibility for my mental state. I was faced with carrying the sins of generations and generations of both fathers and mothers. But, I was given the opportunity to break the cycle, the cycle of madness, fear and delusion, the cycle of Samsara.

As a way of healing and finding my misplaced soul, I finally realised that I had to separate myself from some family members. Without that, the cycle of dysfunction would continue. But this realisation only came after my own complete mental breakdown years later. Complex family dynamics were affecting my mental state. In the cloud of family roles and dysfunctional relationships, I could never access peace of mind.

The question of forgiveness is one that I was faced with as I felt and carried guilt for taking the extreme measure of cutting my parents from my life. Forgiveness cannot be forced upon someone. It comes largely from a religious ideology. As far as I was concerned, I didn't have to forgive and I didn't have to hate either. Forgiveness stops when blaming stops. There is not a demanding God the Father commanding us to forgive another demanding physical father. There is no greater power or law besides our true Self, which is God. Trusting in my own decisions in the course of life turns the question of forgiveness into an irrelevant one. Acceptance is a better goal. Accepting the past and moving on to a better life, a life of love that every one of us deserves is the only way forward. We deserve to be loved but only when we stand up for this right.

Our childhood is a precious time. The gift of timeless love

to us from our ancestors is always with us, all of our lives. It is a love that belongs to us all despite it sometimes being hidden by terrible and abusive situations. It is forever present but it will slip through the hands of any greedy person who attempts to keep it for themselves. It is formless and unconquerable. It is both the fire in your belly and the fire in your head. It is the foundation of your integrity, powerfully untouchable. It is the beautiful madness that drives us to procreate. It is who you really are.

Back in the Legion, it was said that Anglophones make good transmitters. Anglophone is the French term used to categorise those people whose native tongue move English words. I was an Anglophone, although I always felt that Gaeilge was in my blood and spirit.

Generally, for some reason, Anglophones made the best Radio operators in the Legion. I'm not sure why that is but maybe it's because we usually had some brains in our head. I had a "Niveau Général" rating of sixteen out of twenty which indicated that I had some intelligence. At least I had enough common sense to know how to use the radio equipment and an ability to pick up Morse code quickly.

Before being selected to go to the 4RE, we, the potential future transmitters from the 1REG were given a test in Morse code. Eight of us were brought into the CCL Communications station to have a trial run with Morse code. We were being tested on our ability to listen to and decipher the sounds. The CCH in charge was a huge man, an interesting New Zealand Maori. He showed off his ability with the Morse language, scribbling down what he heard from a rapid succession of beeps. And then, by using his thumb and forefinger on a small metal device, he replied with an equally fast succession of beeps.

From my Company, there was Mulder, a small Dutchman if there ever was one, and myself, chosen to go on the next Radio and signals course at the 4RE in Castelnaudary. We left for Castel straight after the annual Camerone weekend (On the 30th of April every year, the Legion commemorates the battle of Camarón, Mexico 1863).

Our training section for the Radio and signals course at the 4RE was comprised of about twenty five of us from different regiments.

Fast forward four months later and it's the day before our passing out parade in front of the Colonel (CDC). A pig faced French CCH pulls me aside. He tells me that I have finished top of the class and that I have been chosen as "Major de Stage." I will be called out of the ranks on the square the next day to be presented with the award by the CDC. I will salute the Colonel and accept the award. Then I will lead the section away, marching. I was very happy with the news. It gave my confidence a huge lift. But hope didn't last long in the Legion.

When the time came the next day, a young polish chap was called from the ranks to receive Major de stage instead of me. I was peering out from the back row with a thumping headache, feeling like shit. There were ten fresh and messy stiches on the back of my head just below the rim of my snow white Kepi. I could detect the scent of both yesterday's beer from the pissup we had and Savon de Marseille from the routine cleaning of my Kepi. I stood there, hidden in the back row, as my spirit faded into a black void. The night before was one to forget.

As customary, the day before the passing out parade, our frustrations were quenched with cases of Kronenbourg, and cases of Heineken. It started early in the afternoon. 1CL Mulder got drunk quickly. That same pigfaced CCH took a dislike to him and insisted that he leave the gathering. Then he told me that Mulder was a dirt bag and that I should not associate myself with him. However, I felt some loyalty to Mulder as we were both from the same Company; the 1CIE of the 1REG.

The drinking continued into Friday evening. Dinner time arrived for those few of us wanting solids. Later that evening, we all had a good cure. Before dismissal for the evening, we were aligned as a section in the corridor of our billets. The CCH and SGT were rambling on whatever stuff they talked about. Then all of a sudden, 1CL Mulder stepped forward out of line for no reason, probably just being smashed drunk and acting the idiot. Without delay, he was grabbed by the CCH and SGT and brought into a nearby room. It appeared to me that he was going to get a beating. I stepped out of line to go and intervene. In the messy haze of events I approached the room and entered, meeting the SGTs disapproval. His two hands slammed into my chest driving me back with a cruel force. I fell back hard, landing on the ground in the corridor. My head, with a splitting thump, opened on the sharp door frame.

After the initial shock, I felt concerned hands carry me towards the shower in one of the rooms as my head was bleeding profusely. With my head bent under the flow of water, and the water rushing in front of my face, I saw red. I felt my body heat up with anger as I mentally processed the event. People now gathered around me including the CCH and SGT.

Pretending to feel better and communicating calmness, I exited the shower with my sports clothes drenched wet and stained in blood. But as I got close enough to the SGT, I unleashed my drunk and wet corpse with fury. I swung desperately hoping to reach his face. The first contact felt hard and instantly satisfying. I needed more.

In the mess of scuffles, roars, and smothering arms, I was wrestled down to the floor and my emotion contained. After some time, the firm hold of many controlling hands relaxed, as I faked my surrender. I was allowed to stand up. Again, I let go of self-control, swinging fists like a brat with a valid excuse.

An innocent Caporal de Semaine who had come to see what all the noise was, tasted my hurt and tasted my fist. But I soon gave up the fight and its lost cause. My body went spent and I surrendered for real.

Finding myself at the infirmary, I was met with a skinhead CCH and his face of disapproval, a face worse than pig face. His rudeness along with what I can only describe as a sourdough face irritated me. With an aggressive and mean tone and in his Slavic accent, he ordered me to take a seat. Then he ordered a trainee LEG on a medic's course to commence the stitching on my head. I felt my own anger heating up.

My thick stubbornness took over and I refused to be treated by the trainee. I looked sourdough in the face and demanded that a medical officer perform the stitches. His face turned from sourdough to beetroot. He screamed some abuse and violent threats towards me. His screams echoed through the shit building like a filthy father. I could sense his desire to assault me.

An Adjudant Chef (ADC) soon arrived in civy clothes, but no doctor, no officer. I compromised and giving his thirty years plus of service, I bowed my head to get stitched up, wondering if the next sensation of pain would come from a needle or his black boot kicking my teeth in. The stitches felt rough but sweet as I let a salty tear reach my lip.

I spent seven days in the 4RE prison before re-joining my Regiment. I was not expecting it, but the ADJ of my section back at the 1CIE in the 1REG was almost hinting at a slight approval towards my attempt to defend a fellow first Company transmitter.

After the short PLD in Ireland and freeing my family from that hell house, I returned to Castel to complete my Caporals Course. My motivation was low but I pulled through.

At two years of service, I got my situation rectified which

meant that Legionnaire 1CL Sims was no more. It took a while for 1CL Stefanazzi and then CPL Stefanazzi to catch on. I would still hear the name Sims echo through the corridors but less and less until he vanished.

I was glad to finish for good in Castel. I was becoming more certain that I wouldn't stay more than five years in the Legion so there would be no reason to return there again.

I was now in a position, and only slightly, of authority being a CPL. My first task was to organize and oversee my section, the first section of the 1CIE of the 1REG, building our Christmas Crib.

We decorated a whole room in the style of our mission to Indonesia. The room was darkened. We put sand on the floor. Two LEGs made a large cardboard model of the Joan of Arc ship, which we had travelled to Indonesia on. We stuck some palm tree leaves around the room to give the impression of Sumatra. There were tools that we used during the operation, like chainsaws, pick axes and shovels, paintbrushes and rollers, on display in the room. A laptop screen had a slide show, showing photos from our time there. The theme music from the movie Gladiator played in the background to add to the atmosphere. In the middle of it all was a little wooden crib waiting for the arrival of baby Jesus.

Our sections crib was impressive. We finished second overall in the regiment, out of twelve cribs. That was my first task as CPL in my section. I enjoyed the creative aspect of it. But as the months passed, it would prove more difficult being a twenty year old CPL and ordering people around who were sometimes twice my age. I was very much on the side of the LEGs rather than on the side of the NCOs and that was a difficult act to balance.

Christmas Eve came and I was officially presented with my CPL stripes during our Christmas party. Christmas was a strange time in the Legion. Every member of the 1CIE got a gift. The Capitaine (CNE) called us up individually, one by one in the dining hall. He gave us our gift and wished us happy Christmas while the whole company applauded.

After the evening meal, the drinks continued. During this particular Christmas party, many guys started dancing around the room in the form of a train. If you can imagine a trail of legionnaires placing their hands on each other's shoulders, kicking out their legs, as they danced around the large dining hall, it was a funny sight. I wasn't really in the mood for such things. I felt the whole thing was a bit silly. The drinking would continue late into the night back at the 1CIE bar. I really just wanted to go to my room instead, and sleep. I wasn't feeling the Christmas spirit.

Just as I tried to sneak off, the LTN ordered me to go and present myself to all the NCOs in the bar and to have a beer with them. This was the standard thing to do after a promotion. I obeyed and went down to the Company bar where everyone there was very drunk. I had a beer with whatever NCOs were still around. It would have been better to do it another time as most of the NCOs had gone home. Those diehards who were still left at the bar were pissed drunk. It was a waste of time.

The next morning was the 25th of December. Traditionally, that morning involved the NCOs doing the cleaning duties for a change. Roles are reversed. They also bring us up breakfast; coffee and croissants. For one morning of the year, the LEGs order them around as they clean the toilets and corridors. It's a bit of fun. But it doesn't last long and the real cleaning up from the night before begins, which is up to us. Until midday we clean thoroughly until there is no sign of the party from the night before. Then we are all free to leave on two weeks PLD.

I remember that particular Christmas day, my third one in the Legion, leaving the base and going into Avignon with a slight hangover. The streets were deserted. It was cold and most places are shut. With no way to fly back to Dublin on Christmas day, I had a pretty sad Christmas alone in a hotel. The next day, St. Stephens' day, I got a flight to Dublin.

My mother now had a place of her own with my two brothers. They were away from the hell of living with my father. Sadly, my older brother was now turning into the bully than my dad was. He took on a role similar to him. Their freedom was too good to be true so he sabotaged it. From one dysfunctional household to another, nothing ever changes. And once again the coward, my mam, enabled this to continue. I had always felt sorry for my younger brother who couldn't just get up and leave like I did. But I was angry too. I felt that I had to take on the task of sorting my family out. It wasn't my job to do.

Christmas became a time of unease and inconsistency for me. Before the Legion and after the Legion, it was a time which I dreamt about. I fantasized of a warm and loving time within a happy family. It became a time that I would no longer celebrate or believe in. I remember each Christmas that I spent in the Legion. Each one was different.

The first one was in the 4RE in Castelnaudary, towards the end of basic training. I was introduced to an Irish CCH who was from Dublin and we had a beer together. The second Christmas was in Djibouti and it was very hot. The third one, I have just mentioned previously with the building of the crib. For the fourth one, I was locked away in the regimental prison. I remember the CNE coming over with presents for the prisoners. It felt pathetic. For the last Christmas, I was doing company service at the reception for a week. I was actually glad to avoid the party. It was unremarkable. The SGT on duty and I were brought our Christmas dinners on a tray. On Saint Stephens' day, we were relieved from duty and free to take our PLD.

During those five years I did not spend any Christmas day back in Ireland. Those from before the Legion had mostly faded in my memory. My fondest part of childhood Christmases was how I used to enjoy my younger brother's excitement in the morning while we opened presents together. He was eight years old when I left him. When I returned from the Legion, it was different.

It was difficult for me, seeing my brother grow up so quickly. My sense of him had remained frozen in that eight year old boy I left behind when I fled to France. He was no longer that child anymore. My parents had separated and my father was no longer present at Christmas which at least made it stress free. But I didn't want to take on the role of playing father either.

Christmas became boring. I had begun to dislike it. It just became a day that I would prefer to get drunk or avoid all together. I hated the hypocrisy of it. Why was I sitting around a table pretending to be happy with a mother and older brother for whom I had very little respect? I owed them nothing. I was only there for the sake of my younger brother and he was a kid no more. Christmas gradually became meaningless to me.

COËTQUIDAN

The most difficult experience of those five years was not serving overseas or the duties which I performed as a soldier. It was an incident which happened during in France. Three fellow CPLs entered my bedroom and beat me up. The psychological effect of that was worse than anything else I experienced in the Legion.

I had just turned twenty one. I had already been a new CPL for a few months. I was attached to a different section of my company for a training manoeuvre. Nobody wanted to be attached to the second Section of the 1CIE. It had a bad reputation. But I didn't have much say in the matter. I was sent to assist them as they needed an extra CPL.

We set off for *Coëtquidan* in the North West of France. It was the home of the Saint-Cyr academy, used for training French cadet officers. We would be at the complete service of the cadets, performing their field manoeuvres.

I was assigned as CPL and infantry team leader. I wasn't happy with this as my real function in the first section was as a transmitter. I had already grown tired of Infantry training. In *Coëtquidan*, we were effectively at the disposal of the Special military training school of Saint-Cyr to be used as pawns. The future officers were completing their field exams in infantry warfare.

Our own LTN, the CDS of the second section was a young skinny Frenchman. He had only graduated from Saint-Cyr a few years previously himself. His eyes had a twisted look and his smile was creepy. I never liked him from the start. He was imposing his own version of authority on our section during our time there. The days spent out on the field were long. In the evenings we had little time to rest back at our billets. Moral was low within the section.

One day the LTN said that he had found one of our trucks unguarded. There were guns and other materials in the back of it. The blame was put on all the CPLs, five of us. He said that we would have to pay for this. He ordered that all the CPLs would bring the Section out that night and pay for two kegs of beer in the local bar.

I refused to go out to the bar with them. I disagreed with the collective responsibility and the blame that the LTN placed on us, that the trucks had been left unguarded. I was also tired and fed up with the Infantry duties. I wanted to rest that evening.

Before I had gone there to *Coëtquidan*, I had also made a personal decision to use those six weeks, to give up alcohol. It happened to fall during the period of Lent. I didn't feel part of this other section. I was only attached to help them to help out for those six weeks. I was looking forward to getting back to my own section in the 1CIE.

We were already three weeks into it at this point when it happened. That particular day was a long day of running around playing soldiers, camouflaged up with all our gear. The hours dragged by. Large amounts of time were spent kneeling on the roadside, hiding, pointing our guns while young officers were tested by older officers. I had already begun to grow tired of the whole thing and the stupid roles we played over and over again. When I refused to go out that night with them to the bar, I paid the price with a vicious assault.

There was an Albanian CCH with the section who took himself as a commando. He liked to show off his skills, running around during the day. He acted as if he was a ninja. He was more like a big kid. When things didn't go his way on manoeuvres, he would curse and throw his weapon on the ground. The rumours were that he was kicked out of the 2REP, the parachutist regiment of the Legion. Our Engineering regiment was known for receiving oddballs from other regiments who had messed up. I had a sense that it was him who put pressure on the three CPLs to "Sort me out." There was one other CPL, a decent chap from Poland who didn't get involved in the attack.

I was in my room organising my gear for the next day. The three CPLs entered into my room slowly. They told the few LEGs who were sharing the room with me, to leave. The LEGs left. I knew then what was coming. I was cornered in my room and I felt sick. In that trio, there was a sly arrogant French chap who was taller than me. There was a big fat German guy who kept his head shaved bald. And there was a dark-haired slimy Slovakian. He was the quiet one, easily influenced. I was only twenty one years old and they were all in their thirties. They were gutless to have done what they done.

As they approached me, the French guy first, he said something like "You owe us money for the kegs of beer but it's too late now." For a split second, I saw in his eyes and by the tone of his voice, a confusing mix of anger and nervousness. Then the three of them pounced. I made a futile attempt to defend myself but they surrounded me and I was knocked to the floor, followed by a flurry of kicks and punches. I did my best to cover my head during the assault. I was punched stamped and kicked all over for what felt like an eternity. I felt my body seize up, rigid with fear. Eventually they left, and I laid there for some time.

After the feeling of relief that I was still alive, emotion flooded my shocked body. Feeling sore, angry and disgusted, I slowly realised what had happened. I felt betrayed, vulnerable and worthless. I felt utterly ashamed of myself when I became aware of my soiled pants. The Legion, its promises and ideals, amounted to nothing. Its camaraderie was built on fear with a code of honour that I no longer believed in. The myths of the Legion that were built up in exaggerated French glory were now but a dirty lie. The Legions fake ideals all came crumpling down as they beat me up and I shit my pants. That was the end of my Legion Loyalty.

As a Legionnaire, you are expected not to think, just do. That's exactly what they done. I had the shit kicked out of me literally.

Sore and helpless, I picked myself up and made my way to the shower. I binned my soiled underwear, took a hot shower, and changed into fresh sports clothes. With the adrenaline still flowing through my bruised body, my temper rose. I felt at that exact moment in time, if given an opportunity, I could really kill those three men regardless of the outcome.

There were several rooms for the soldiers. Each room had one CPL and three to four LEGs. The CCH shared a room with the SGTs and SCH. The LTN had his own room. Downstairs there was a small club bar set up in a hall where you could watch television.

I went downstairs and approached the club bar where all the NCOs were gathered. I asked the SCH at the doorway if I could speak with the LTN. The LTN came out to me in the corridor with his twisted grin. I attempted to explain how I had just been beaten up and that it was unacceptable. He dismissed everything I said with no acknowledgment whatsoever, as if I was speaking a different language. He diverted the conversation, informing me that the following morning I was on duty and that I was to have everyone ready for assembly at seven forty five a.m.

I felt belittled and helpless. I had lost any faint amount of confidence in these people. As far as I was concerned, they were all scum, just like the shit in my pants. I was hopeless.

Returning to my room, broken mentally and physically, I felt that, if they were going to beat me up then they should go all the way. I wanted to die. In that hopeless state of mind, I had nothing more to lose. Fuck it. Let's see if I can get those cowards back one on one.

Although younger than all three by a good margin, I felt I could take them on one at a time. I approached the Germans room and peered inside. He was alone with two LEGs. Here's my chance. Storming into the room I ordered the two Legionnaires to get lost. Now it's my turn. He reminded me of a fat NAZI pig. I landed a punch straight in and we danced around the room like it was a boxing ring.

I felt faster and ready for a fight to the death. Then suddenly out of nowhere, I felt hands around my neck. The Slovakian CPL had sneaked into the room and grabbed me from behind. The Nazi used this opportunity. He ran at me, rugby tackling me to the ground. I found myself again powerless and receiving a second beating. The Slovakian kicked and kicked me in the head as the German, while holding me in a tight headlock, screamed into my face with his foul breathe. "I'm going to cut your balls off with my combat knife" He growled. He sounded as if he meant it too. The Slovakian sneaked away and the Nazi let go of his tight neck hold just before I passed out. I was truly beaten.

I crawled back to my room with more bruises, helpless and numb. My shame had only slightly eased by my attempt to get them back. I sat on my bed. I escaped into a world of imagination to avoid the pain of reality. I imagined myself with live ammunition and holding my FAMAS. I wondered would I really do it and blow them all away. Then I imagined and fantasized another scenario. This time I had no ammunition. I was standing over them as they slept in their sleeping bags out on the ground. In that fantasy, I used the butt end of my rifle and pounded their faces into a mushy pulp with all my might. I couldn't decide which one would be first.

For some time, I indulged in the small comforts that such imagination provided. It was the only form of escape I had of dealing with it. Regrettably, I did nothing about that attack. With hindsight, I should have gone directly to the Police that night and filed a complaint against those three men. But at twenty one years old, I was unaware of my rights. As a Legionnaire, I felt that I had none, or so I believed.

That evening was a major turning point in my five years in the Legion. I was only half way through my five year contract. Fast paced Legion life continued and I never had the chance to process that event effectively. It sure left an emotional scar.

Many years later that event would resurface in the form of twisted nightmares. It is something that never leaves me. It manifests through an everyday anxiety that appears unexplainable. As a result of that trauma, I learned to avoid macho male personalities. Any sniff of aggression and I feel my body going into flight or fight mode. Emotional numbness and difficulty experiencing pleasure have been further side effects of that attack.

Only a few days after the attack, a French SGT started getting on my case. He was probably involved along with the Albanian CCH in influencing the attack on me. He pulled me aside one day. With a load of insults in his best French slang, he told me how bad I was at my job. In a mean voice which expressed his twisted satisfaction in my suffering he said "I don't need to get three CPLs to kick your head in, I'll do it myself."

He was a thin ragged looking French man. I hated him so much. The sight of him alone made me sick. Usually I could avoid him as he was in the second section. These were the kind of people that gave that section its bad reputation. I was glad to finish those six weeks of hell at Saint-Cyr in *Coëtquidan*, and return to my own section. But one day months later, that same SGT and I were assigned to twenty four hour guard duty together.

The guard duty was to begin on a Saturday morning. He came to see me on the Friday afternoon, letting me know that he would be inspecting our uniforms at five p.m. that evening. The three 1CLs and I had our uniforms ironed perfectly when he arrived for the inspection. I could smell the drink off him as he staggered into our bedroom. It was clear that he'd been on the piss since lunchtime. He had a reputation for being an alcoholic and a "Chiffon."

The lads were looking forward to getting off base for the evening before our guard duty started early the next morning. Five p.m. was dismissal time on a Friday for the whole regiment. Some of the guys had girlfriends in town. But the SGT was only interested in getting pissed drunk in the club bar and giving us as much hassle as he could.

He pulled the perfectly ironed uniforms off their hangers, trampling them on the floor under his boots. He called me aside, spitting insults into my face and threatening to kill me if the uniforms were not ready by nine p.m. He left us and staggered off to the club bar to continue drinking.

My body had filled up with adrenaline. I didn't care anymore. We spent a quick half hour getting another set of uniforms ready. After that, I told the lads to do what they wanted. They could go out in town if they pleased. I would take responsibility.

I waited in vain until nine p.m. preparing myself for a scrap with that rat of a man. I was mentally preparing to leave him in a coma and then face the consequences which could be my own death. I had a Hurley stick in my room that I was really considering using on him. But of course, he never turned up. The adrenaline of anticipation which built up inside me meant that I hardly slept at all that night.

Early the next morning, myself and the three 1CLs were all perfectly dressed and waiting at the armoury. We were there earlier than usual to collect our guns. We were supposed to meet the SGT there. Half an hour went by and he never showed up. We could not wait any longer. We had to go change the guard without him. We took our guns and went towards the guardroom at the entrance to the base. The other SGT who was coming down off guard duty that morning was not pleased. He had to stay on for an extra two hours until the ragged French SGT eventually arrived.

The "Chiffon" eventually arrived to the guard post smelling like a rat and his clothes in tatters. He made no eye contact with me. He looked pitiful as he handed me his badges, asking would I pin them on his jacket. We sat together in the guardroom that morning without saying a word to each other. At one point I played again with the thought of going over and kicking the living shit out of him. But I knew I would never get away with it.

ANTARES

Around halfway through my five year service, Legion life had become a real struggle for me. Since getting attacked at *Coëtquidan*, it was impossible for me to maintain any enthusiasm or motivation. I lived in a constant state of fear and anxiety but soldiered on. I wasn't aware of this at the time but it became clearer years later. My drinking got heavier and heavier as time went on. It is likely that I was suffering from PTSD as a result of getting beaten up in *Coëtquidan*. As this remained untreated, it later developed into psychosis and eventually schizophrenia.

As I was still the newest CPL in my section, I was assigned a lot of duties. I was often asked by my LTN and CNE if I would be interested in re-signing for another contract and go on my SGTs course. I tried to avoid giving them a straight answer. I knew well that the five years would be my limit, if I even managed to reach that point. Surely they could sense that I was already starting to look forward to finishing my contract. But I didn't want to say it. I remained ambiguous around the topic of an extended contract. It was a known in the Legion that those who are not resigning a new contract generally get fucked over with every extra duty or assignment that comes around. But I was also concerned that I may not be sent to the Ivory Coast if I had made it clear to them that I had no intention of staying one day more than five years.

After all the training, I wanted to at least serve on an OPEX tour of duty (Opérations Extérieures). I might even get to use my weapon for real. Even though I had lost interest in the Legion and every day felt like a penance, I was still prepared and trained to use my weapon for real if it ever came to that. I even wanted to use it. At least then I might be able to feel something inside. It might even force me accept my role as a soldier. Maybe it would help me deal with the disgust and disillusionment I held towards the Legion. Maybe it would be the making of me. Maybe it would be the spark my soul needed to give up all my mental struggles and submit mind body and spirit to the Legion. Maybe if I used my weapon for real, all doubts would vanish and my brain would be washed clean of any weakness, any civilian mentality. Then there would be no way back. This would be the rebirth, a real Legionnaire.

But in those five years, I never used my weapon in combat. I might have come close but I never actually pulled the trigger or had to. I just wonder would it have changed things.

That summer in France I was close to three years of Service. Our company were due to go to the Ivory Coast for four months. Before leaving France, we went on a week's training manoeuvre in Antares - a military training zone. The idea was to practise our operational capacity there.

One of the SGTs in my section started to get on my case that week. He had risen quickly through the ranks and with less than five years of service, he was already SGT. He was only recently promoted. As a new SGT on the block, he was quick to prove himself. He was fully committed to the Legion. At least it seemed that way. When he became SGT, it was as if a whole different person inhabited his body. When he was still a CPL, I used to admire him. I thought he was a decent guy. That view was shattered along with my own consideration of a Legion career. A small, dark-haired chap from Turkey, he always excelled at sports and he finished high up on his SGTs course. He was full of himself and the title of SGT turned him into a right asshole. During that week in Antares, I became an easy target for him. People could already sense that my moral was broken since the recent attack. I was easy prey. In Antares he used me as a target to show off his new authority as SGT.

I was the only transmitter in the section as well as being the CPL de Jour - the main CPL on duty. One evening we were all preparing our gear for a long twelve hour night marche and infiltration exercise. We were told that there would be some mock casualties and to prepare ourselves for carrying someone on a stretcher. I knew by the sounds of it that it would be a long night. The exercise would continue well into the next afternoon before concluding. I was pretty certain that we probably wouldn't sleep at all.

I was hoping and expecting that a LEG would carry the radio instead of me as I was now CPL de jour. I will admit that I wanted things a bit easier now that I was a CPL, selfish as it may sound. There were many times as a new LEG when I had to carry the extra load of a radio and I wasn't the section transmitter.

The SGT was annoyed at me when I suggested this selfish idea. He ordered me to carry everything myself. It was not that I wanted to offload everything onto a LEG but more that I needed to be able to access the radio quickly while on the move. If it was on someone else's back I could do any necessary adjustments as we were moving along rather than continuously stopping and taking off my backpack to adjust it. Also, when the radio is placed inside a backpack, some of the dials can get turned by accident. This disturbs the signal. I had intended to share around our loads as evenly as possible. For example, someone else would carry the spare batteries which were heavy. But I wasn't even given a chance to explain this idea. The SGT didn't care. He didn't give a fuck how heavy my load was. In fact, he would relish in the idea that I would be struggling with a huge load. We had half an hour to prepare before assembly and setting off on the marche. We all went to our quarters and got geared up. All I could do was help myself.

With my full kit, rations, water, radio and batteries, the whole lot would weigh far more than anyone else had to carry. It was early summer and even though the nights would be chilly, I was sure we wouldn't be sleeping that night. We really didn't need that much gear.

To lighten up my load I didn't take my full kit. Instead, I packed the minimum that I needed into the large pockets of the harness that held the radio. The harness itself was designed with back straps and pockets so it could to be used like a sac à dos - backpack. I intended to use it as such so I left my backpack behind with anything else I didn't need. It was much better having the radio on the harness as it was easier to adjust any of the settings when necessary. The other more common option was to not use the harness but put the radio into the backpack with just the antenna sticking out. The problem with this is that every time you need to adjust the radio, you have to open up your bag to get to it. By doing this, the cable of the hand held emitter would be shortened, making it more awkward to use on the move. It was hard to keep the radio standing upright inside the backpack. It would bounce around and the antenna would get twisted, affecting the signal. Using the harness was a lot more practical. After all, the harness was designed for this reason.

With the harness, the radio was clipped in and fixed rigidly to my back and the large pockets were enough to carry all my essential kit and supplies. The antenna could extend freely and the batteries could easily be changed. Of course, the radio was waterproof and there was no problem with it being exposed to the elements. Into the large pockets of the harness, I stuffed some extra layers for the night. I had a fleece, a rain jacket, my poncho, enough rations and water for the marche. I also had four large spare batteries for the radio in the harness. In my combat vest, I had four magazines of blank ammo and two smoke grenades. Even without a full kit, it was still a heavy enough load.

We were all lined up outside in the early evening ready to set off. I noticed the SGT's disgust when he saw my ingenuity. "Où est ton putain sac à dos, Stefanazzi?" he shouted at me.

"I've all the kit that I need inside the harness. The radio signal will better like this and it's easier to make adjustments on the move" I replied. The SGT was furious. He ordered me to immediately run back to the dormitory, get my backpack, put the radio inside and leave the harness behind. His face was red and his eyes dark. He clearly didn't like my creative idea.

I went along with his orders but ignored them at the same time. I knew he just wanted me to suffer with a huge load on my back. I went back to the room as if to change my gear. But instead, I just went to the toilet for a piss. And I took my time. Any minute we would be setting off on the marche. Just as we were about to head off, I returned. I still had the harness on my back, completely disobeying his order. Nothing had changed.

In that instant, I had prepared myself mentally for an attack from the SGT. I had made my mind up that if he did have a go at me, I would unleash myself like a wild animal. I was traumatised from the beating a few months before. The next time it would happen, they would really have to kill me.

But it didn't happen. He just gave me a dirty look and said slyly "We will see about that later, Stefanazzi." At least the adrenaline I had built up would help with the marche but I was already in bad form starting off that night.

As the section transmitter, I marched alongside the LTN who was the only one who used the bloody radio. Now and then he would just demand "Radio" and I would give him the handset while I marched right beside him. The night was long with lots of stopping and starting, running here and there. I felt useless, just there to carry the radio for him. I was reminded of my idea to offload the radio onto a LEG and for a moment, I hated myself. This was turning into a bad night. On top of that, I also knew that they had something in store for me as punishment when the week was over.

At one point I stopped to change the battery. It was about four a.m. I was in a foul mood. I knew, with the new battery and a full charge, the radio would last until around midday which should be enough time. The other two batteries, I took out from the pockets of the harness. Along with the used one, I threw them away into the bush when nobody was looking. I had stopped caring. I had a sense that I was going to get some shit duties or punishment on return to the 1REG. They can add on few lost batteries to the list for my punishment. I set off again, five kilogrammes lighter.

The Turkish SGT said nothing more about my disobedience until that week in Antares was over. Arriving back to the 1REG tired, hungry, and filthy, we cleaned our guns for hours as usual. Afterwards, the SGT used cotton wool buds to inspect them. He poked in any little corner or crevice of the gun. If it came back even a little dirty which it always did, he would return two hours later. We were looking forward to the relative comfort of life at the barracks once the guns were back at the armoury and we were dismissed for the evening.

Eventually when the guns were cleaned to his liking or he wanted his own downtime, we headed over to the armoury. Queuing up outside the armoury to leave the guns back, I had almost forgotten and I hoped they had forgotten too about my run in with the SGT a few days earlier. Not a chance.

He came up to me and smiled. "You can keep your FAMAS out, Stefanazzi. You're going over to the Second Company (2CIE) to go to CENZUB for two weeks with them. They need a transmitter. You have one hour to prepare your kit and head over to the reception of the 2CIE," he said. I felt sickened. I was exhausted. Furthermore I hated that place CENZUB after the first time I went there with the 1CIE only back in January.

I completed yet again two weeks with the 2CIE in CENZUB. I was burnt out when I returned to the 1REG. Never again did I want to go back to CENZUB. Twice was enough for me.

I knew that our company would be given ten days PLD very soon before departing for the Ivory Coast. I was really looking forward to that PLD. Damn, I needed it too.

This was a very short PLD before an OPEX and we were all unhappy with that. The CNE tried to convince us that we had so much preparation to do before we left for the Ivory Coast as the reason for our short leave. But I think it was more the case of him purposely not giving guys too long a holiday. Some of us might get too comfortable on PLD and start to doubt if we really wanted to go to the Ivory Coast. But I was genuinely interested in going on a real operational tour of duty. I still needed those ten days of PLD to chill out and rest.

We had all undergone a standard full medical check-up and a round of vaccines before an OPEX. Then the week just before we could go on PLD, I got a call back to the infirmary to repeat my blood test. The doctor, a COL, informed me that my iron levels were a little low and they would need to repeat a blood test. This was on a Tuesday. They would have the results by the end of the week.

It wasn't surprising that my levels were low, having returned from three weeks out on the ground and being completely exhausted and run down. I told the COL doctor about the ten days PLD for all the 1CIE that were starting from that Friday onwards. He said "If your iron levels come back normal, I've no problem with you going on PLD, but if they are low again we might need you to stay here on the base just as a precaution. Call the infirmary Friday morning and we will have the results from your blood test. If the new results are ok, you can go on PLD."

I had already booked a flight for the coming Saturday from Marseille Airport, to go back to Ireland for ten days. Friday morning came. I went over to the infirmary nervously, to get my results. "Your results came back, CPL Stefanazzi, and your Iron levels are OK. No need for more tests. You are fit for OPEX" they informed me.

Immediately I rushed back to my sections office and informed my Chef de Section, a Polish ADJ. But I was shocked when he said that I couldn't go on PLD. I was to stay at the base and rest in my bedroom for the ten days as a precaution. He was usually a good NCO and I always looked up to him. I tried in desperation to explain to him how I had just been to the infirmary.

"My blood test came back OK this morning and the COL doctor has given me the all-clear" I said. Obviously there was a lack of communication and misunderstanding somewhere. I repeated again as clear as I could in French that the infirmary had given me the all-clear. But he wasn't even listening to me as if he had already made up his mind. Eventually he did agree to seek clarification with the CNE of the 1CIE. He said impatiently "Wait here in the office, Stefanazzi. I'll go and check with the CNE."

He came back after just two minutes and said "I just met with the CNE briefly. The CNE says that you are to stay here while the company go on PLD. Also, you have been assigned to weekly duty at the reception, and it starts this evening at five pm. Be sure you are there on time, Stefanazzi! C'est tout, tu peux disposer!"

I had looked him straight in the eye, attempting to show my disgust before I left his office. But I swallowed my frustration and remained silent. Only in my head did I say "Fuck this. What a lot of bollocks. They have been giving me crap for weeks on end. Do I really want to go on an OPEX with these people where there is a real chance of actually using our weapons?" But I said nothing except for "Oui mon Adjudant" in a flat defeated tone. My respect for him was beginning to dwindle. He was one of the only NCOs left that I actually looked up to. He usually stood up to the CNE and looked out for his Legionnaires. Overall, he was a very good CDS. The CNE however, was a right dickhead. The CNE had known of my assault a few months back at Saint-Cyr. My Aussie friend had gone straight to the CNE and told him all about it. The CNE didn't want to know. That same CNE would go on to become COL and Chef de Corps of the 1REG.

That Friday evening, the 1CIE was dismissed for PLD at four forty five pm. The lads were jumping into the showers, loud music was pumping out from our bedrooms. Everyone bar me was getting into their civy clothes; mostly jeans and t-shirts. It was a beautiful sunny evening outside. The air smelled of freedom and lynx aerosol. Everyone except me was in good form. They were going on holidays.

I sat on my bed, still dressed in my combats. I was feeling shit. In thirty minutes time, I was due to relieve the CPL downstairs who was finishing a week of permanence duty at the reception. I would be sitting there with a SGT for ten days while the building was empty and everybody else was on holiday. It seemed pointless.

Then all of a sudden, it felt like someone stuck a needle of heroin into my arm as a powerful surge of warmth flooded my entire body. Fuck it. I changed quickly into civy clothes without taking a shower and sprayed deodorant all over myself, nearly choking in the spray and the excitement of my compulsive idea. It took me less than a minute to gather some stuff for ten days PLD into a small backpack. I took my wallet and phone. I put a baseball cap on and I went down the two flights of stairs and out the back entrance of the 1CIE building so nobody would see me.

I walked straight across the square towards the main gate. Other guys were walking out too and I mingled in with them. I listened for and expected the dreaded shout from some NCO in the 1CIE who might see me - "Tu vas où là, Stefanazzi!" But it never came. I had the feeling of Déjà vu because there had been so many scenarios like this where I lived in anxiety and expected the worse. My imagination didn't help it. Neither did my compulsiveness.

At the main gate, there was a queue outside the guard's room. Every Friday evening was the same. LEGs, 1CLs and CPLs had to present themselves at the guardroom with their permission slip of paper. The SGT on duty that evening came outside and said "All the CPLs can go on ahead, you don't need to present yourselves." Four of us walked straight out the gate, leaving a long queue of legionnaires behind us.

There was a good crowd of lads from different companies gathered outside the main gate. Some were getting lifts from their girlfriends, some sharing taxis, and some just waiting and smoking. The seriousness and stress of Legion life had left their faces. They all looked very different on the other side of that large metal gate, a lot more relaxed.

I myself noticed a pattern over the years. Every time I left the base and got on a TGV- Train à Grande Vitesse, the first thing I would do was go and take a shit. Then I would walk through the aisles of the TGV towards the bar, while looking at the faces of civilians who were snug in their seats. I would think how they took for granted the safety, warmth and security of their lives. I wanted to be one of them. And I never wanted to take that security for granted once I got out of the Legion. The Legion itself was a TGV. It kept moving at a fast pace and I was seriously struggling to keep up with it.

I kept my head down as I waited outside the base. As soon as I saw that there was a spare place in one of the taxis, I jumped in immediately. Some other lads were going to the train station too.

I knew that I was going to get in a lot of trouble when I came back after the ten days. But I would deal with the consequences then and take it on the chin. I had my permission slip that was signed and stamped by the CNE the week before the decision was made that I had to stay on base. For that reason, I knew I wouldn't be declared AWOL or deserter. Having that signed piece of paper officially declared that I was on PLD.

After the ten days back in Ireland trying to relax but mostly with the aid of booze, I returned to face all those who were very annoyed and affected by my disobedience. I upset a lot of people. I was lucky not to get a few punches in the head. If it had been in the eighties or nineties I'm sure I would have gotten a few slaps all right. The CNE sentenced me to seven days in prison commencing immediately as there were only seven days left before our flight departed for the Ivory Coast. Well worth it, I reckoned.

The CNE said that he would have me released from prison right before they were leaving the base to go to the airport. I was to prepare my bags for OPEX immediately and leave them with my section. He said I was lucky that I was still going to the Ivory Coast. He would have left me behind, only that he was short a transmitter for the OPEX. I didn't really believe that but maybe it was an effort to build up my self-esteem which was rock bottom. I knew that he knew all about how I had been viciously attacked some months before but he did nothing about it. The whole 1CIE knew what had happened in *Coëtquidan*.

It is easy to say with hindsight that I should have gone

straight to the Police after the assault. But just shortly after my twenty first birthday, I was a clueless young CPL. The incident was a major turning point in my life. The fast pace at which the Legion moved meant that I was unable to effectively process it. I was traumatised. The next two and a half years after that was a major struggle. I felt myself trapped in a constant cloud of depression. Little had I known, the real struggle would continue outside the Legions gates. That was unexpected and it caught me on my blind side.

LA COTE D'IVOIRE

The Irish national flag is the same as the Ivorian flag but in reverse. The other similarities between the two countries are that their coast line is also on the Atlantic Ocean, the Catholic Church is well established there, the landscape is beautiful and they drink Guinness. Besides that, the two countries are worlds apart.

The Ivory Coast was hot and very humid. There was a large France presence there. On arrival, we stayed in camps for the first few days, set up by the French regular forces in Abidjan. Then we were assigned a specific mission. My section was posted to a small camp near the city of Bouaké.

We set off in a convoy traveling north from Abidjan. On the way up, we took in the landscape; a lot of bush, rich vegetation, some hills and some open pasture land. The earth was red; the roads were bad and the air, sticky.

As the burning orange sun was low in the sky that evening, we arrived at our camp. The previous French regular army Engineers and Infantry had recently left. Now it was the Legions posting. The 3CIE from the 2REI along with our section from the 1REG took over the camp. The base also had some personnel from the Air Force and from Logistics. The troops rotated every four months. It seemed that the camp had been up and running for a few years by the time we arrived.

Just outside the base, locals had set up little stalls, selling all sorts of handmade stuff like leather wallets and bags, African style clothing and carved woodwork. Some trusted locals were allowed onto the base. They traded with the soldiers and others helped in the kitchen. One local Ivorian visited our section regularly and always replied "Oui Chef" to any demand or whatever we asked of him.

One CPL in my section was particularly fond of the drink, and often he had the local bring him cheap bottles of whiskey. Maybe it was the fact that the CPL was from West Africa himself that caused him to drink hard while he was there. Being on duty in a neighbouring country similar to home probably wasn't easy for him.

I asked that same local chap to get me a machete made, with my name sewn into the leather casing. He got it made for a reasonable price. But years later it went missing during a period when I was mentally ill. My parents must have gone through my possessions and hid it away. I never got it back, or asked for it. Since I left the Legion, I've slowly given away, donated, or discarded items that I first brought back with me.

I donated many items to Collins Barracks Museum in Dublin. A good friend of mine who served five years in the 2REI told me that the curator of the museum was interested in a Foreign Legion uniform. But my friend wanted to hold on to his uniform as it held sentimental value for him. Instead, I was happy to donate mine. It was a proud moment when I went in to the Museum one day to see my uniform on display behind a glass panel. Looking at my uniform with my name badge still on it, mounted upon a headless mannequin, it gave me a sense of separation with that past life and my old self.

All that I'm left with now are some photos, my memories and a few medals. The medals look nice but because I never fired my gun, I sometimes feel they mean nothing. Five years in the Legion and it has taken me another ten years on the outside to get my head straight. So I can only guess what twenty five years of service would have done. Probably my head wasn't straight before joining anyway. A good friend once told me; whoever joins the legion probably wasn't right in the head before and would surely not be right in the head afterwards. But I eventually had to come to terms with my time there and accept it as part of my life journey. If not, I would probably end up drinking myself to death or committing suicide, whichever came first.

Despite sometimes regretting my time there, I still needed to accept it as a chapter in my life. I became a member of the French Foreign Legion Association of Ireland as a way of accepting it as a defining chapter in my life. It was good to meet with others who had moved on and made something with their lives after the Legion.

Sometimes, I count myself fortunate that I've actually pulled through, when I hear the sad news of an ex-Legionnaire that has committed suicide. There is a saying "Once a legionnaire always a legionnaire." Even though I try not to buy into that, there is a certain amount of truth to it. It points to the struggle of redefining oneself after having lived such a structured and definite lifestyle. An environment which is very black and white, fast-paced and dislikes uncertainty or ambiguity becomes the norm. The aim of the Legion is to transform men into soldiers who are willing to die for the Legion. When one exits the Legion this transformation must be dismantled if possible. It's not that this transformation must be reversed in order to move on from it, but rather that it must be seen for what it is. And maybe it will remain forever, that depends entirely on the individual. But in the Legion there are no individuals.

Dealing with uncertainty in civilian life and the immense freedom and possibilities it offers, posed a threat to my Legion conditioned mind. My mind was more sensitive than average and incapable of dealing with the unknown. Even though I rebelled in the Legion, I had still unconsciously adjusted to the regime where I was not required to think but just obey orders as a legionnaire should. Once I found myself on the outside, there was no one ordering me around. There was nobody for me to rebel against. There were only societal norms and expectations to live up to. There was too much freedom.

Maybe it was easier back in the Legion. This disturbing thought did affect me at unexpected times whenever I had the blues. A "Don't Think Just Act" way of life seemed appealing once more. Another sad aspect was that I felt the status of Legionnaire seemed better than the status of ex-Legionnaire. And an ex-Legionnaire felt better than a Nobody. I really had no clue who I was. And I couldn't return to the eighteen year boy who joined the Legion.

But let's get back to the Ivory Coast and Operation Licorne. The challenges and sculpting of my identity continued. Four months in the Ivory Coast saw us regularly go out on patrols in the local area to assess what help we could provide to the local community. One job saw us spend two weeks repairing a bridge near a small village. We also spent some time reinforcing the surrounding guard posts back at the camp. We carried out any other maintenance work. We carried out some more patrols in the greater region.

I had a dual function as a VAB driver and as a Transmitter for the section. Much of my time was spent controlling and maintaining the radio equipment as we were constantly coming and going from the camp. I felt that I needed to focus on my role as transmitter. I went to talk with the SCH about this. I asked him "Could someone else be the VAB driver? I need to focus on my job as the Section Transmitter." The Chef was from Austria. He had piercing black eyes and bushy eyebrows. He had a reputation of being an arsehole towards CPLs. I was no exception. His insults felt genuine and struck hard.

A short time before going to the Ivory Coast, I was in the NCO's office one afternoon. The SCH was giving me orders about preparing some things for the training camp in Antares. Instead of replying constantly "Oui Chef Oui Chef Oui Chef" I let out of a few informal "Ok Chefs" instead, trying to create a team friendly atmosphere. He stopped talking at once. Then in a very threatening manner, in a flat gentle voice which didn't match his words, he said "If you say 'OK Chef' one more time to me, I'm going to smash you to bits." It wasn't a great thing to hear from someone you were trying to respect and work with, and especially when it felt that he meant it. I felt helpless just as I did when I was beaten only a few months before. It was as if my body had stored that feeling and it flooded back into me instantly. My body held a confusing mix of adrenaline and fear that couldn't be used.

Since then, I had started to lose all respect for the SCH. I actually began to really hate him. Little by little, I started to mentally group together all the people I hated. It began with the three CPLs who beat me up. Gradually it grew, containing more and more of the Legion as my trust was vanishing and my anxiety grew. Soon it would be the whole Legion against me. A battle I would surely loose.

The sight of the little smirk on the Chefs neat face disgusted me as he hid behind his rank of SCH. On this occasion in Ivory Coast when I requested that I could focus on my transmitter duties, he replied with another line of insults, "Tu es inapte commandant, Tu es nul à chier." Maybe he is right, I thought, I am incapable of leading. I felt that as a CPL, I was too easy on the Legionnaires. Even if a LEG stood up to me or challenged me I don't think I could have punched him. Maybe I was too soft and not mean enough to be a CPL in the French Foreign Legion. So be it. Nevertheless there I was in the stinking heat of the Ivory Coast and I knew damn well that I was a good transmitter. I took pride in keeping all the gear in good working order and ensuring communications where maintained when we went out from the base. That SCH couldn't even turn on his own radio.

The NCOs all shared the same big tent at the camp. There was the ADJ who was Chef de Section, one SCH and three SGTs. We had no Officer there and that was a good thing. Every one of us had all began in the Legion as EVs. The polish ADJ was the type that didn't forget that. He was a fair man and we did have a good respect for him. He overheard my request to the SCH about balancing my two jobs as both VAB driver and Transmitter. He spoke over the SCH. "Very well. We will get someone else to drive the VAB. You just focus on your Transmitter duties, CPL Stefanazzi," the ADJ said.

BOUAKE

After that near run in with the SCH, I was left alone for most of the four months, to do my job. Twice a day, I had to submit a daily report to the logistics centre of the base. I was well organised; I kept an inventory of all our equipment, and I set up a storeroom in a metal shipping container. I checked all the equipment daily. Each time that we went out on the ground, I ensured that all the gear was operating to the best it could. I gave a basic class on the use of the Radio equipment for the section.

It felt good having a specific role within the section, and knowing that the section had a certain dependence on me. But the SCH didn't ease up on his bullshit and was quick to jump on my case whenever he could.

Before leaving France I had invested in a pair of black Magnum combat boots which I purchased from a military store in Paris. They were more comfortable and breathable than the standard-issue boots. One day, the SCH saw that I was wearing them. He ordered me to put them away, saying that I should only be wearing the standard boots. I just said "Oui Chef" but I ignored this order. Two days later he approached me again over my nice boots. I had my excuse ready for him. I said that for the past couple of weeks I had an ingrown toenail and that the standard boots were aggravating it. I needed to wear the Magnum boots. He said he didn't care unless I had a note from the doctor. The next day, one of the SGTs confronted me "Why won't you do as the Chef ordered you Stefanazzi and change your boots?"

"I have an ingrown toenail" I began, attempting to explain. The SGT didn't even wait to hear me out. He shouted in anger "Je n'ai rien à foutre, va voir le Chef tout suite!" and he stormed off. I went to see the SCH, expecting to get some form of punishment, maybe even a box in the jaw. My own head was turning into that mess of familiar numbness I call mushy peas, when I didn't care about anything anymore. It's as if the uneasiness in me spills over and I lose all feeling. But I still had a slight useless anger which at least pointed to the fact that I wasn't a complete zombie. I thought to myself "Why can't we just focus on the OPEX mission we are here to do, and stop fucking around with stupid stuff like this?" Of course, I didn't have an answer to that.

I marched up to the NCO's tent and I presented myself to the SCH, "CPL Stefanazzi, a vos ordres Chef." He said nothing as he sat back into his chair. Then a little mean smile appeared from the corner of his mouth.

"OK Stefanazzi, this is what you're going to do. After lunch today when we are all having a siesta, you're going to take one of the hack saws from the storeroom. Out the back of the camp there's a stack of old iron railway. I want you to cut me a nice section of iron railway, ten centimetres thick. And don't come back here until you finish it."

"Oui Chef" I said loudly and marched off. No fucking way was I going to start doing this bullshit. I was on a serious OPEX mission in the Ivory Coast. He wants me to start cutting a piece of railway because he doesn't like me wearing my Magnum boots. This was absolutely ridiculous. I returned to my tent after lunch and waited it out. I was expecting to get a beating from the NCOs. My body was building up adrenaline to face it. Two SGTs came to my tent after an hours time. I sat on the edge of my fold up bed, looking at the ground waiting for the punches to come. "Stefanazzi" one of the SGTs said, "If you don't act like a CPL anymore, we're not going to treat you like one."

For the next two weeks, I was treated as a LEG. I done all the guard duties and cleaning chores that the CPLs were usually exempt from. I did more chores than the Legionnaires themselves. I just got on with it but I had enough of the stupid mission we were on. OPEX, my arse. I was fed up and exhausted.

One night, I had a good few beers at the bar in the Logistics base across the road from my camp. I was the only Legionnaire that went across there. It was away from my section. I went over there regularly as a transmitter to the central Transmissions office so it wasn't unusual that I could be around there. It was good to get away from my section for a while. This was one of the benefits of being a transmitter. I spent the evening over there. I killed a good few ice cold beers.

That night after lights out, I was lying in bed unable to sleep despite the exhaustion and the beers. I really hated it there by that point. The beers had helped me relax just a little. I felt the need to go take a dump. The toilets and showers were over the far side of the camp. It was dark and nobody was around. Everyone was sleeping. The numbing effect of the few beers was wearing off. I could feel again that I hated military life. This whole OPEX mission wasn't amounting to anything. The closest it came to action was when I had loaded my shotgun during guard duty one day and pointed it out over the sandbags. Some local teenager had thrown a rock at me. He ran off quickly. I could have shot him in the back. That was about the only pathetic smell of action I had. And how pathetic would it have been if I shot him?

As I crossed the assembly square in the dark of night on the way to the toilets, I stopped to look at the large painted emblem on a concrete slab. The slab was about one metre squared. The emblem was painted on a flat sheet metal plaque fixed on top of the slab. Every four months, the arriving Commanding

Company would repaint their emblem onto the plaque. Every morning, we all assembled section by section on that square around that emblem. A wicked idea shot through my mind. This time, I didn't think. I just acted.

I knew it had to be done quickly in case someone was out having a late night cigarette and spotted me. Plus, if I had time to think I might of rejected the impulse. I scanned the whole area. Not a soul to be seen in the darkness or even the little red glow of a cigarette. In less than five seconds, I had whipped down my shorts, squatted, and squeezed out a huge mound of soft shit. My aim was perfect and the pile of poo was exactly symmetrical on the middle of the emblem. Instead of going to the toilet, I continued on to the shower. As I stood in the shower washing my arse, I knew by the satisfying feeling of achievement that I was experiencing, that I must be a bit twisted in the head. Nobody would know and nobody would find out. This would be my inner way of regaining control. It was my own little piece of action on OPEX, that would justify getting two more medals.

The look on the commanding Captain's face the next morning at assembly was gold. He slowly walked up to the plaque to investigate the nature of some alien matter. I relished in the three confusing seconds he spent looking down on it. His brain stalled, trying to comprehend the mineral content by sight and then by smell. I relished even more in his loud threat that echoed out over the assembled crowd towards the unknown perpetrator. Some laughter sporadically broke out among the crowd of two hundred French soldiers and Legionnaires as everyone slowly realised what the little mound of brown was. The colourful painted emblem of a Unicorn representing Operation Licorne was covered in shite.

The Silver Unicorn soon saw light again when urgent orders ripped through the ranks to remove "La Merde." But maybe it was Unicorn shit that had magically appeared as a sign of good luck for our mission. Nobody could figure it out.

I did feel sorry for the LEG who was ordered to run quickly out and gather it up on a spade. But that pity was not nearly enough to cancel out the immense inner satisfaction that couldn't be taken from me. For most things about the Legion, I didn't give a shit anymore. But in that case, I did.

In a strange way, it actually boosted moral for a few days, giving the guys something to laugh about. But it was forgotten quickly. As the end of our tour was in sight, the idea of magical unicorn shit was less interesting than thoughts of their upcoming PLD. I wanted to use this next PLD to travel. Instead of going back to Ireland, I was planning to go to South Africa on PLD. But there was still about four weeks left to go there in Cote D'Ivoire.

The ADJ ordered me to teach one of the LEGs, a French guy, everything that I knew about the radios. He had pulled me aside one day and said that there was some bad news from the Regimental Command back in France regarding my future as a Transmitter. I had asked for a transfer on returning from the Ivory Coast to the Regimental Transmissions section within the CCL. Only then would I consider a career in the Legion. It was more of a story I had made up to get them off my back about resigning. But it was really a possible career option I had once entertained, before I was assaulted.

The decision was made not to give me security clearance to operate as a Transmitter any longer. Something about not been granted military security clearance - Secret Défense, he said. I wondered was it because I was still in the FCA before I joined the Legion. But more likely it was because of my rebellious behaviour over the last year. I never found out why, but this was bad news for me. I was no longer being recognised as a transmitter. They even omitted it from my Service Certificate when I left the Legion. The ADJ said that despite this decision, it was ok for me to continue to be a transmitter in the 1CIE but that I would not be able to progress to the CCL Regimental transmissions section.

The French 1CL who I instructed on the Radios was the driver of the ADJs Peugeot P4 Jeep. I didn't like the sound of this order from the ADJ, to teach him everything I knew. They were looking to erase any dependence they had on me as a transmitter. This would only mean they could fuck me around even more.

By this time my ingrown toenail was getting worse. It became slightly infected. There was a little pus oozing out where the nail was digging into the skin. I knew I could hold out until I got back to France but I thought it might get the SCH off my back if I got it treated there and then. Also, the way things were going, it wouldn't surprise me if, arriving back in France, everyone is granted four weeks PLD and I'm sent to the Infirmary to get my toenail taken out. Then I'd be stuck in the infirmary with my foot in a bandage for a few days and it would ruin my PLD.

So fuck them, fuck this shit mission and fuck the whole bloody thing. I was the true Major de stage for my Transmissions course back in Castel and they took that off me, now they can have my smelly toenail too. I went straight to the Infirmary there at the camp. I exaggerated the discomfort pain and smell that was coming from my ingrown toenail. I said it was troubling me, that flies kept landing on it and that I had a numb feeling in my foot. Half of this was true. The doctor on duty operated on my toe straight away. With a local anaesthetic, he cut out half of my big toenail from the root up. Then he bandaged it and gave me a supply of antibiotics and painkillers. I hadn't told anyone in my section before the treatment because I knew they would try and talk the doctor out of doing the procedure.

I took pleasure in the disapproving look from the SCHs face when I appeared back from the infirmary that evening. My foot was in a bandage. I held one crutch to help take the weight off that foot. I presented him with a little piece of paper signed from the doctor. It said "CPL Stefanazzi is to rest for 10 days. No heavy duties, he is to stay in sports gear. Also, CPL Stefanazzi has permission to wear his Magnum boots for the remainder of his tour as they will allow his toe to heal better. Signed, COL Unicorn, from the Flying carpet Brigade."

They left me alone for those ten rest days. I did instruct the French 1CL on the basics of operating the radios, but I kept some important stuff to myself. I needed to keep some power to survive those last four weeks in the Ivory Coast.

MANKONO

Another section from our company called Section Travaux were building a new road about two hours away from Bouaké in the bush. They had heavy machinery for doing roadwork. The project would take a few weeks to complete. Some of us from my section, myself included, were sent over to help them out.

When we arrived we could see that they all looked tired and fed up being stuck out there. It was the first time we saw those guys since leaving France. They had already being there for some time, working on the new road.

They had cleared a large spot of land the size of half a football pitch for their temporary camp. It was somewhere in the bush, in the middle of nowhere. Barbed concertina wire surrounded the camp. Inside the perimeter were all the vehicles and the machinery. There was a makeshift shower and toilet. There were many large tents with the usual fold up beds inside. There was another tent with tables and chairs set up as a dining area.

In the parking area, there were two diggers, a road roller and a loader truck which were used for the daytime work. There were two jeeps, one VAB and a passenger truck. Work was seven days a week from dusk till dawn. A roster was set up so that everyone got a day off after every four days of working. Those on their day off would maintain the camp and help with the cooking. They could also look forward to something else.

Each night, a LEG stood guard around the camp. We quickly noticed a seedy routine that occurred at night. The cool dark nights provided a relief from the stinking daytime heat. When it was late and darkness fell, some figures appeared from the bush to the edge of the barbed wire perimeter. But these figures never alarmed the guard. The opposite was true, they were welcomed. The LTN had always retired to his tent by this time.

Every night these young girls appeared and provided temptation to the tired and frustrated Legionnaires. The first night I saw the girls appear I was surprised. How is this happening? The lads are getting away with it? The LTN was always gone early to his tent. We knew that he was just turning a blind eye to what was happening with the girls. But we were grown men, capable of taking responsibility for our own actions. We didn't think though, we just acted.

By the time me and the others from my section had arrived, the evening process had become routine. We didn't know what age these girls were. We didn't want to know. A legionnaire would pick out a girl that he liked, stand on the barbed wire and help her over it. For some little local money, or even a couple of ration packs, the girls sold themselves.

I felt disgusted the first night when I saw one girl brought by the hand of a legionnaire up into the back of a truck. But I was more disgusted at my own unexpected intrigue. Another CCH didn't go to so much hassle and he just laid his poncho on the ground behind the digger. Their frustration and boredom was released into these young girls.

Every night was the same. After a long, hot day working in the hazy red dust, having progressed further along with the road to nowhere, we retired back to our isolated camp as the sun melted on the jungle horizon. Dinner consisted of improvised ration packs cooked up with some local ingredients. With enough garlic and onion, black pepper and chilli, anything from a tin was edible. Showers were taken in a corner of the camp. We took turns going there. Metal Jerry cans of musty water were lined up, still warm from the day's heat. We used a plastic scoop to pour the water down over our bodies.

Standing on a wooden pallet, feeling the warm water run down my body, washing the dark brown dust off me, I felt a bit cleaner, but inside I thought about those dark figures appearing from the bush each night. And like the other legionnaires, I gave in to the dark half of my soul.

I chose my girl. I stood on the barbed wire, took her hand and helped her over. I led her over to an empty truck and up into the cabin. With her head between my legs, I too released my frustration and boredom into her. To ease the shame, I gave her a little more money than usual and a ration pack. I led her back towards the darkness and stood again on the barbed wire helping her over. She went back to whatever life was like for her, to whatever place she vanished into the darkness to. In a pathetic attempt to dismiss my shameful act, I reminded myself of what one legionnaire said to me - "Those girls are passed freely around all the men in their villages, don't worry about it."

ABIDJAN

Waiting on our military flight back to France from Abidjan, our whole 1CIE was gathered with other soldiers from different Corps of the French regular forces. We waited in the loading area, close to the aeroplane. There was a mix of Legionnaires, French regular soldiers and Gendarmerie separated into various groups. There was a long delay to board the plane. I didn't mind about the waiting. I was just glad to be going back to France. I was also looking forward to a long PLD of five weeks. My toe had just about healed too. All was good.

It was my plan to get a flight to South Africa once we were free in France. I would visit a good friend of mine who had deserted back when we were both new legionnaires. We had done our Regimental training together at the CCL in the 1REG. We had about one year of service each, when he left. He had told me that he had enough of the Legion and was deserting.

I also had second thoughts about sticking out the five years. I admired his view that he didn't have to prove anything to anybody. He left his bank card with me in case he still got paid at the end of the month as that bankcard wouldn't work outside of France. He was very grateful a few weeks later, when I posted him a book with lots of fifty Euro notes stuck in between the pages. The monthly payment had been made to his account and it was still active. I took out as much money as I could before his card was swallowed up by the ATM. I believe he bought himself an old Volkswagen Beetle with that money in South Africa.

Back at the airport in Abidjan, I waited in whatever shade I could find, to board the plane. Eventually there was a roll call. In alphabetical order our names were called out. We each walked up to a desk to collect our boarding passes. It took some time before the names approached the letter S. I listened and I prepared to walk up to collect mine. Soon I heard "SCH Stefanazzi" and then "CPL Stefanazzi" as the names continued on. There must have been a mistake, I guessed, as I walked up to collect my boarding pass. They had called "Stefanazzi" twice.

Looking at the others who walked up, I attempted to identify who was this SCH Stefanazzi. Then as I got my boarding pass at the desk, I met a SCH from the French regular army who was collecting his. We both looked at each other. I saluted him, saying "Bonjour Chef." We both paused, looking down at each other's name tags. I looked carefully, making sure all the letters were there. He done the same.

"Is that your real name?" he asked. Then before I could reply, he said "I heard that legionnaires never use their real names anyway."

"It is my real name" I told him. I explained that I had gotten rectified. I had been called Gregory Sims before that. I explained to him that I was from Ireland. He took a moment and then he became more interested, claiming that there were cousins of his living in Ireland. He had grown up hearing this but had never met them. He said when he was sixteen years old he went on a school trip to Dublin. His father in France had told him to check the phone directory while there. He did get his hands on a phone directory and saw that there were indeed three "Stefanazzi" names in the Dublin region. I told him that those "Stefanazzis" were my family. We smiled with excitement but still doubting the possibility.

Then I remembered my Aunt back home who had wrote me a letter during my basic training in Castelnaudary. That letter had cost me one hundred push ups. In the letter, she mentioned an old lady, a first cousin of my deceased grandfather living in the Southwest of France. My Aunt had written down her name and address and pointed to the fact that "you never know when it might be useful."

I thought for a moment. Then I remembered the name. "Montori, Denise Montori near Biarritz," I said. The SCH's eyes widened.

"Je la connais Denise," he said. "Elle est la tante de mon père." We stood there, both shocked and excited. Then we smiled and laughed in amusement. What an unlikely chance meeting. We sat together and chatted on the flight all the way back to France. In turned out that we had both found a third cousin, and in some way reconnected a link that was severed almost a century ago. Both of our great grandfathers were brothers who had fled Italy together for whatever reason. One of them, Luigi, had settled in France. The other one, Ernesto, had gone to Ireland.

Our meeting was a rare coincidence, especially in the Ivory Coast on the last day of a tour of duty. This encounter meant a great deal to me. The last two years in the Legion were difficult. It was important for me that I finished the five years. Had I not found my cousin Emmanuel, maybe I wouldn't have returned to France after my PLD in South Africa.

KRUGER PARK

Time seemed to drag by in the Legion after my return from South Africa. I had a good long holiday there. I did wonder though if there was something wrong with me during a five day Safari trip. The excitement and vivid interest of the group of tourists on seeing Elephants, Lions, Buffalos, Giraffes and even Cheetahs in the wild, I did not share. As I looked at these amazing sights of amazing animals, it was difficult for me to feel much excitement or any pleasure inside. Soon, I would just sleep in the back of the Safari Van. I did not bother to get up after a while when I heard excited voices signalling the arrival of more elephants. Sex or Alcohol was about the only two things that could motivate me.

The months ticked by slowly at the 1REG just outside Avignon in the south of France. I lived for every bit of free time I could get. I continued to get in trouble and I spent more and more time in the Regimental prison. Altogether, I would spend about two hundred and twenty days "En Tôle" over my five years. I almost felt safer inside the prison then dealing with people I hated from the 1 CIE and having to see those cowards that beat me up, every day. There was many a Sunday night at the end of a weekend off the base, when I dreaded returning.

One particular Sunday night, I was in Marseille with the same American chap that I had visited the brothel with in Spain. He was now in the process of trying to get officially discharged from the Legion. His knees just couldn't cope with Legion life anymore. There was another LEG from Slovenia drinking with us that Sunday night. He had injured his spine in the 2REG. He was on sick leave. We were all in an apartment, drinking Diesel - cheap bottles of red wine mixed with cola. They didn't have to go back the next day but I did. The more of that cocktail I drunk, the more I knew I was going AWOL on another one of my three day benders.

I already had a routine for this stunt. I would call my Chef de Section on Monday afternoon, inform him that I would be back on Wednesday night and to make sure that there was a hot dinner waiting for me.

Arriving back to the base that Wednesday night, the Military Police (MP) came and searched my locker and belongings. I had forgotten to leave my spare passport back to the embassy in Paris after my trip to South Africa. It wasn't like me to forget such things. The MPs found it and confiscated it. Although I had my name rectified and was now entitled to apply for overseas PLD, there was still a process to go through. Passports had to remain at the OPSRs office. The following day, I was sentenced to twenty days for my unauthorised absence.

I had become immune to being in prison. The sad thing was that I always felt it was actually worth it every time I went AWOL for a few days. The countdown was on to my Fin de Contrat. If I had a choice, I would have been happy to just be a gardener for the last year. I was already planning my next PLD. I wanted to go and visit some distant cousins in Canada. There were a number of "Stefanazzis" living there too and a good few around my own age. I had never met them before. I had lost hope in the Legion family. I wanted to discover my real one, my extended one. Maybe my ancestors were calling me from someplace deep in my psyche.

Just before I started those twenty days in prison, I was called by my CDS to go and see the OPSR. I had heard about this new OPSR as being a right arsehole. I learnt that truth quickly when I met him for the first time.

"I see from a stamp in your passport, Stefanazzi, you spent four weeks in South Africa. You didn't have authorisation for an overseas PLD. What were you doing there? Eh? Were you trying to become a mercenary or something?" the big chunky CNE said in a suspicious voice.

What on earth was he talking about. I was just on holidays there in SA. I was in a bad mood and because I was going to prison anyway for twenty days, I didn't feel like giving in to his power trip. So I said back to him "Ça ne vous regarde pas, mon Capitaine." I refused to tell him anything more. He certainly didn't like that response. That was the start of a battle between my stubbornness and his pride which would continue for another year.

A few days later I was enjoying a little daydreaming while out doing some hedge trimming around the base. The prison guard came and told me that he was escorting me back to the 1CIE. I had to go and put my number ones on immediately. I was being escorted by the ADJ Adjoint OPSR to the 1RE in Aubagne. I didn't think that the CNE was serious a few days before when he said with a smirk "If you won't talk to me, damn you will talk with the Gestapo in Aubagne, Stefanazzi."

Arriving at the 1RE, the ADJ was still silent. He hadn't said a word all the way there in the car. Up two flights of stairs we went and he knocked on a thick metal door. A small hatch slid open and two eyes fired towards me. A large bolt was unlocked, the heavy door creaked open and a man jumped out. With his fist clenched above my face, he roared some insults at me, as his spit sprayed into my face. I slouched, looking at the ground without moving. I could feel the familiar cocktail of nausea and adrenaline mixing in my body. After his dramatics were over, he looked at his watch. It was just after midday. We were both to come back at two p.m.

Arriving down to the bottom of the stairs, the ADJ spoke

to me for the first time. "Stop fucking around, Stefanazzi, you better talk with them at two o clock" he said impatiently.

"Oui mon Adjudant," was my automatic reply. But I could already feel my mushy peas defensive mode coming on. I couldn't believe it when he then said that we would meet back at that same spot at one forty five pm. I had an hour and a half on my own, great. I resisted an urge to just walk out of the 1RE and go into the Irish Pub in Marseille. Maybe it was really time to desert. But I had nothing with me.

The ADJ just wanted to have lunch himself and he didn't want to be babysitting me for the whole time. I went off and had lunch myself at the legionnaires canteen. Then I hung around the Foyer area having a coffee until it was time to go back.

I thought about the situation. Maybe their idea was to frighten me and then give me some time alone to think about their ultimatum to me. Before we left for lunch they made it clear that I had a decision to make on returning. "You have two choices, CPL Stefanazzi" I was told. "A - You explain what you were doing down in South Africa, or B - You sign a letter saying that you want to denounce your contract and the discharge process will commence immediately."

At two pm. I was back up in the Gestapos office. The ADJ waited outside. This time there was a bit of pushing me around here and there. I was ordered to sit down at a desk. A few of them walked frantically around the room as if they were in a rush someplace. They all looked like they needed a good shit.

The door was slammed shut unnecessarily. The same lean mean air dried fella that sprung from the door earlier like a gazelle, pushed a pen into my hand and squeezed it shut. He looked like a piece of cancerous biltong. Another bully pushed my head from behind down towards a printed letter that had been typed up for choice B. Then he slapped me across the back of the head. It was ready for me to sign. There was a blank page too, that was choice A.

I could either write a Compte rendu to their COL explaining what I was doing in South Africa or I could sign the printed letter that they had prepared. But I had already made my decision during the lunch break. It was outside their ultimatum.

I looked up at a fat baldy SGT. For a moment it felt like a hallucination. He was a crossbreed between the Nazi pig who attacked me in Coetquidan and the CCH medic who ordered my head to be stiched up in Castel. Then in a similar sour Slavic accent, he showed off in front of the others. "Remember Stefanazzi, your Compte rendu has to be done exactly with the right spaces and margins. Use the ruler to measure the spaces or ill use it across your fingers" he said. I stalled for a few seconds.

Then the Gazelle shouted at me "Stefanazzi, tu as deux choix. Soi tu écris un compte rendu disant ce que tu as foutu en Afrique du Sud, ou, tu signe ce document que tu veux partir au civile. C'est simple, en avant!"

I continued to stall. He grabbed me by the shoulder and shouted in my face again, "A ou B?" I could smell from his breath cigarette and the Langue de boeuf et ses petits légumes that had been on the lunch menu earlier. He could have done with a few more of those cow tongues to beef up a little. But then he probably wouldn't fit into his tights and high heels on the weekend.

"C" I said calmly and quietly as I placed the pen flat down on the desk and crossed my arms. Bowing my head, I then said my last word - "Je ne fais rien." I entered mute mode. It's not that I was feeling particularly brave; it was more that I was feeling nothing at all.

After another round of failed drama auditions and bullying, I was standing to attention in their COLs office next door. The COL was talking and talking at me incessantly but I had zoned out long ago. I had left my body. The voices got louder and louder. Then the ADJ pushed me back outside the office and into the corridor.

"Arrange ta putain de cravate, putain de merde" he shouted at me. I was like a lifeless mannequin. My tie and uniform were a big mess. I purposely gave no effort to my presentation in front of the faceless Colonel. I had remained mute so the COL didn't get his presentation that he was so used to. A quick effort by the ADJ to fix my tie and straighten my uniform up and I was back in the office again. Another rant by the COL and I tuned in this time for the sake of it. I understood something that sounded like they were going to end my contract and send me back to civilian life where I belong. Great news at last but why don't they just fucking do it?

On the way back to the 1REG, I was thinking that it might not be so bad if they end my contract and I can walk out with about four years of service. I wouldn't need to stay another year. Discharged sounded better than deserted. I could have signed that paper I suppose, but I didn't want to give them the satisfaction.

I found myself back in the prison with an extra-long sentence added on, the days merged into weeks. I waited in vain to be discharged. I was eventually released from prison. I continued on with the 1CIE. Nothing more was ever said about that trip to see the Gestapo in the 1RE. My hope of being kicked out of the Legion died. It was as if that trip to the1RE never happened, nobody mentioned it again. But now I wasn't just a Legionnaire, I was a South African mercenary too. My four week PLD to Canada was on the horizon and I looked forward to it desperately.

ALGOQUIN PARK

My trip to Canada was in some way an attempt to reach out and connect with distant family. The Legion family wasn't giving me the connection I needed and I was still unsure about my birth family back in Ireland. But it was also just an opportunity to visit Canada for the first time.

It was during the month of July and the temperature was scorching in Toronto when I arrived. I met up with all the extended family. There were cousins of mine around the same age whom I had never met before.

On one of the weekends, my cousin Rory and his girlfriend invited me to a wooden cabin on a lake a few hours North of Toronto. It belonged to his girlfriend's family. A bunch of their friends who were staying nearby joined us.

On the Saturday evening, we were sitting outside and drinking, around a campfire at the lakes edge. As a way of forgetting the Legion, my drinking was getting heavier in Canada. It was becoming hard if not impossible for me to relax without alcohol. I was feeling bored despite their friendly company and I decided to go for a swim in the lake. Perhaps if I was willing or able to open up to them about what was going on for me in the Legion, the boredom wouldn't have been there. But it seemed like a swim was the answer.

The water was flat calm and even though it was dark, the lake felt inviting. Once in, I felt my body's limit dissolve into the water. I became part of the lake itself. It was comforting to feel fully submersed in the warm water, like an unborn baby, unaware of its separateness with the world. I swam out a little, then a little more. I swam out further until I could see the others, now distant figures, sitting around a little glow which was the campfire. I could see them and hear their voices across the water but I was invisible in the darkness. I decided to keep swimming. I swam parallel to the shore past the neighbouring property and the next one and the next. I felt like a swimming version of Forest Gump, half-drunk too.

As the alcohol and boredom was sucked out of me, I began to tire. Not feeling like swimming all the way back, I swam towards the water's edge at the next lakeside property. The large house looked vacant. There were no lights on. The neatly kept lawn which kissed the lakes lapping edge, was inviting. I swam towards it. I was looking forward to lying down on the soft grass. And I did just that for a short while, looking up at the stars, until my body began to chill and I felt cold. I got up and walked across the lawn towards the main entrance, exiting the property. My plan was to walk the mile or so along the road back to my cousin's place.

All of a sudden, the whole place lit up and a dog started barking loudly inside the house. The dog was soon accompanied by two middle aged faces peering out the window. I was ready to run to the lake once they released the dog. I stood there like a rabbit in headlights. Luckily, they kept the dog inside. Then one of them shouted out the doorway "The police are on the way." I shouted something back in a vain attempt to explain my unexplainable situation.

I left the property quickly to start walking the road back. But I only got out the gate when I realised that the road was not tarmac but covered in small shingles. They cut into my feet. I would probably only get a couple of hundred metres anyway before the police car would come. So I just sat outside the entrance of the property. I sat down on the side of the road, mentally preparing my story for the cops.

Within only a few minutes, the squad car arrived. Two huge officers with their big hats from the Royal Canadian Mounted Police got out. I stayed sitting down. My excuse was simply that I had too much to drink and went swimming up the lake. I told them that I was on leave from the French Foreign Legion. They told me to jump in the back seat. I got a lift back to my cousin's place. They just laughed and said "No more swimming for you tonight, mister Legionnaire." They were surprisingly easy-going about the whole thing. I got off lucky.

LOURDES

When I got back from Canada to the 1REG, it was a difficult transition back into Legion life at the 1CIE, along with the withdrawals from alcohol. I had pretty much drunk every day of my PLD. It was midweek when I bumped into an American pal of mine on the base. He remarked on how sad I looked to be back from PLD. I told him about meeting up with my cousins in Canada and the great trip I had there. But I think the sadness was also related to the fact that in one month's time, I was due to return to Djibouti for a second period of four months. Unconsciously, I didn't want to go. One trip to Djibouti was enough for me. But the usual training and preparation before deployment was already underway.

Two weeks before the 1CIE's departure to Djibouti, I repeated another of my long weekends by going AWOL on a Monday and returning on the Wednesday evening. But this time the situation was a little different. They had told me on the Friday morning that I was on weekly duty at the reception starting that evening. I was also assigned to do guard duty on Sunday. But I ignored this and left the base that evening.

The week leading up to it, I had been looking forward to that weekend. Ireland was playing France in the Rugby World cup that Friday night. But it turned out to be a disappointing night as the French beat us well. I remember the disappointment I felt standing in the middle of the main square in Montpellier that autumn evening. There was a large screen set up showing the game and a big crowd had gathered. I found it odd that everyone sat on the ground instead of standing up. Alone, I drank a few cans of beer and watched the game. My other pals from the 2REI couldn't make it out until the next day. I felt terribly lonely watching Irelands defeat, as young French students celebrated all around me.

When I returned to the base on the Wednesday, I already knew somehow what was in store for me. I had my formal uniform on and I stood to attention in the CNE's office. This time, the CNE did not claim that he needed my transmitter skills in Djibouti. My departure to Djibouti was cancelled and I was sent to prison for twenty days. He told me that I was finished with the 1CIE. I would be sent to the CCL on my release from prison. By that time, the 1CIE would already have left for Djibouti.

Before I went to prison, I packed up all my belongings and left them in the cellar of the CCL. I had just ten months left to serve in the Legion at that point. I was glad to be finished with the 1CIE. The only reason I was interested in going to Djibouti again was that I could have saved up a lump of money while over there. But the potential ten thousand Euros that I could save in four months wasn't appealing enough. I didn't want to return to Djibouti. That was in the back of my mind when I went AWOL. Something also told me or warned me too that the second time in Djibouti wouldn't go well with the pattern of things that had been going on for me during the last two years. Maybe I would never return from Djibouti. I could easily disappear out there, my death covered up as a training accident. I did live in fear for my life, whether that was irrational or not. And they knew that I was finishing up at five years of service so I would be given every possible duty that came up.

So I went back to the relative security of the prison. Ironically, it was the only place I felt safe in the Legion. I had plenty of time there to reflect on life. I performed my gardening duties each day. I enjoyed those solitary moments away from the anxiety of the 1CIE. Then the day arrived for the 1CIE to depart for Djibouti.

I was alone with my bare combat uniform sweeping the first autumn leaves to accumulate in the drains around the main square. I stopped sweeping. Leaning on my yard brush, I watched two coaches full of Kepi Blanc's drive past me. I could see guys from my section at the back end of one of the coaches. As they peered out from the windows, there were some smiles and one or two waves. I gave them a salute. I smiled silently to myself and felt relieved. But I also felt a touch of unexpected sadness too. I had finished with serving in my combat company, the 1CIE. This change meant that I was getting closer to the end of those five years.

On release from prison, I settled into my time serving in the CCL. I visited my French cousins and extended family in Paris and in Bordeaux, during my time off. I spent two nights with Emmanuel and his family at the end of December, just after my last Christmas in the Legion. I had become close with them since meeting my cousin, SCH Emmanuel Stefanazzi, in the Ivory Coast.

That night we walked around Paris and saw the Eiffel tower lit up. The air was cold and crisp and I felt happy. I had just begun three weeks PLD and I had a flight to Dublin the next morning. I was sure that the hardest part of my five years was over. The previous two months in the CCL had been relatively stress-free. I was assigned to the transport section. I assumed that this relative ease would continue for my last eight months.

I had recently put my name down for the Fiftieth International Military Pilgrimage to Lourdes - Pèlerinage Militaire International (PMI) taking place in the coming month of May. Things were looking good. It would be an interesting event with members of Armed forces from all over the world attending. Perhaps I would meet Irish soldiers there and have some Craic.

I had already visited Lourdes myself one weekend during my CPLs course two years previously. Lourdes wasn't too far by train from the 4RE in Castelnaudary.

One Saturday I went there. It was a cold clear day in November. There were very few people around at that time of year. I wandered around. I had seen the famous grotto. Even though I was raised Catholic, I didn't know how much I believed in that version of God. What I did know was that I had been suffering and I was unsure of the reason for that. Maybe religion could help me accept it. During my time in the Legion, I had got my first tattoo. It was a small black cross. I got it done on my ribs and it hurt. I didn't know why at the time I got it done. Maybe I thought it would force me to believe more in Jesus.

As things turned out, I wouldn't return again to Lourdes and the 50th PMI. There was more suffering to come before those five years were up. And there would be even more after the Legion too.

SISSONE

The days were a lot more relaxed in the CCL than in the 1CIE. I could often choose in the mornings, what kind of sport to do. Work usually involved maintaining the transport vehicles, manning the fuel station or going on transport runs. I would sometimes have to drop off or collect officers or NCOS to and from the train station. There was still the odd twenty four hour guard duty to do but overall I was glad to be in the CCL. The work didn't bother me once I was away from the bunch of Rambo's in the Combat Companies.

I felt that I would finish off my contract there in the CCL without too much hassle. But I still knew that those legionnaires who were coming to the end of their contract got all the extra duties. I wasn't surprised therefore when I had to spend Christmas week at the CCL reception, on permanence duty. It didn't bother me as I never got home to Ireland for Christmas anyway and I wasn't a fan of the Legion celebrations on Christmas Eve.

I thought I had avoided most other duties until one sickening day in February. I had just over six months left to do before my end of contract. The SCH in my section said to us all that the 2CIE were going to do training at CENZUB in the north east of France for two weeks. I got a fright when I heard that word. They were low on men. They needed some back up from the CCL, specifically a VAB driver.

Le *Centre* d'*Entraînement* aux actions en *zone urbaine (CENZUB)* is a mock village set up in a military zone in the French countryside. It is used for training in urban warfare. I had been there twice before with the 1CIE. I hated the place.

"Stefanazzi," the SCH called me. "I heard you are an excellent Pilot VAB." I almost begged him not to send me. But there was no bargaining with him. Immediately, I was unhappy that I had to go on this duty. The SCH said as I was the only one available with a VAB licence, I was chosen to go. I didn't believe that. He also said that I would only be required to act as Pilot VAB for the duration of the two weeks. He assured me that my function would be strictly as a driver because I was from the transport section of the CCL.

I had already completed the CENZUB training on two occasions with the 1CIE. I really did hate that shithole. I felt it was just an exercise for officers and NCOs to attempt manoeuvres and work on their commanding skills. I knew exactly how it would go. The officers would be busy giving commands over the radio and positioning their troops around the village. We would run around like lemmings.

I started feeling hopeless again. I felt that I no longer wanted to be a soldier. I remembered the whole thing was just a big pathetic mess, the two previous times I was there. It usually involved not sleeping much at all, and a lot of waiting around in the freezing cold. As legionnaires, you would be left standing or kneeling on one knee for ages waiting for another stupid order. It was nothing more than an officer's playground.

At least, being a VAB driver would not be too big a deal. I had done it before both as a VAB driver and as a 1CL soldier on the ground. I knew I could put up with the monotony of sitting in the VAB driving around the camp for some very long periods. I could have the heating going as much as possible in the cabin. I could just about bear that. I knew I could eat whenever I was hungry in the cabin of my VAB, behind the wheel. I knew I didn't have to listen to their shit tactics either. I just had to shut my mouth and drive.

But for the lads out on the ground, it would be freezing cold, boring and extremely frustrating. If I had to do that again, I would have a serious pain in the bollocks. The thoughts of putting up with that shit for two weeks would drive me insane.

So I agreed to go as a VAB driver but I made it very clear to the SCH and my Chef de Section - an ADJ that I would not be operating under any other function other than VAB driver while at CENZUB. I didn't really have a choice about going but I wanted to make myself clear before I left anyway. I had a sneaky suspicion that something was coming my way. I could sense that something sinister was in store for me. I didn't trust the dogs in the 2CIE either. In fact, I didn't trust anyone at that point. There had been a bad story circulating about a LEG in the 2CIE who nearly died after two SGTs attacked him. A small metal stool was smashed of his head in Djibouti that same year. He was left in a coma for a long time.

I gave in to the idea of going as a Pilot VAB, hoping that I would be left alone to drive my VAB and look after its maintenance. There was a few of us from the CCL assigned to the 2CIE for the two weeks exercise. We made our way over to the 2CIE for a briefing on CENZUB and to help organise the materials and vehicles needed for the trip.

Under the command of an ADJ from the CCL, we the designated drivers were assigned to our different vehicles. Once the vehicles were prepared, we drove them by convoy to a nearby town. There, the vehicles were loaded onto a special freight train. It then made its slow trip north towards the small village of Sissone where CENZUB is located. We returned to the base. We all left on coaches the following day, direction: Sissone. It was long trip north of about nine hours.

The first day, on arrival at CENZUB, involved unloading the materials and vehicles off the train and installing ourselves into the barracks. The materials went to the store rooms. Each driver then installed his vehicle with sensory equipment. At CENZUB, laser equipment was used. This sensory equipment was attached to each person's gun, combat vest and helmet, and to all the vehicles. A small box is attached to the barrel of each gun, which emits a sensory beam when the gun fires blank rounds. Each person has a receiver box on their jackets and helmets. A sound is emitted like an alarm when a direct hit is made.

There were P4 Jeeps, Trucks, and VABs being used. There was also a group of French regular army who were involved in the joint operation. They had both Infantry personnel and a Cavalry section with some Leclerc Tanks. A few high ranking officers, including a General were there as observers. Lots of photos would be taken of course. All together the operation included about two hundred troops.

Every one of us, even the drivers were given sensory equipment to attach to our combat vests and to our helmets. I tried to explain to the ADJ that I didn't need any for myself as I'd only be in the VAB driving the whole time. But I was ordered to get it anyway "Just in case." I didn't like the way he said that.

That afternoon, we all went out to the mock village of CENZUB to familiarize ourselves with the terrain, before commencing the operation the following day. There would be a few days of training before longer manoeuvres of twenty four hours duration. Finally, the joint exercise would finish in a long seventy two hour siege at the end of the two weeks. I remember doing those long operations and how I had a serious pain in my bollocks during them. The last one I completed with the 1CIE, I swore to myself that never again would I go through it. But here I was back for more fun.

The Camp of Sissone itself covered a vast area. The barracks and mock village of CENZUB were a few kilometres apart. As the camp is not considered an operational one, but for transitional regiments to come and train, there is no real controls on access by the back roads. It's a relatively open camp.

That night, the ADJ came to see me in my room. I was surprised but suspicious to see him looking for me. He called me out to the corridor. He told me straight up that plans had changed. The whole organisation of the operation was being altered. It was now above and out of his control. They were short a CPL to function as infantry team leader - Chef d'équipe. I was the only possible one that could fill it, he insisted. Someone else like a CCH would drive the VAB instead of me, he explained.

I went into nervous shock. I felt that all too familiar sickness in my core. Tomorrow, I would not be a Pilot VAB anymore but I would be on the ground as a toy soldier. Someone else would take over responsibility for my VAB. Inside, I felt disgusted but I was also in denial. The shock I was feeling was related to the fact that I had hit a dead end. I saw nowhere to go with this impossible future laid out before me. The news itself from the ADJ wasn't a big deal anymore. It was this new internal state that felt foreign and weirdly interesting. It felt otherworldly, or was it just insanity waking up.

Either or, but there was no fucking way on this earth that I was going to do anything other than drive my VAB. They had taken my function as Transmetteur away from me. They had taken my title of Major de Stage. They had taken my dignity by beating the shit out of me. Now, they are not going to take away my function as Pilot VAB. I had spent ages getting it ready for this exercise. It was my VAB, my baby.

Although I knew it was useless to express my unease to the ADJ, I gave it my best shot. I told him that I was assured and promised beforehand that I would only be operating as a VAB driver. My elevated tone of voice did communicate my unease. Somehow, I knew his response even before it came as if everything was working like clockwork. He shrugged his shoulders like he wanted to say I don't give two shits. But he just said simply "C'est comme ca, Stefanazzi, c'est tout," and he walked off. That's just the way it is! C'est la vie.

The following day was only preparation and training for the first long siege on the village. I was in foul mood and barely spoke to anyone. I was more disappointed with myself that I had given in to my change of function. I stood there with all my gear and camouflaged up, along with my section. I looked with envy towards the drivers who were snug in the cabins of their vehicles. Then I saw some stranger CCH from the 2CIE in my VAB, smiling out the window at me. It was a cold foggy morning and we were all done up like toy soldiers: Helmet, gun, camouflage, combat vest, and backpack full of engineering equipment. Our engineering equipment included mock plastic explosives and detonating chord, a small shovel, tape and other crap. I was usually organised but not this day. All the gear was stuffed into my bag, in a big tangled up mess. I could not have cared less. Hopefully it would fall out as we ran around the place.

I decided to at least give it a go for a day. It wasn't as if I had another option. But I was still curious about the possibilities of insanity. Did it even exist, I wondered. Be careful what you wish for mister Legionnaire, you might just get it.

That day was spent doing an attack on the village. There were times when nothing was happening for over an hour. Just as I tried to get something to eat, we would have to move on. To say that I was in a bad mood is an understatement. I was so disinterested that I spoke very little the whole day. At one point a SGT asked me about what equipment my team had at our disposal. I looked at him straight in the eye but I couldn't even muster up any form of response. I wore a dejected expression on my camouflaged face. The whole thing was just a big joke. Then he asked me a second time while we were on the move again. "On a tout ce qu'il faut," I shouted back at him, in a voice that sounded alien to me, yet interesting.

In the fogginess of the smoke, frozen mist and my dark mood, I recall a moment when we were all kneeling down at the side of a house on entering the village. The attack was just about to begin. Along the road two officers who were not partaking but observing the manoeuvres, strolled past us in their pompous style. I think one of them was a General. The lower ranked of them, probably a COL, looked at us. He shook his middle aged bourgeois head in disapproval at our positioning. He made a gesture with his hand for us to move back further. I saw him but I ignored him and looked away. Then he came over. "Reculez, Reculez, Reculez" he snaps.

Our positioning was not to his liking. It made my blood boil. Like puppies to their master, we all shuffled back a few meters. I wondered right then, what would happen if I ran over and kicked the General up the arse. It might actually be my ticket out of there.

That ingenious thought only lifted my mood slightly. It signalled to me that I was becoming desperate by even considering such drastic action. But my head was still tormented. It was growing itchy with frustration under my helmet. Only considering radical action was not enough. My dark mood surrounded me even deeper. I needed some real action to calm my agitated mind. The festering curiosity of insanity would not leave me alone until I gave in. I had opened a portal that could not be closed.

Soon after that, it was the brink of the attack. We found ourselves on the ground floor of one of the buildings awaiting further commands as usual. Suddenly, there was a flurry of shots and smoke grenades going off outside. The whole village had erupted in fake gunfire. Seemingly unsure what to do, the SGT panicked like a school kid caught picking his nose. The command was given "Out the window Out the window, Allez Allez Allez."

It was a messy affair with guys banging their knees off the window ledge, tripping, cursing, falling and tumbling out onto the ground outside. Their FAMAS guns were banging and falling everywhere. Luckily we didn't have live rounds. The lack of composure annoyed me. Immediately, I grabbed a nearby metal locker. Using it as an outlet for my frustration, I slammed in on the ground under the window. It now acted as a step. The rest of us exited the window with a lot more ease, rapidly and composed.

As that day ended, I just knew that there was no way I could put up with the same crap again the next day. It had only been a few hours. Both my head and balls were going to explode. Even a piss up and a brothel wouldn't solve this one. Something inside me just said "No, no, no. I can't. I just can't. I'm losing my mind." But losing one's mind was just a figure of speech, as far as I was concerned. I didn't know that it could actually happen.

After dinner and showers, everyone was in their rooms relaxing and getting ready for a longer operation the next morning. I decided I would ask to see a doctor because I felt something was wrong in my head, whatever that meant. I went and knocked on the ADJ's door. It was late. He opened the door, looking surprised but slightly alarmed to see me. I requested that I consult immediately with a doctor on duty at the camp. The ADJ asked what the deal was and if I could not wait for tomorrow. I had very little facial expression, but I managed to point at my head and say "Problème dans la tête." I did have a slight frog in my throat and I wanted to cry. But no way was I getting teary eyed in front of him. He looked in disbelief and asked me "Où mal? Où mal?"

I replied "C'est n'est pas mal, C'est problème dans la tête!" With that, he gave in and said to go on over to the Infirmary.

To my surprise, one of the medics at the Infirmary was an American who had been my training buddy on our CPLs course more than two years previously. He was from the 2REI and it was nice to see him again, a decent chap. He told me to take a seat. I waited for some time before the doctor on call arrived. Again, to my surprise it was a doctor whom I knew from my regiment who had moved to the 2REI. But I wasn't so glad to see him. Memories flooded back of when I had a hernia operation as a young LEG. He had refused to extend my sick leave. Initially I was granted two weeks to recover at the Malmousque, a Legion home in Marseille for legionnaires on PLD or convalescing.

The surgical operation to repair my hernia at the Laveran military hospital was done in a way that nobody even informed me of the mechanics of the procedure. I felt like a piece of meat. After the surgery, I had demanded to speak with the operating surgeon but nobody came. I couldn't move from the bed for a few days and I was in a lot of pain. I heard horror stories of how they performed some botch jobs in that place. It was said that legionnaires were operated on by trainee surgeons. I heard of one LEG who had surgery performed on the wrong knee. I saw no officers getting treated at that hospital.

After a general anaesthetic, I had woken up with a four inch scar and large metal staples in my groin area. I couldn't get out of bed for five days and when I did, I was hunched over for the next week while trying to walk straight. When I was still in pain following two weeks of sick leave, this doctor at CENZUB refused to extend it. Instead, he granted me an extra two weeks confined to my bedroom on the base. He thought that I was faking it. This meant that I was exempt from all duties but I was stuck in my room all day. Now, surely he would think I was faking it again.

Here I was four years later but with a different type of 'pain in my bollocks' other than a hernia. I knew straight away when I saw him that evening, that it was useless trying to explain my situation to him. There was no bargaining with him.

In my head one thing was sure. I knew that no matter what, there was no way I was going to continue on tomorrow as a pawn in the big officers war-games. I was hoping for the impossible; that somehow he would grant the possibility that I could regain my function as VAB driver. He arrived, dressed in Jeans and a checked shirt. He said "Qu'est ce qui se passe avec toi Stefanazzi?" but his tone translated to "What are you doing bothering me at this time, I have better things to be doing than listening to your winging, I could be masturbating to gay porn with my thumb stuck up my arse."

I could read the look on his face. He thought I was faking it. At that point, I was past even attempting to explain anything. I went silent. I did not say a word but stared into space. He waited a while. Then he posed some standard questions to which I gave no response.

Eventually, his patience ended and he said out straight and clear "Ok, it's simple, CPL Stefanazzi, you either tell me what is going on in that head of yours or we will organize a Jeep and escort you to the Military Psychiatric hospital in Paris." I was being given another Legion ultimatum. I remembered the first one I was given back Aubagne with the Gestapo. There was always another way out.

Looking back, it would not have been a bad option if I had just remained mute and they did escort me to Paris. But I was afraid of madness, it was unknown territory.

I decided to break my silence in the desperation for some compassion or understanding that he might be able to express. I stood up and full of emotion, I blurted out "It's all rubbish. It makes no sense." I acted out the infantry movements like I was on a stage. "The lads are jumping out of windows, banging their guns, banging their knees, it's all a big mess. The officers don't care. Nobody cares. I can't do it anymore. I was sent here as a VAB driver. I was guaranteed by my CDS that I wouldn't have to do anything else."

I sat back down, breathing heavily. I waited for his response to my dramatic explanation of "Problème dans la tête." Looking at the floor, the tiles seemed to offer a different reality, their shape more intriguing than the obvious. I felt that I had expressed my concerns and now I must wait, desperately hoping for an outcome. But the doctor simply replied "You are a Legionnaire, you have to be flexible. You have to adapt to the situation."

On hearing this, I stopped listening to what he said. I zoned out completely as he continued talking. This was going nowhere. I regretted even opening my mouth. I should have kept going with my silent protest and let them bring me to Paris. Then, with his voice nothing more than background noise, something clicked in my head. Something came alive in there, something new.

There was no more room for 'should haves' or 'could haves.' My focus became clear like that of a Tiger. My senses suddenly heightened to full capacity. I was taking back control, taking back power. For the first time in my life and there would be further times, I had a moment of clarity, a blend of madness and epiphany. I knew crystal clear, the only person that could help me was me, and only me. With this moment of clarity came a twisted humour. I had to restrain myself from laughing out loud in front of the doctor.

He was surprised to see my desperation slowly turning to a large grin. I knew then that I would just play along with the game of life. I stood up straight, pushing my chair back. He looked a little startled. I felt immensely confident. I gave him an impeccable stand to attention, putting on my béret vert and saluting him. I was on fire. "Oui mon Commandant, Merci mon

Commandant, Je peux disposer a vos ordres mon Commandant"
I belted it out in a tone that would make Muhammad Ali shiver.
That was it. I stepped through the portal. I had lost my mind
and I loved it.

As I was marching out, he asked me, with more uncertainty
in his voice, "Are you sure everything is Ok, CPL Stefanazzi?"

I turned at the doorway, facing him briefly. With my two
thumbs up, I eyeballed him and startled him with my response,
"Impec mon Commandant, Impeccable!"

As I walked back towards the dormitories in the dark, I felt
adrenaline building inside my body. I had no choice but to act.
I had to get out of there tonight.

I went straight to the ADJ. I calmly confirmed to him that
everything was okay – pas de problème. I returned to my room. I
sat on my bed, my head racing. I then remembered some story I
once heard about a Finnish Legionnaire who while in Djibouti,
took a P4 Jeep and drove away during a desert manoeuvre, in
the middle of the day. I secretly admired his courage for that
crazy act. But now it was my turn. I was going to beat that with
an even better story.

I thought about leaving on foot, but we were too far from
anywhere. The equivalent in Ireland would be being stuck in
the Glen of Imaal, in the Wicklow Mountains.

Anyway, the decision was made. There was no time for second
guessing. Already my blood was nice and warm with a steady
flow of adrenaline and I didn't want to waste it this time. My
brain was sparking off some pleasurable microscopic fireworks
too. It was a natural cosmic high. My decision to enter the
otherworld meant that my brain was probably creating a new
row on the Periodic Table of Elements. I could see the future
clearly; I will use my VAB. I knew it without any doubt. Anyway,
that was my assigned function. I'll show them, that bunch of
French and Foreign rejects, who the real Pilot VAB is. I was

angry at the Legion and angry at the whole world.

With the surge of beautiful adrenaline through my body, I felt a mixture of fear, excitement and even pleasure. "Okay" I instructed myself. "I need to remain calm about this." I lay on my bed for a while trying to centre my thoughts and slow my breathing. I then prepared my kit along with the other Legionnaires, giving the impression that I was getting ready for the long siege tomorrow. I didn't want to arouse any suspicion in them. I chatted with them. Then I checked with my team that they were all ready for the twenty-four hour long siege starting the next morning.

I behaved as normal as I could despite my secret plan to leave, once everyone fell asleep. I felt the LEGs noticed my shift in mood from a silent and depressed state to an elevated and energized enthusiasm. They probably thought I was either Bipolar or I had just taken a big line of Cocaine.

I took my time to have a long hot shower. I looked in the mirror while brushing my teeth, giving nods of encouragement to the bearded maniac looking back at me. I had been growing a small beard as I was preparing to be a pioneer at the upcoming Camerone Parade. Every year on the thirtieth of April, the Legion commemorates the battle of Camarón, Mexico from 1831. Traditionally Pioneers came from the Engineering Regiments of the Legion. During parades they wear a leather apron along with an axe placed over their shoulder in line with traditions. Anyone willing to parade as a Pionnier was allowed to grow a beard in the months leading up to Camerone.

But now I had a feeling that I wouldn't be parading as a Pioneer at my last Camerone in the 1REG. I no longer cared about it anyway. I was going to break out a trail of my own that night. I didn't need an axe or a leather Apron to do it, just the use of my own VAB instead.

Little did I know then that the clearing of obstacles is never finished in the outside world, which we perceive as separate from our introverted Self; the biggest lie of humankind. Only when the mess inside our heads is conquered, can we see the beautiful clear light of our Soul. But try telling that to a twenty three year old Legionnaire who was traumatised and addicted to adrenaline in order to avoid his pain.

That night I waited and waited until about one a.m. when everyone was asleep, before I left. I devised an alibi in case I met with someone outside and they questioned me. I had also prepared the same story for the guard at the vehicles when I would arrive there to take the VAB.

There was a large parking area were all the vehicles were parked up. LEG's from my section took turns walking around guarding the vehicles during the night. The guard changed every two hours. Not to arouse any suspicion, I would tell him that I was preparing more material to load into the VAB for the manoeuvre tomorrow and I needed to take it closer to the dormitory. I would tell him that the VAB was leaving early the next morning to start the operation.

I dressed in my long sports track suit. I took my small backpack called a Musette. Inside my musette, I had a fleece jacket, a wool hat, a change of socks and jocks. I had Savon de Marseille, my wallet and phone, my toothbrush and toothpaste. I left all of the rest of my gear there in the dorm, packed up inside my bedside locker. I didn't need any of it.

I did not want to be seen on the corridor by any NCOs so I chose an alternative exit. I climbed silently out through the bedroom window in the darkness. It was the second window I climbed through in the last twelve hours. It crossed my mind that this time was in contrast to the situation earlier that day when people were tumbling out the window in CENZUB. There was great panic and noise with sounds of gunfire and shouting. But now, it was dark and silent, except for some erratic snoring coming from tired bodies in the dormitory room. I should have been tired too but the situation kept me wide awake and alert. I was now doing my own infiltration – Infiltration nocturne. I still didn't need any night vision either.

.Once I was outside, I carefully closed the window. I was on a mission of my own direction and responsibility. There was no hierarchy here. My own Alpha team was made up of me myself, 1CL Sims and CPL Stefanazzi. I was The General, SCH and 1CL all at once.

The Alpha team walked slowly as one in the darkness. Using the cover of nearby trees, it progressed with stealth towards the parking lot.

A LEG from my section was standing guard around the vehicles. He was surprised to see me walk up towards him slowly. I acted as if I was checking on him to see if he was doing his job well and not dossing. I commended him for being alert and doing a great guard. I then put on my helmet and told him that I needed to park my VAB close to the dormitory to have it ready for the morning. I asked him to help direct me as I drove my VAB out of the tight parking. He did so without question. All he was concerned with was getting back to his warm bed.

I drove off slowly as if I was going to park the VAB next to our dormitory building. Then once I was out of sight of the parking and the guard, I turned away from the dormitory buildings. I drove towards the back roads that led away from the camp.

That was the point of no return and I felt a turbo booster of adrenaline pump into my body. I exerted self-control not to speed up with the VAB. I drove steadily along small country roads, not exactly sure where I was going. I was hoping for some sign posts to a bigger national road. Despite the time being close to two am, I was wide awake. I knew that I would eventually arrive at a national road and then on to a motorway at some later point. I had a full tank of fuel. I couldn't believe I was actually pulling this mission off.

I wasn't intending on deserting. I was just getting the hell out of there. I would go back to the 1REG near Avignon before the seven day grace period was up. I knew how the system worked at this point. If I was gone over seven days, my status of AWOL would change to Desertion. Then all my belongings would be packed up and given to the military police. My pay would be stopped. It would then be more complicated to return.

Relief came over me when I got onto a national road. Soon after, I saw a sign for the motorway. My alert eyes caught the familiar city name of Reims on a road sign. It was only forty seven kilometres away. That's where I was going. I knew it immediately. The city of Reims would have a decent train station with regular service. I felt giddy.

Once I was on the motorway, I brought the speed up to one hundred kilometres per hour and I stayed in the slower lane. With the hum of the VAB close to its top speed and the excitement in my body, many thoughts were scattering around my head. Thirty minutes more and I should be there. But I needed to have a proper plan. I decided that before arriving at Reims, I would pull over and get myself together a bit and try to calm down. I reached a rest area just off the motorway about ten kilometres before Reims and I pulled over for a few minutes.

There were a few large trucks parked up. It was quiet there. I took a couple of minutes to breathe slowly. Then I checked over the whole VAB from outside to inside. I had already done so at the parking but I verified again that there was nothing important such as any armoury or radio equipment on board. I then prepared all the inner secure locks for when I arrived in Reims and I kept them beside me in the cabin along with my musette. At this point I was almost talking to myself, trying to remain calm and composed. When I was sure all was good and organised, I took a piss behind the VAB.

"Ok c'est bon" I assured myself. I need to get into Reims, park up the VAB some place secure and get to a hotel for the night. That's the plan. "En avant là!" I started up the engine again and drove back onto the motorway. Rolling along nicely, I was feeling more confident of my plan and my thoughts were in order. The cockroaches in my head were back in formation.

There were very few cars on the motorway at that time of night. Then suddenly, I saw blue flashing lights in the tiny wing mirror and I got that sickening feeling through my body once again. But I kept the same speed and ignored it. A Gendarmerie van overtook me at speed in the fast lane. It was followed by a second Gendarmerie vehicle. Shit, that's it. I'm done here. But to my surprise, they kept going and going. Then I realized it wasn't got to do with me. An almost orgasmic feeling of relief flooded my body. It put a smile on my face. I did wonder what had they thought of a lone VAB driving on a motorway in the middle of the night without an escort.

Not long after this I saw a road sign for an upcoming toll. I had some cash in my wallet. I slowed down and drove up to one of the toll booths. There was a woman at a hatch. Usually in a car, the driver is looking up at the cashier. However with the VAB, we were sitting at exactly the same level. I opened up the side armoured door of the VAB and looked directly out at the woman who was less than a meter away. "Bonsoir Madame," "Bonsoir Monsieur," we both greeted each other. She looked understandably surprised. The toll was around four Euros and twenty cents so I handed her a fiver. "Gardez la monnaie et passez une bonne soirée Madame," I said.

It would have made more sense to accept the change and not arouse suspicion but I was anxious to keep moving. I was pleased when the light turned from red to green and the metal bar went up. I drove on. Soon, I took the exit for Reims – Centre

Ville. I slowed down on entering the city. I saw some road sign about large vehicles and weight restriction but I just ignored it. I needed to get into the city and park this thirteen tonne can of beans up. I didn't want to be doing detours all over the place and drawing any unnecessary attention to myself.

The streets of that old city were narrow and pretty. At a slow pace, I recall driving around a nice fountain as the VAB bounced gently along on the cobbled road. For a second, it reminded me of Temple Bar in Dublin. I certainly looked out of place to the few people still strolling around the centre of Reims at this hour. There were still a few late night revellers sitting outside a bar having a drink and smoking. Their heads turned in bewilderment when I crept past them in the VAB. They were well wrapped up in big coats, hats and scarves. It was a freezing night. I was hot and cosy in my VAB with the heating on maximum. But it was the last time I would be inside that armoured womb. Soon I would leave it for good.

Continuing on for a little while further, I scanned the area for a good spot to park up. I drove onto a quiet street. Just outside some sort of boutique there was a parking spot. That's it, that's my spot. I stopped. I took my time to park it well, in off the road. I locked up all the doors from the inside and exited by the pilots trap on the rooftop, happy that nobody besides someone experienced could enter the VAB. I left my helmet inside on the steering wheel. It was a great feeling walking away from that hunk of metal. Mission complete. I would ring the ADJ at CENZUB the morning and let him know where the VAB was.

REIMS

The first hotel I came across was full, but the night porter directed me to another one. I hoped that I didn't look too suspicious in my dark green track suit, army green fleece and scruffy beard.

I was delighted that there was a room for me at the next hotel. I paid immediately for one night with breakfast. I went up the stairs and dropped my bag into my room, sensing the forgotten feeling of warmth and security that hotels offer. I put on my winter hat, took my wallet and went back out for a few beers in a late bar to calm my nerves. Every small event since I had left the doctor's office a few hours earlier felt like a roller-coaster of emotion, alternating between immense anxieties to immense relief. There was no way I could sleep without a few drinks.

The next morning, I got up and had a steaming hot shower. I took my time having breakfast at the hotel while I thought about my plan for the day. I checked my mobile phone and saw that I had threes missed calls from eight a.m. that morning from a certain mobile number. I guessed that they were already looking for me. I had missed the morning Assemblement. Surely they knew the VAB was missing by now.

I finished my breakfast and checked out of the hotel. As I was walking down the street, I called that number back. It was the ADJ. He asked where I was, and why I missed assembly that morning. Without waiting for me to reply he asked me if I was still having breakfast at the cafeteria back in Sissone. On hearing that, I was surprised. Little did he know I had just finished breakfast at a hotel in Reims, fifty kilometres away. He then said "Hurry up Stefanazzi. We are going out on the ground very soon to start the Operation."

From what he said, I knew they hadn't got any idea what I had done the previous night. The Alpha team had done a great job. They didn't even know the VAB was missing. This was confirmed to me when I heard the panic in his voice after I explained the real situation. "Écoutez bien mon Adjudant," I began. "I am in Reims now. My VAB is here also. But don't worry; it is parked up safely in the city centre. It is locked securely from the inside out. There are no weapons or radio equipment on board. I'm taking a little holiday down South at the seaside. I'll return to the 1REG next week. Send someone right now to pick up the VAB."

"C'est quoi ca? C'est quoi ca?" He sounded very alarmed. I tried to clarify the situation for him one last time, "Listen, mon Adjudant, the situation is simple, you need to send somebody straight away to go to Reims city centre and collect the VAB. It's parked on Rue Cérès. I'm already on the train now, heading to Nice. C'est tout."

I heard the anger in his voice before I hung up, "But, but, but, but."

"Sorry" I said, "I have to go." And I turned off my phone. I knew then that they wouldn't be too long to arrive. The Police or Gendarmerie would most likely be involved too. I immediately regretted making that phone call so early. I should have waited till I was really gone out of there. I couldn't risk being seen now so I decided not to go straight to the train station. Then an idea just came to me. I would go and hide inside Reims Cathedral for a few hours.

No one would look for me there. I thought it would be safe there too, in the house of God. I bought a few cans of strong Bavaria beer on my way there. Looking back, my mind was definitely starting to crack a little. Although it felt like I was pulling off some great act, and that I was fully in control, deep down I didn't recognise myself. I felt like someone else.

I had been sitting in one of the pews in the darkest, dimly lit area of the cathedral for over an hour. I had to hold off for another hour to be sure they weren't still looking for me around the city. By then, they would have recuperated the VAB and returned to Sissone. I was growing impatient and bored. I cracked open my last can of beer and hid it at my feet. Now and then I would kneel down as if to pray but instead I would take a long gulp of the cold fizzy liquid. How disrespectful, I thought, drinking in such a magnificent holy building. What would God the Father think? Would he be angry or amused, I considered. But this was the house of God and Alcohol was my God.

All the former respect I had held was being questioned, being examined; my respect for the Legion, for Religion, for my parents. Maybe this was the start of taking back control of my own life and finding out for myself, what the world was all about. What does respect actually mean? I thought. It meant nothing. Everything meant nothing. Words were useless and shallow. I remembered a quote that my uncle in-law once wrote on a birthday card for me. I always felt there was a certain truth to it.

"Life is a jest and all things show it, I thought so once and now I know it" John Gay (1685-1732).

I suddenly got a strange idea. I would pretend that I was carrying out some form of research. I would have my own little private joke. I had been in Our Lady of Reims for two hours by this stage. I approached some of the visitors who wandered around the cathedral. They were mostly middle aged, French retirees. "Bonjour Madame Monsieur," I said on approaching them. "I am carrying out a survey. There is only one question that you must answer. It requires simply a Yes or No response. Are you ready? Oui? Ok. Do you think that Catholic priests should be allowed to marry?"

I got both definite Yes and No responses. I thanked the participants but I gave no sign of having my own opinion. I clearly felt that catholic priests should be allowed to marry. I didn't really care about their responses. I was just bored, a little drunk and going mad. I was getting a kick out of being odd and I was feeling good in a weird way. But it was time to leave the Cathedral, now that my survey was complete.

I started walking towards the train station. But I wasn't really feeling like a train journey. On the way, I continued with my survey for the buzz of it, stopping people on the pavement and asking the same question. I stopped a French girl and she gave a definite yes, which I liked. I also liked her. I was feeling confident too. Then I asked her or told her that I would buy her a drink. She was a student in university and I thought to myself "What the hell am I doing in the Foreign Legion?" I just wanted a normal life like any other twenty three year old.

She invited me back to her small flat that evening after a few drinks at a bar. The train could wait for the next day. I was glad. My behaviour must not have been too weird for such good luck to strike. Or maybe she liked my weirdness. Either way, I was feeling great that I may have scored here. With the surplus adrenaline in my body from the last twenty four hours, the thought of sex with this beauty would be the cherry on the icing. This was definitely better than being stuck out in CENZUB, playing soldiers.

My need for real intimacy was something that was not met during my time in the Legion. The closest it came to it was visiting brothels. That night, after the beautiful student girl from Reims made us some nice dinner of Ravioli in her cosy studio apartment, we climbed up into her loft and into her warm bed. We lay there. The Alpha team and I were ready for action. But just as we were closing in on the village church she broke our advance, "Do you have a condom?" Of all the gear the Alpha team carried, a rubber wasn't one of them. My mind froze, and I scratched my head.

"Je n'ai pas de préservatif," I confessed. So thinking I would solve this dilemma easily, I said "I'll go and get one." Jumping down from the loft and throwing on my clothes faster than I done in basic training, I ran outside into freezing Reims. Hoping there would be a late night shop or condom vending machine nearby, I searched the area.

The streets were empty and dark. After half an hour spent desperately searching in the bitter cold for a condom vending machine or a late night épicerie, I became frustrated and admitted defeat. I ran behind some bushes and masturbated violently. Jesus Christ, what the hell am I doing? Was this revenge for drinking in the Cathedral? I looked up to the sky as I tugged desperately. Is this what priests get up to? Ok fine, I said out loud, I accept the penance but at least give me a hand here, it's bloody freezing!

When I got back to her flat and up into her bed, she was asleep. I slept beside her warm body. In the morning we had a hot chocolate drink and brioche with strawberry jam for breakfast. We walked the streets together. At some corner, in some part of Reims, we kissed and bid each other farewell. She went to University and I made my way to take the TGV down south. I felt like a failure but I blamed it on the Alpha team. It was a Friday morning so I was going to hit Montpellier and go hard on the beer.

MONTPELLIER

That Friday night in Montpellier, I met up with an Irish CCH and a Welsh 1CL. I had texted them on my train journey, on my way down. We arranged to meet in a Rock n Roll themed bar that we knew. I arrived while they were already sipping their second round of beers at the bar. I noticed there was a painting of a Native American Girl with a feathered headdress looking straight at me from behind the bar. I felt there was some meaning in that picture. It was calling out to me. I also knew that I was probably going mad.

The lads were surprised to see me in my Legion sports tracksuit and with a beard. It had been a couple of months before we last met up. We shook hands and laughed.

"What the hell are you doing in Legion sports gear Kev, have you deserted or what?" the Welsh guy said, sounding puzzled but amused. I ordered us a round of beers and I filled them in on the story. We had a good few pints and a good few laughs that night and the night after.

They went back to their regiments on Sunday evening. I spent the next two days in Montpellier alone and trying to make friends with civilian strangers. I kept drinking. By Wednesday I had to face up to the reality of going back to my regiment. At that point, my beard was shabby. I looked in a rough state from the few days of heavy drinking.

For some reason, and I thought it might help show that I was losing my mind, I decided to present myself to another Legion regiment, the 2REI in Nîmes. It was closer to Montpellier than the 1REG. I didn't care what the outcome would be.

All those feelings from CENZUB came flooding back upon me. I took the train to Nimes and walked to the gates of the 2REI. There, I told the SGT on guard duty that I was looking for a bed for the night as if it was a hotel. He saw my Legion sports gear and I showed him my identity card. He was confused. He didn't understand why I was there. Either did I.

I waited while he went off to the guardroom with my identity card. A short time afterwards, a CCH from the military police opened the gate and brought me through the guardroom and into their office. There was still confusion amongst the MPs until they phoned the OPSR of The 2REI - the officer in charge of Regimental Security. I waited and waited.

The lieutenant OPSR eventually arrived in his civy clothes. He came in like a bull, shouting and slamming the door. He screamed at the three military police who had all jumped to their feet, "Put him in the corner facing the wall. Put the handcuffs on him straight away."

The OPSR was an Italian LTN. He went on a big rant about how much trouble I was in. He explained that the Chef de Corps of the 1REG, the Colonel, had pressed charges with the Gendarmerie against me for "Stealing his VAB." I didn't bother try explaining how that VAB was really mine. I remained silent with my head on the wall.

The LTN phoned the military police from the 1REG, ordering them to come and collect me ASAP. As I waited, he started saying how the Irish and the Italians make the best Legionnaires. To my surprise, he commended me on how I carefully parked and locked up the VAB from the inside out. He said that just like in a war time situation, I had done it correctly without leaving a mess behind. But he emphasized that I was still in some real serious trouble now.

After a long wait facing the wall and with the handcuffs cutting into my wrists, I heard the LTN shout, "Gardez-vous."

It could only be one person, the big Capitaine OPSR from the 1REG. I heard his distinctive eastern European voice. "Ahhhh, Stefanazzi, you've come back to us," he said sarcastically. The previous year I had a run in with this CNE when he questioned me about my trip to South Africa. He was a heavy man who liked to bully others and throw his weight around. I knew he was going to give me as much shit as he could get away with. He reminded me of my father.

I was brought back to the 1REG in the back of a P4 Jeep and put into the prison there. They devised a fake story they could report about why they went to Nimes; the military police of the 2REI had caught me out in Nimes while visiting my girlfriend and they had arrested me. That was a load of rubbish. The truth was that they didn't want people to know they had to come all the way over late at night to pick me up from the 2REI. It was basically a free taxi ride.

I was causing them a lot of inconvenience just because I couldn't be bothered making my own way back to the 1REG. The 2REI was closer to Montpellier, so I just went there. It was also the case that I really no longer gave a shit anymore. I would use any opportunity I could just to piss them off. I wanted them to discharge me from the Legion. As an alternative, I would have been happy to do as many days in jail as they could give me and finish off my time gardening, now that CENZUB was out of the way. There was only about six months left on my contract. I knew that I would also have about thirty days of PLD which I was entitled to. They would have to grant me that PLD before I finished up the contract in August.

I spent that night in the 1REG prison. The next day I was escorted to the infirmary to see the head doctor, a COL. I guess it was routine for him to attempt some sort of psychological assessment after such an incident. He said what I had done was "Absolument fou!" But the COL was extremely rude and he didn't want to hear any of my reasons for taking the VAB. I was told to go and pack a bag of clothes from my room in the CCL. I was being sent to the Laveran military hospital in Marseille, to the psychiatric ward.

I was escorted by a CCH medic to my room in the CCL. He was an easy-going and friendly guy. He waited in the corridor and said to take my time packing up whatever I needed for hospital. Luckily, I still had my wallet and phone. The military police had forgotten to confiscate them with the all the confusion of the previous night. I packed up some spare clothes, toiletries, my wallet and phone into a backpack. Then we went for lunch in the canteen before hitting the road to Marseille.

I still wanted to finish off the five year contract or at least be discharged on mental health grounds, anything besides deserting. I felt that deserting would be a failure on my behalf. More so, I felt that my desertion would be a win for the Legion and a loss for me. That's what they were hoping for.

In my head it was me against the Legion. That was some battle for a twenty three year old to take on. It was likely that I might have had grounds to seek compensation if they discharged me and I could prove that I developed a mental health illness as a result of my service in the Legion. But I was never told anything about their assessments of my mental state or of any diagnosis. It would save them a lot of bother if I just deserted but I didn't want to give in. That was what they wanted, to clean their hands of me, to spit me out. They had broken me down but I could still fight on a little more. There was more of me left to chew.

I had given my youth to the Legion and busted a gut literally in doing so. I lost all respect and honour for them the day I was beaten up by my so called "Frères d'Armes." The other two and a half years after that, I felt like a corpse wearing a Képi Blanc. Any enthusiasm and trust I once held was now wiped out. My suffering would be in vain if I deserted. I had gotten this far. Just like a stubborn and rebellious Jesus, I couldn't just leave and walk away. I stood my ground as if I wanted more suffering. It was the hypnotic madness of the otherworld which the suffering can produce, that kept me playing with fire.

But on the way to the hospital that day, I didn't know that two weeks from then, I would attempt to desert for real. I would be so sick of everything that I would actually give in and attempt to go back to Ireland.

MARSEILLE

At the Laveran hospital, I shared a room on the psychiatric ward with a young LEG from Bosnia. He was only twenty years old. I was twenty three.

He had attempted to slice his wrists back in his regiment while locking himself in his room. He talked about how he had seen people get blown up back in Bosnia when he was a child. But he had a different mind-set than me in that he was hoping to continue with the Legion. He was worried that he would not be allowed to return to the 2REI to continue on with his Legion service. That was the Irony of my situation, I couldn't get discharged no matter what I done and he probably would get discharged even though he wanted to stay.

We were not in a locked ward, but there was a curfew at ten pm every night. In the afternoons we would go down together for lunch in the dining hall pretending that we were just day patients at the hospital. We were supposed to eat the food that was brought to our rooms by the nurses. The food was plentiful and better at the cafeteria downstairs, and we drank a load of the small wine bottles there.

There was not much to do up in the ward. It was boring there. We didn't get to see a psychiatrist very often. In the evenings, instead of the hospital food, we sometimes got pizzas from a pizza truck that was parked outside the hospital. They sold wine too. We would sneak a bottle or two of cold Rosé under our jackets up to the room with our pizzas and watch TV.

One day I was called to meet with the psychiatrist but I didn't pay any attention to what he was saying to me. For me he was on the Legion's side. I was suspicious of him. I had prepared a handwritten A4 page to give to him, clearly stating my needs. It read something like this: One, I want to go to my cousin Emmanuel's wedding next week near the Pyrenees. Two, I want to be discharged from the Legion right away. And Three, I want to go back to Ireland. Signed CPL Stefanazzi. He just smiled when he saw it and folded it up, never to look at it again. But I was deadly serious. I mean, a year ago the Gestapo were trying to kick me out but I wasn't ready to leave. Now I was ready to go, so they could surely arrange it.

I grew restless each day waiting around for something to happen. The days got longer and more boring. I attended an activity class one day with other patients in the ward. The nurse who was giving the class was pretty. The activity involved choosing an image from many images spread out on the table and talking about why you choose that image. We all sat around the table. My turn came and I chose one image of a bird flying across a clear sky. I said "I chose this image because I want to get the hell out of here."

I developed a crush on that same nurse. I chatted with her whenever I could. I thought she had a cool style about her as well as being sexy. She had dreadlocks and she had a motorbike, while still being really cute and feminine at the same time. It was a curious mix that lit something inside of me. I chatted with her one day outside the hospital. She was having a cigarette before going off on her motorbike, back to whatever life she lived. I tried to get her number but she wouldn't give it to me. I longed for her and I longed for intimacy. When I couldn't get it from her, my inner child was hurt. I was walking on the edge of sanity.

One day soon after this, I did a very strange thing. Although I was a patient in a psychiatric ward, and strange behaviour is to be expected, it still appears very odd.

After having a good amount of red wine during lunch, I wandered aimlessly along the hospital corridors. I found an empty wheelchair. For some reason, probably boredom mixed with alcohol, I decided to sit into it. I pushed myself around the hospital corridors for some time. I enjoyed the feeling of it. I enjoyed pretending to be crippled but being able bodied. I got a little injection of adrenaline. Then I decided for the buzz of it, I would go out of the hospital. It was a nice sunny day.

I knew that I would probably be stopped by the security guard if I tried to go out on the wheelchair. Instead, I left the hospital, walking. I pushed the wheelchair as if I was going to collect somebody from outside the hospital. I said to the security guard "I'm just collecting my friend, he's arriving in a taxi down the road." The guard nodded and I went out past the exit and down the road, smiling to myself. Once out of sight of the entrance, I hopped into the wheelchair and pushed myself along the pavement. I felt another injection of adrenaline as my new acting career took off.

I pretended to be a cripple. But then I thought of the Irish film made about the great Christy Brown. I felt guilty. As I was going down the streets, I saw a young lady. She waited next to me at a set of traffic lights. I greeted her and told her how I was so tired. In a pitiful manner, I asked if she would push me along for a short while. She agreed.

In silence, she pushed me along the pavement for almost half a mile. Then all of a sudden I said "Stop, stop." I got up out of the wheelchair, on to my feet and I turned to face her. Hunched over and looking down at the ground in shame, I put my hand out to shake hers. "Merci beaucoup" I said. She left me standing there with my outstretched hand hanging, waiting. She expressed her shock angrily, with an insult, and walked off.

I sat back on my wheelchair and continued pushing myself along the street. I knew I was cracking up but that I was still in control somehow. I liked the possibilities of craziness.

I arrived at a bar. I wheeled myself up to the step at the entrance. I turned the wheelchair around and before I could ask for help, two locals from the bar were already lifting me over the step and inside. I thanked them with a nod and wheeled myself up to the bar. My head was at the same level as the counter. I looked up at the barman and ordered a beer – "une pression, s'il vous plaît."

I drank a couple of beers as a cripple on his own in the corner of the bar. Then I felt the need to take a leak. I had an idea. Using my arms, I pulled myself up out of the wheelchair with the support of the bar top. Using the bar and then the wall as a support, I shuffled along to the toilet. It would be easier to act as a semi-cripple with some limited movement rather than faking complete paralysis. I felt I was doing a good acting job of it. Nobody seemed to suspect that I was a charlatan at that stage. And anyway, why on earth would someone do such a strange thing?

I wanted to continue on down to the busy port area of Marseille. I could go to a couple of Irish bars along the quays. So I asked the barman at this bar to order me a taxi. I knocked back the last mouthful of 1664.

The taxi man soon arrived at the bar. "Taxi" he called out. I wheeled myself towards the exit and again with the help of some locals, I was helped over the step. I wished them and the barman, a good afternoon. With the wheelchair positioned alongside the car, I shuffled out of my wheelchair and onto the back seat. Lying on my back, I grabbed and lifted my two legs inside. I declined any help that the taxi man offered me. I slowly sat up on the back seat as he closed the door. He then folded the wheelchair away into the boot.

"Direction, le Pub Irlandais au Vieux Port," I said and we set off. Arriving in front of the Irish pub, the driver helped me out and into my wheelchair. I was probably hoping there might be some Irish Legionnaires I knew inside and we could have the Craic, but there wasn't anyone I recognised there.

I ordered my pint of beer and scanned the bar for a place to sit. Near the entrance, there was a bunch of younger French people my own age, probably students. They looked friendly. I wheeled myself up to the table next to them. I sipped at my pint and listened to the fun they all seemed to be having. I wished again that I could just have a normal life as a student. I wanted to be part of their group.

It was early evening by now. There was already a security guard working at the bar. I called him over and asked him for help. I wanted to climb out of my wheelchair and onto one of the benches as I intended to stay there for a while. I asked if he could fold up the wheelchair and put it aside until I was leaving. He obliged. I also thought that if I was going to score a French girl that night, I was less likely to do it in a wheelchair. Eventually, I got chatting with the group of students near to me. I shuffled along the bench to join them.

I was getting on well with them as the evening progressed. There were a couple of cute girls in the bunch too and I was chatting with one of them. I gave her money and got her to go to the bar for me when my glass was empty. I bought her a drink too. All was good fun until I started getting dirty looks off one of the guys in the group. Then at one point he just said, "You're a fake. There is nothing wrong with you." He was right. I had nothing to say back to him. I just ignored him.

I didn't even know what I was doing or why I was doing it. I knew I was lonely. Yes, I was getting an adrenaline kick out of it and as far as I was concerned, I was hurting nobody with my little game. But I didn't bother trying to explain myself to this guy. I continued sipping my pint. Then he got annoyed that I was ignoring him. He began insulting me. He said that he had a sister who was a genuine cripple and would never walk again.

I got annoyed too and fed up with the whole fucking situation. Why is he bringing his poor sister into this? I wasn't going to take any shit off this guy. I stood up firmly to my feet, pushing the bench away. The group looked up, surprised and confused. I had enough adrenaline and was pumped, ready for fight or flight.

I shouted at him "Let's go outside, toi et moi maintenant!" The bouncer came over and told me to leave. He brought me my wheelchair. Insults kept flying between me and the true cripple's brother as I was leaving the bar. I waited for him outside on the street. I was ready for action. I wanted to fight, I needed one. But it never came. I opened up the folding wheelchair again. I slouched back down into it, feeling spent as the light grew from twilight to darkness around me. The adrenaline wore off and I fell into a sombre mood.

I bought a red rose from a gypsy woman and stuck its long thorny stem down my back. With the rose flower coming up over the back of my head, I pushed myself around the streets for a while looking like a weirdo. Not even wanting any more drink, I wandered around aimlessly feeling down and miserable. I eventually took a taxi back to the hospital. This time I folded the wheelchair and put it in the boot myself.

Back at the hospital, I was pushing myself along in the wheelchair on the empty and dark fifth floor corridor towards my room. I had my earphones in and I was listening to music. Then out of nowhere, I felt two sets of forceful arms come from behind and lift me up out of the wheelchair. "Let's go Stefanazzi." The military police from the 1RE in Aubagne had come to get me. What are they doing here? I was surprised. They had already packed up my gear from my bedroom while I was out.

They drove me straight back to the 1RE. They gave me plastic cups of water to help sober me up from the days drinking. I suspected that this was the end for me, at long last. I am being discharged finally, I hoped. Why else would they bring me to Aubagne? I couldn't figure it out.

Maybe playing the cripple had really paid off. It really did look as if I was mad. Maybe it worked. But my hopes died as soon as they said that the MPs from the 1REG were on the way to pick me up. They told me that the hospital had called them to take me away because I assaulted a female security guard. Bullshit, I thought to myself. Then I remembered back to an incident the night before. It didn't seem like such a big deal.

I had gone out with the Bosnian guy in my room as usual to get a pizza. As the temperature was mild out, we found a small park nearby were we had our pizzas and drank some Rosé. We came back to the hospital a bit late. It was after the curfew. As we were going back in through the entrance, we were fooling around. We had a two litre bottle of Coca-Cola that we passed to each other. We used it like a rugby ball. There were two security guards at the entrance who gave out to us as because it was past the curfew. One of the guards was a woman. She grabbed the bottle of Coca-Cola off me. She thought that there was alcohol mixed inside. But it was only Coca-Cola. She even smelt it to make sure. She refused to give it back to me.

They were escorting us back towards our ward when the incident happened. Walking in the corridor, I slowed a little so that the security guards walked in front of us. She was holding the bottle of Coca-Cola by the lid, down by her side. Here's my chance to get it back. I ran up and kicked the bottle out of her hand. It skidded down the corridor. I grabbed the bottle and ran up the corridor, pretending to be playing rugby again. She never appeared to be hurt in any way. But apparently, I hurt her finger when I kicked the bottle. Now the military police were saying that I attacked her, which was an over exaggeration.

It appeared that I had just acted without thinking when I took the VAB in Sissone. Now a couple of weeks later, I was being taken back to the 1REG in the back of the jeep with the military police. The CNE, OPSR was agitated and confused with what to do with me. It was the second time that they had to come and collect me from another regiment. I was really getting on their nerves.

They took a wrong turn on the way back. It had been a silent trip apart from the hum of the engine. Then I broke that silence when they took the wrong turn off the motorway. What I said to him from the back of the P4 Jeep, made him even more furious. I said loudly in a slow but confident tone, "Il faut réfléchir avant d'agir, mon Capitaine."

I almost enjoyed the disgust in his voice when he replied, "Oui, Oui, et tu as réfléchi avant de tailler la route avec le VAB? Oui, c'est ca, Conard de merde!"

He was implying that I stole the VAB without thinking. It would seem like that. But the strange thing was that I did think about it. And I would probably do it all over again if I had to. It was very likely that I had lost my marbles but I still felt in control, in a strange manic sort of a way.

LAUDUN

While driving back to Laudun where the 1REG is located, they brought up the accusation again that I had assaulted the woman security guard at Laveran Hospital. But any excuse would be enough for them, that's all they needed to bring me back to their prison. And the big OPSR was happy to use this as an excuse to put me into the isolation cell. From a hospital psychiatric ward to a Legion isolation cell, they were pushing me towards real madness. Arriving at the prison compound, it was only then that they opened the isolation door. They kept that surprise till the last moment.

The OPSR and two CCHs escorted me into the isolation cell. I didn't resist physically. But I pleaded with them not to put me inside, that my head wasn't right. The other legionnaires who were in prison were asleep at this time but one guy came out to see what the noise was. He pretended to go to the toilet so he see what was going on. He stood in the courtyard looking on. It was dark but I saw that it was a 1CL from my section in the CCL. We shared the same room at the CCL. I was surprised to see him "En tôle." Just as I was being brought towards the cell, my eyes met his. I caught a ray of compassion in that glance. He said something like "Don't put him in there, come on." But the military police shouted at him and told him to get lost. They bolted the door shut.

I was happy enough to be in prison like the others but just not in the isolation cell. There were no windows in that cell. The room was tiny, only about six metres squared. Inside there was nothing but a single mattress on the tiled floor.

I lay there on the mattress, looking up at the blackness, feeling like shit. I was annoyed at my stubbornness. I could have just deserted when I had the chance back at the Laveran hospital in Marseille. How bad are things going to get before I give in? Was I prepared to die just to finish those five years? I asked myself. Then I realised that the questions made no sense. But nothing made sense. Maybe I was already dead inside. My soul had died and I needed to retrieve it somehow. I no longer cared about finishing the five years or what anyone else thought about the Legion. I had enough. Now, I just wanted to leave. I had nothing to prove to anybody. This was my life after all and I needed to take back control over it. Right there and then, I really hated the Legion. I had no honour, loyalty or respect for the Legion. I felt the same way about my father. If I had any once of fidelity left in my soulless carcass, it was reserved for the Legion dead. I closed my eyes and slept.

The prison compound was composed of two bedrooms with about six beds in each room, toilets, a shower room, a room for clothes, and an isolation cell. They all opened onto a small enclosed central courtyard. There were two more doors leading off the courtyard that were locked. From one of them, the military police could enter the compound and from the other door, the men on guard duty had access to us. There was a wire mesh high up over the central courtyard to prevent prisoners from climbing out.

From inside my isolation cell, I could hear other prisoners walking around in the courtyard. I could guess what time of the day it was from that. They came back in from gardening to polish their boots for lunchtime and dinner time. They had relative freedom to go from their rooms to the courtyard and to the toilets and showers. Only basic items, such as toiletries and spare clothes were allowed on entering the prison. The military police carried out regular checks and confiscated any

172

items found, such as mobile phones or cigarettes or money. You risked getting an extra seven days if caught with these things.

When they had put me into the isolation cell, I had no idea for how long it would last. I wasn't expecting it. The OPSR CNE ordered it. It had been late in the night when we all arrived back at the prison courtyard. He ordered the military police, "Put him into isolation, straight away!"

Now, the next day, the OPSR was back again to see me for some reason. He entered into my cell and closed over the door behind him. Two MPs waited in the courtyard. It was just the two of us in that confined space. He was right up in my face, intimidating and insulting me. I simply looked at the ground without moving. I knew all he wanted to do was find any excuse to lay into me with punches. Then he left the cell but just before the MPs locked the door, the OPSR asked me if I wanted some books to read. I didn't understand his twisted thinking. One minute I was close to getting a beating, the next I was being offered some books to read. Was this some sort of bargaining? To get me to play ball and just go along with the isolation for a few days. I couldn't be sure. I said yes to the offer and they brought me some books later that day. What kind of psychological tactics were they using here?

That first morning when I woke up in the cell, I had the uneasy feeling of waking up and not knowing where I was. I was disorientated. I had a very deep sleep. My door opened three other times the first day besides the OPSR's visit. It opened for breakfast, lunch and dinner. Each time, my food was brought on a plastic tray. There was a plastic spoon and a plastic cup. The food even looked plastic too in the dim light of my dark cell. I asked the CCH from the military police when he brought my dinner, if I could have a shower. He said that maybe tomorrow I could. That sounded promising at least. I asked how long would I be kept in here and he said he didn't know. He bolted the door shut again. It was only six pm in the evening and I hadn't even completed twenty four hours yet.

My body was getting itchy with nerves and built up energy. I had no idea how long they would keep me in there. I did some push-ups to try and burn up some of that anxiety. I glanced through the three books they had brought me. But I couldn't read anything in the dim light and my head was sore. It was not just sore from the drinking spree in Marseille the day before but it felt sore and full, full of annoying thoughts running around. I started to feel the same disgust as I had felt back in CENZUB. And once again I knew something with crystal clarity. I knew that I could not stay inside that cell. The otherworldly sense was coming back upon me.

But my imagination found it hard to think outside this actual box which I found myself in. This time it would not be as easy as just jumping into my VAB with the Alpha team. I might need someone else's help here.

But I still had a little fight left in me. I decided that I would stop eating the food they brought me. I also decided that I wouldn't drink any more water. I was unsure what the outcome would be but I knew it wouldn't be easy. I remember asking an English LEG once what would happen in the British Army if a soldier went on hunger strike in an isolation cell. He told me that they would wait for him to pass out and then force feed him with a glucose drip. I was curious to see would it go that far in the Legion. I made the decision to stop eating. That night I slept with my demons.

The following morning, I woke feeling hungry and surprisingly fresh. I heard the bolt on the door opening. Fresh bread, butter and jam and a bowl of coffee on a tray were slid into the corner of the room. The CCH just said, "Bonjour Stefanazzi," in an almost friendly tone. I replied, "Bonjour, Caporal Chef." The door bolted again. I had second thoughts about going through with the hunger strike after getting the whiff of coffee and fresh bread. But my stubbornness got the better of me and I threw a blanket over the whole tray. This was the start of the end.

I was entering unknown territory and I was afraid. The hours passed and I grew hungry. I heard the other prisoners talking outside. I knew it was lunchtime when they came back in from work to polish their shoes in the courtyard. In the evening, I heard them chatting and the showers running. I even smelt the cigarettes they managed to smuggle in. Lunch and dinner came that day, and I put a blanket over the food each time. No words were exchanged between me and the military police any more. They silently replaced the trays each time. I refused to eat. I was extremely hungry, but more determined to continue with my little rebellion.

The next morning, on the third day, the CCH from the military police asked me why I was not eating anything when he brought breakfast, this time with a croissant. I remained silent. I had also stopped talking when I stopped eating. I was using the tactic of going mute again. But sometimes I wasn't sure if it was a tactic or if I was really unable to speak.

Lunchtime came. They saw that I was continuing not to eat and I had stopped drinking water too. They saw that I had poured my water bottle over the ground. The tiled ground was all wet. They refilled the empty plastic bottle with water, handed it to me and said, "Boire Stefanazzi." I poured it out again as soon as they bolted the door shut. The puddle of water flowed out under the door and onto the courtyard.

That afternoon, I began to feel quite desperate. I knew the seriousness of not drinking water. I lay on my mattress beside the large puddle on the floor. I lay on my side and peered into the puddle of water and at the man in the reflection. I cried when I saw him, I saw Jesus Christ.

I lay back and stared up at the ceiling. I took a few deep

breathes and surrendered. "God" I said, "If you can get me out of here, I swear to you, I will never drink alcohol again." I meant it at the time.

That was a hard deal for any Irishman to make. But I could see no possible way out of there. Even with the Alpha team, it seemed hopeless. There were no windows or anything that I could break. The room was bare except for the mattress and a plastic bucket in the corner. Since I hadn't been eating, there was only urine in the bucket. Then I considered that when I would take a shit, I would rub it all over the walls in the form of a dirty protest. It didn't come to that, thank God. Not at that point, at least.

I looked at the only item in the room that might spark something in my imagination. The small radiator was fixed solidly to the wall beside the door. I looked at it for some time. In the silence and boredom of my isolation, my mind went into creative mode. Then, an idea just came to me. The fact that the radiator was close to the door was important. I noticed that the large solid bolt on the door was only in the middle. There were no other bolts at the bottom or top half of the door. There may be a little movement at the corners of the door. The radiator was also to the right side of the door, close to the side of the door which opens. I needed to test my idea.

I got down and lay on my back close to the door. With my feet at the bottom of the door I lifted my legs up and bent my knees into my chest. Using my right hand, I made a strong grip on the solid pipe under the radiator. Luckily the pipe was only lukewarm. This grip prevented me from sliding backwards. The radiator and pipe were just the perfect distance so that I could pull myself up closer to the door. I still had my runners on my feet but without any laces. They had only taken the laces out. Without my runners this idea would have been useless.

I gave one kick with the heel of my right foot on the bottom right corner of the door. To my delight, I felt how the door shuddered and moved ever so slightly. The position I was lying in was similar to those gym machines where you push a weighted platform while lying on your back. Like some sort of squat machine. Only here I wasn't pushing a platform but kicking the corner of a door with my right leg. I had strong legs. I was always good at using that machine in the Legion gym.

I kicked again, this time a little harder. The force of my kick spread through the door. I could feel the large bolt and the fixation on the door frame absorb the force. Those kicks made a lot of noise.

With the next heavy kick, I felt the first hit of adrenaline in my blood. I continued at a steady pace, giving powerful, stamping kicks to the door. The loud noise shuddered through the whole building. It sounded like some sort of deep tribal drumming. Each heavy kick, I followed with three light ones to build momentum... BOOMdududuBOOMdududuBOOMdududu... it grew louder and louder.

One of the prisoners became alarmed and called from the courtyard "Stop! Stop! What are you doing Stefanazzi?" I recognised his voice. It was my roommate from the CCL. It was the same chap that I saw late the other night. He had come out to have a look and our eyes met just before they put me inside the cell. He was a small dark guy from Nouvelle Calédonie. He reminded me of an Australian Aborigine. He too was growing a beard for Camerone. We were going to be Pioneers together but not anymore.

I ignored him, although I was pleased with the concern in his voice. It actually encouraged me and gave me strength to go on. I knew that very soon the military police would be in. I expected that I might get a punch or two from them. But I was desperate to get out, so I continued stamping...

177

BOOMdududuBOOMdududuBOOMdududu…

A plan of action came into my mind for what I would do if they came and opened the door. I would stop my stamping and immediately lie back on the tiles, motionless in a crucifixion type pose, in the puddle of water. This would pose no threat. To beat me in this Jesus like position would seem wrong.

I soon heard the angry voices of the military police as they rushed in to the prison courtyard shouting. They were coming towards my hell. "Arrêt, Arrêt, Putain de merde" they shouted at me to stop. But I continued even harder with my kicks.

There was now a constant flow of adrenaline pumping in my muscles. I heard them unlocking the big bolt on the door. I stopped, laid back on the wet floor, motionless and silent in my crucified Jesus pose. The door swung open, the two CCHs grabbed my arms and legs and lifted me back to the corner of the room and onto the mattress. The SGT from the twenty four hour guard stood outside the cell, along with another CCH from the military police. They all screamed at me and threatened me as best they could so that I would not continue. But I found their insults pathetic. I remained silent and motionless on the mattress. They slammed the door shut and bolted it again. The noise they made was nothing compared to my super-bass beats. They didn't know that Stefanazzi was gone.

It was now early evening of the third day in isolation. I had caught a glimpse of twilight outside when they had come. This was my chance. Darkness is coming. I knew that I would do whatever was necessary. I'd been beaten up already in the legion, and I was prepared to take another beating if necessary. I felt like a caged animal. I had stopped caring about possible outcomes. I felt both in control and out of control, a sort of outer body experience. I wondered was I possessed. If so, then that demon, angel or ancestor was very welcome to inhabit my body.

All the former anger, fear, disgust, excitement, and pleasure had turned into numbness. Mentally, I was in a mess, and I needed to communicate this visually. The next plan entered my head and it wasn't me who put it there.

I stripped bare naked except for my runners. I lay on my back on the cold floor in the wet puddle of water. I shivered. Goose bumps created a new skin on my body. I poured out the bottle of drinking water they had refilled again when they threw me back onto the mattress. I emptied the bucket of dark yellow piss onto the floor, mixing it into the puddle. The liquid seeped under the door and I heard it dripping onto the courtyard outside. I started humming some strange sounds which were out of my control.

Sliding around in the wet floor, I took those three books I had been given. I began pulling the pages off one by one. Some pages I stuck to my body, some I crumpled up and some I scattered anywhere. My humming got louder and stranger. It sounded nonsensical. It reminded me of some sort of Native American chanting, something from deep in my DNA. The chanting was healing the inner turmoil that I was experiencing. I felt I was going into a sort of trance.

I slid around the wet floor in that mess. I wet my face and hair and stuck pages on my neck and head. The chanting was building in speed and volume and that creature inhabiting my body slid up again towards the door. I took my position, arsehole, balls and cock in the air, ready for war. The creature stopped chanting suddenly without me knowing why. There was a brief ten seconds of silence, of oneness, of bliss, before the thunder of the kicks. Twilight had ended.

This was the war. There was no going back. I stamped and stamped and welcomed the warm rush of adrenaline through the creature's veins...DOOMbububuDOOMbububuDOOMbububu...

Soon again, I heard the shouting of the military police and

the guards outside in the courtyard. "You stop right now," They angrily demanded. But it fell on deaf ears. This time I didn't stop. I couldn't stop. I was gone.

The regular rhythm continued. They tried to open the bolt but it was jammed shut. They couldn't open it as long as I kept kicking the door. The loud thuds shook through the building and echoed deeply in the courtyard. Those sounds spoke for me. They were dark sounds and defiant in their regularity. They ran deeper than my awareness. They carried ancient hurt and ancient power.

Small cracks appeared all along the doorframe. Pieces of plaster and chunks of cement fell outside on the ground. Ever so slightly, the door began to weaken and the bolt started to give way. The pounding continued. The bolt shook more and more, and the echoes grew louder through the whole building. More lumps of the wall fell off and the cracks grew deeper. White plaster and dust fell on my face and covered my whole wet body. I wasn't cold anymore. My heel was aching and possibly injured but the adrenaline helped.

After a long period of silence on their part, I heard the voice of the military police again. But their tone was different. "C'est bon, C'est bon, C'est fini, C'est fini. The doctor is on his way," one of them said. But I continued anyway. My mind was slow to process any information. I didn't want to acknowledge anyone anymore. Nor did I trust anyone.

In many ways, I was broken. The feeling of complete indifference was present. But something which is broken can always be broken down into something smaller and smaller, until like sand it becomes formless.

I eventually stopped. The door was opened and the doctor, the COL, stood there in blue jeans and a check shirt. The military police stood behind him peering over his shoulder. For a brief moment, they looked puzzled at the sight before them. I was some sort of animal covered in a wet paper and white dust. "Stefanazzi, put on some clothes." the CCH threw a blanket over me.

The COL asked "What do you want, Stefanazzi?"

"I don't want to die in here!" I shouted back at him.

"You won't die in here," he said. "But you need to eat something and drink some water. Will you eat?" Once again, I felt language to be useless in dealing with them. Just like before, I replied, "Oui mon Colonel."

He turned and signalled to one of the guards holding a fresh tray of food and water. I sat up on the floor, pushed myself back to the wall and spread the blanket on my lap, ready for a feast. Covered in shreds of paper and white powder, I felt that I was an Aborigine from Australia.

Reaching out with grateful arms I took the tray. I smiled and thanked them for the food. I waited for the guard to walk back out of the cell. The COL stood in the doorway with the military police still peering over his shoulder. They all looked on in hope and silence as I slowly sprinkled two sachets of salt on my dinner. I crossed my hands as if to say grace, but instead I roared out as loud as I possibly could "Bon Appetitttttt!"

The COL nearly fell over backwards. With the last drop of power left in my naked body, I flung the whole tray of food up towards the ceiling. Some bits of ravioli and red sauce stuck on the ceiling and walls. The tray crashed down, adding to the mess of the torn books on the wet floor. It was a right piece of artwork. But I didn't feel like the artist.

They closed over the door without bolting it. Outside I could hear the COL say to the military police that I was to get dressed and brought to the infirmary. I was surprised that the stunt had worked, although it didn't entirely feel like a stunt. I was thankful to the creature for its help getting me outa there.

At the infirmary, I was shown to a room and told by the

medic on duty to take a shower. There was food in the kitchen that I could reheat in the microwave. I was left alone.

The place was silent and felt safe. I wondered what would happen in the next few days. I slowly took a hot shower, noticing the pain in my right heel as the adrenaline wore off. I felt exhausted and completely drained. I put on some fresh clothes. Oddly, I didn't feel hungry but I knew I should eat something and get some water into me.

I looked at myself in the mirror. I still had a beard at this time which I had forgotten about. I saw some hints of red in it. I thought about my Celtic roots. Then it occurred to me that the next day was the seventeenth of March, Lá Féile an Phádraig. I imagined that a millennium ago, Paddy must have suffered a lot more than me during his time as a slave. I wondered did he ever crack up in the head just a little bit too.

I made my way to the kitchen. There was no one around. The infirmary was silent. I reheated some more Ravioli in the microwave. I got some baguette, cheese and a glass of water and sat down to eat in peace. I felt guilty for whoever had to clean up my mess in that cave they had put me in for the past three days.

This was my first food in forty eight hours. It definitely wasn't any record as hunger strikes go. I felt relatively safe there in the infirmary, but that didn't last long. Just as I had a couple of mouthfuls of Ravioli and I was starting to enjoy the food, I heard loud and fast footsteps from a bunch of people coming up the long corridor. I could sense this was bad so I ate faster to get the food in while I still could.

"Where is he?" I heard the angry voice of the big fat bully. I was sitting at the table, eating, when I saw them entering the kitchen in the corner of my eye. All of a sudden, I braced myself as the big CNE came running at me. It was an attack. He grabbed me and flung me backwards out of the chair while shouting abuse at me. I tumbled on the floor against the wall. "Move and I kill you!" He said, in an evil voice. "Now, you are fucking eating, eh? Tu me rends fou, Putain de merd! Tu ne bouge pas ou je vais te tuer tout suite!"

I lay rigid in a heap, like a piece of shit in the corner of the room. I felt weak and pitiful. I still had a mouth full of ravioli that I was now afraid to chew on. I breathed through my nose. There were two CCHs there from the military police pretending not to see anything. They stood with their backs turned and talked to the medic outside the kitchen in the corridor.

I anticipated a beating, but it never came. I wondered would any one of them stop him if he did start to inflict serious kicks and punches. He stood there with his fists clenched, towering over me. He was a heavy man, probably eighteen stone.

After a while he backed off and went out of the kitchen. He was ordering the others around. He had the military police wrapped around his little finger. I overheard him say, "Stefanazzi is to stay confined to his bedroom, he cannot leave the infirmary. Keep the blinds shut and check on him regularly."

They all left. I remained in that same hunched up position on the ground, but I chewed up my mouthful of ravioli. My sports top was torn and there were a few scuff marks on my shoulder from the attack.

Soon I heard the reassuring voice of the medic telling me to go to my bedroom and stay there. I grabbed some bread and cheese and went to my room. "I'll clean that mess up later," I said to the medic.

"Don't worry about it," he said. He was a decent bloke. There was a mess of food splattered across the table, wall and floor. The 1REG had now two pieces of contemporary Ravioli artwork.

The next day, during a review with the COL doctor, I told him what had happened. He shrugged his soldiers and ignored it. He just said that I would continue to stay in the infirmary for the foreseeable future. No mention of returning to Laveran in Marseille.

I was now confined to my room in the infirmary all day except meal times when I could go to the kitchen. It was better than the isolation cell at least. I pulled the window blinds up despite the CNE's orders to keep them shut. I could see the inviting clear spring sky outside. The idea of civilian freedom seemed like a paradise.

I got stuck into lunch and dinner when it came. I done some push ups in my room and took two hot showers. I sat there, thinking what was next or what my next move could be.

It was a beautiful crisp St. Patrick's Day outside. I thought how it would be great to be out in an Irish bar having a pint and having the Craic. I regretted again not deserting while I had the chance at Laveran in Marseille. I no longer cared about finishing off the stupid contract. My stubbornness was beaten and so was I. The Legion had won and they could now spit me out like a piece of Ravioli.

I thought to myself about why I was so stubborn to finish the contract. Even though there was only five months left, I hated this place. "I hate this whole fucking thing," I thought. "I've lost any respect I once held for those in power. I don't need to prove anything to nobody or to myself. I couldn't care what people will think if I desert. I have enough."

I sat up in my bed in the infirmary that afternoon and made the decision. That was it. I would leave that St. Patricks night. This would be one last adrenaline hit for the road. I felt excited that I would be going back to Ireland and never returning there again. It was time to start a new life. I was deserting.

The Foreign Legion offers people a new home, a new family. I never felt at home in the Legion. In fact, I never felt at home in Ireland with my own family. It took years for me to understand this as being an unconscious reason for joining the Legion.

Returning back to a dysfunctional family was madness. Hoping to fix my childhood was a delusion. The past was the past. I took for granted the second chance of a life which the Legion offers to people. Many would give anything to become a Legionnaire. I turned down a potential career with the Music section of the Legion.

The truth was that I had options outside the Legion. Knowing that had contributed to some of the misery I endured. I never fully committed myself to the Legion. Eighteen was definitely too young for me to join. Some things are not meant to be. But still, everything has its function strangely enough. I wasn't just fighting against the Legion, I was fighting against myself. And that fight would continue with or without the Legion.

The CPL medic on duty that St. Patricks day was a genuine good guy. In the evening time it was just him on duty at the infirmary. There were only three patients including myself, staying overnight at the infirmary.

He was a North African, from Algeria I believe. Algerian Legionnaires must have had a hard time justifying their Legion status to themselves. The Legion was created for Frances hold on North Africa. Many men had died fighting there. The Legion headquarters was once in Sidi Bel Abbès, in Algeria.

It's often said that the Legion was created not to spill French blood. On the surface, I understood this, but when I thought about it more, it appeared meaningless to me.

The word, Meaning, itself is a concept that I sometimes don't understand. Life is experience. Meaning separates us from life. Meaning creates I, the eye within The I. This is how wars begin. Any dream of a utopian earth without conflict or wars, can only come into fruition with a break down in the Meaning of I.

However, I'm not sure how things would go if everybody went psychotic at the same time. It would definitely be confusing. And who wants a utopian earth? How God damn boring would that lie be? Perhaps the possibility lies in a gradual emergence of a singularity across the earth, rather than a bolt of lightning from east to west.

Until we become experts of our own self, I'm not sure if this can ever happen. The bold of lightning is an internal flash of truth. The Japanese call it Satori. The religious call it Grace. Jesus called it the kingdom of Heaven. The Buddhists call it Nirvana. The Celts called it Tír na nÓg or Mag Mell. The doctors call it a Psychosis. Modern Spiritual writers call it Oneness or a mystical Experience. I simply call it home. Once we go home, there is nowhere else left to go, because it's everywhere.

For some reason, I knew I could count on this Algerian Medic who was on duty in the Infirmary that St. Patricks night. I approached him that evening and explained my situation. I told him I was desperate to leave, but that I had no money. I asked if I could borrow fifty Euros. I promised that I would post it in a letter back to him. He gave it to me.

I told him that I would leave by the back exit of the infirmary just after midnight. I would have a taxi waiting for me outside the base. I told him how I would climb over the perimeter fence in a dark area shaded with trees near to the infirmary.

He would alert the military police when he did his next regular two hour checks and found that I was gone. This way, nobody would presume that he had helped me. I was very grateful to him. And I did keep my word and post him back a fifty Euro note a couple of days later from Paris. But he was the sort of guy who didn't expect it back. He knew that I was really desperate to leave and he was decent enough to help. I found it ironic that the last guy I would speak with in the Legion would be a good soul. But who knows? Maybe the whole situation was set up to facilitate my desertion attempt.

AVIGNON

That night I prepared my small bag - musette. I felt a sense of déjà vu come over me. It seemed similar to my night time escape from CENZUB.

I phoned a taxi and told the driver to wait two hundred meters past the main entrance. There was a place where he could pull in at a side entrance to the base which is kept shut. It is a quiet and dark place there. Surrounding trees provide shade along the perimeter fence.

I was ready by midnight. I waited at the rear exit of the infirmary. I was looking out the window towards the side entrance. I was watching for my taxi to pull up on the other side of the fence. My heart beat grew faster.

Just as I saw the taxi pull up, I was about to leave the infirmary but I heard the sound of the military police P4 Jeep. Talk about bad timing. I felt my heart jump. I stood still, looking out through the glass door of the infirmary. Through the line of trees along the perimeter fence, I saw the Jeep speed up. They drove past the taxi. They were just going on their routine patrols outside in the local area.

As I heard the noise of the military police Jeep, fade into the distance, I pushed open the door. I walked at a normal pace so I would not alert anyone who might be walking in the vicinity and see me. I went directly to the trees, scanning the area as I went. There wasn't a soul in sight. I was over that fence in no time. The warm addictive feeling of adrenaline was pumping once again through my tired body.

I greeted the taxi man and hoped that he would start driving quickly. "Avignon, centre ville, S'il vous plait," I said calmly as I sunk into the back seat. Two kilometres down the road and away from the 1REG, I felt a smack of collective emotion engulf my body. Relief was entangled within a ball of other emotions. Happiness was even in there someplace.

I had a friend called Martinez from my section in the 1CIE. I had served with him for the last four years. He was Chilean. He lived off base, in an apartment in Avignon. He had less than five years of service and he wasn't supposed to have a place other than his room at the 1CIE. I phoned him. He was surprised to hear my voice. I asked him If could crash at his place that night. No problem. I told him I would get the TGV to Paris early the next morning.

As it was St. Patrick's night, the Irish pub in Avignon was full. The taxi dropped me off at the square nearby. I saw a large crowd gathered around on the square outside the pub. I walked past the pub as it was on the way to Martinez's apartment. I didn't want to take the chance of going in with my Legion sports clothes even though I was dying for a cold pint. There was a high possibility that there would be someone from the regiment inside. The word had spread across the 1REG and then the Legion about me and the VAB. Never mind the Legion, people right across the French armed forces had heard about it. There were lots of made up variations of the story circulating.

I missed out on having a beer at the Irish pub to celebrate both St. Patrick's night and my desertion, but my Chilean friend had a cold one waiting for me when I arrived at his place. I had already forgotten about the promise I made to God. More likely, I just pretended to forget about it. But I could never forget how I got out of that isolation cell. I was unsure whether it was from my own efforts, or from divine intervention. Could it be both?

Martinez was hoping to stay living in France, with his

girlfriend in Paris, after he would finish with the Legion. Like me, he looked forward to finishing his five year contract.

He had some left over paella. He heated it up in the microwave for me to eat. I got stuck into it and cracked open a second beer. We chatted for a while and we both laughed at the fact that I was now a deserter. We had been to Djibouti, Indonesia and the Ivory Coast together. I crashed on his Sofa that night.

I was up early the next morning. I borrowed hair clippers from Martinez. Getting rid of that beard was a good feeling. As the wiry red tinted hairs collected in the sink, I then saw an eighteen year old Dublin boy in the mirror, a boy who ran away to join the Legion, his age frozen in time. I took a moment to accept him and then whispered "Common Kev, let's go home."

I dressed in a pair of blue jeans, a grey hoodie and runners. The hoodie had a Fighting Irish logo from NOTRE DAME University, on the front. But I admitted defeat. I was finished fighting.

Martinez made us a quick coffee. We left his studio apartment and went outside into the cold crisp air. With the smell of that morning air, I thought of legionnaires at the base preparing for a long run through nearby rocky trails and bare vineyards. I threw away my legion sports clothes into a rubbish bin on the street.

A friend of Martinez, another South American chap, picked us up with his car. He was a CPL from the CCL and had over five years of service. They dropped me at the TGV train station in Avignon before continuing on to the base.

I thanked Martinez. With a strong handshake and a rare hug, we promised to keep in touch. But like many others, we never did. I knew that he hated the Legion but at the same time, he was the sort of guy who may stay there. He may even have become a CCH with thirty years of service. You just never can tell what goes on inside a Legionnaires head.

189

At the TGV train station in Avignon, I was anxious that the military police would be looking for me there. I didn't want to hang around. I kept my eyes open while I was buying my ticket at the machine. I then went straight up to the platform. There was a twenty minute wait for the next train to Paris. That wait felt like an hour during which I imagined two MPs coming up the escalator and onto the platform. It never happened, they never came for me.

I took my seat in a nice quiet cabin. My anxiety melted as the TGV departed. Its speed crept smoothly up to almost 300km/hr. like many times, I went and sat in the buffet cabin looking out at the landscape speeding past, the same landscape that Legionnaires would be doing their long morning run. But I was no longer a Legionnaire.

It was too early for a beer and I didn't want one. I didn't have to numb myself anymore as I wasn't going back to that dreaded place. I looked out at the fleeting landscape while I dipped a Pain au chocolat into a hot coffee. I tasted what I thought was freedom.

PARIS

On arriving in Paris, I went to the post office bank. I somehow managed to withdraw money from my account after explaining to them that I had lost my ID. I went to an internet café and booked a one way flight to Dublin departing the next morning.

I had been issued with a few new passports over the previous five years. The Irish embassy in Paris was very helpful. There was an old lady working there who I got to know over the years. The first time I went there, I explained how I was in the Legion and that they had confiscated my passport. The old lady issued me with a one way emergency document. It was really just a piece of stamped paper with a photo on it. They issued these for a single trip to Ireland. She told me to declare my passport lost when I got back to Dublin. This was the only way I would be issued with a new one even though it wasn't true because it wasn't actually lost. It was being kept by the OPSR of the 1REG. Bureaucracy couldn't handle that possibility.

The first time that I flew back to Dublin, I had completed about one and a half years of service in the Legion. For the next two years I used to travel home on this new passport I got issued. On returning to France, I would leave it at the embassy in Paris. The old lady kept it in my file there. I could collect it whenever I was flying out.

The time came when I got my name rectified from Sims to Stefanazzi. I could now officially request to spend PLD outside of France. Each time I was granted PLD abroad, I would collect the old passport from the OPSRs office and I would leave it back there upon return. This was the normal procedure.

But I also collected the new one at the Embassy in Paris. I was unsure if the old one was still valid to travel with.

Returning to France from my trip to South Africa, I had forgotten to leave the new passport back at the embassy. Then a few weeks later I had been AWOL for three days. On my return, the military police did a routine search of my belongings. They found my second passport hidden in my locker. They confiscated it. At this point the OPSR's office had two passports of mine.

Soon after that, I again flew home with a piece of paper issued by the embassy in Paris. In Dublin, I went through the same process of getting another passport. But with this third passport, I was penalised. They limited its validity to two years but it cost me the same price as the standard ten year one. I decided to leave this one off base with an Irish friend of mine. He was a CCH and the only other Irishman in my Regiment.

But now I needed that passport. I had left the infirmary to desert from the Legion and go back to Ireland. I couldn't get in touch with him to collect my passport.

I was back at the embassy in Paris requesting another emergency document to fly home. The old woman had recently retired and the new people were not as supportive. They reluctantly produced the piece of paper once again that would get me home. But because my flight was the following day, I had to come back and collect it in the morning. I went off and booked into a small hotel in central Paris.

It was a basic hotel. I had stayed there many times before. It was quiet and modest. There was always the same old Arab man at the reception when I arrived. We greeted each other. He knew me by now, and I checked in for the last time.

I wandered around the cold streets of Paris that day. I bought myself a nice warm winter coat and gloves. I walked through an amusement park, filled with the sounds of young kids and their parents. Twilight fell and for some reason, it felt like Christmas time. It was probably the smell of hot wine being sold at a little street market. I took a glass and sipped in the rich flavour.

Nearby, I watched a Ferris wheel going around silently. I felt lonely and sad all of a sudden despite the warming drink. For a moment I wished that I was one of those French children, joyfully innocent and feeling loved. But I was in no man's land, torn between a dysfunctional family in Dublin and the Legion family I now left behind.

I wandered through the dark streets of Paris and stopped at an English Pub near my hotel. I didn't feel like drinking but I went in and had two pints of ale, quietly at the bar. I was happy to sit and think and drink. There was a lot to process. I went back to my hotel room and fell asleep while watching some old French film on the television.

The next morning, I had breakfast and took the bus to the airport. I phoned my father while I was on the bus and told him that I had enough of the Legion. I was coming back to Ireland for good. He said "Ok" without sounding surprised. He said that he would pick me up at the airport in Dublin.

My parents had separated. He was retired. I felt like staying a few days with him before going to live with my mother. I wished that somehow things would be different. Maybe we could all get on like a happy family. But I was leaving the authoritarian regime of the Foreign Legion to return to an Authoritarian father. This was the reason why I left for the Legion in the first place. Going back to that was just as insane as joining the Legion.

It was a dull morning in Paris. I was on the bus going to the airport. It was cold too. It reminded me of the gloomy Irish weather which I left behind. It now felt a little sad to be leaving France. I watched people outside the bus living normal lives. I felt that, although I was in France for four and a half years, I was living in a sort of bubble, a soldier's life. It was mostly a lonely existence. I wondered how much of that fact was determined from my own life choices.

My anxiety of being stopped by the military police had faded since leaving Avignon on the TGV. It now seemed guaranteed that I would be back in Dublin in just a few hours' time, starting my new life. I had started to accept that I was really a deserter now. I could live with that. But if someone had said to me, right there and then, that I was destined to complete the five years, I would have said, "Absolutely not. That's not possible! I am about to fly home in two hours."

BEAUVAIS

I checked in my bag and got my boarding pass for my flight at the Ryanair desk. I was at the small Beauvais airport, north of Paris. I walked calmly towards border control and joined the queue with my emergency document from the embassy in one hand. My mind was elsewhere, thinking of Dublin, as I approached the hatch.

The officer in the cabin looked at my document for a moment and then ran a check on my name in her computer. She hesitated for a while, focusing on a screen in front of her. I thought to myself, has she never seen an emergency passport before. That must be why she's taking a bit longer than usual. But then she looked up at me and said calmly, "Attendez Monsieur." She signalled to her colleagues nearby. They came over and into her little cabin. The three of them looked at her computer screen for a short time. They whispered something to each other. Then they came out to me and said, "Can you come with us please sir?"

They escorted me back to the nearby police station within the airport and told me to take a seat. I was still unsure what was happening. I waited for some time and then I slowly became concerned. There was bunch of police in that office doing administrative work. I saw then that one police officer printed out some paper and looked at me as he was reading it. Then he asked me if I was in the military. The penny dropped.

That sickening feeling I thought was gone forever hit me in the stomach like a punch. In an instant, I felt once again, weak and broken. "Oui," I replied and giving into the lump in my throat, I cried.

Crouched over with my head in my hands, I sat there feeling helpless. The legion had put an alert out when I took the VAB, to prevent me from leaving the country across a land border. Apparently, a notification had been sent to all the French border controls.

"Where is the VAB right now," they asked. I didn't have the energy to explain the whole situation to them. I wanted to get that flight.

"That was weeks ago," I said, in a defeated tone. "They have the VAB back, it's all over now," I sighed. The alert was still on their computer system even though it was now almost a month since that night in CENZUB.

When I saw one of the police officers bring me my bag which I had checked in earlier, I knew for sure that I wasn't flying home to Dublin. After a long wait, they told me that this was an issue for the Gendarmerie and not the Police, as I was a soldier. They escorted me out of their compound, across the parking lot of the airport to the Gendarmerie station.

The atmosphere there was different than with the Police. It was regimented. The guys looked strict and mean. I was told to sit down in an office. The ACH on duty said, "Do we need to handcuff you? If you will be nice with us, we will be nice with you."

I felt I was back in the Legion already. I had no energy for this bullshit so I just went along with anything they said. I replied, "Oui mon Adjudant chef, pas de souci." He said the SCH would take a statement from me, and he left the office.

A younger man entered the office. He was clean shaven with black hair. He wore an obedient look on his face. He sat across the room behind a wooden desk. I sat on a plastic chair against the wall three metres back from his desk. I wore a depressed look. My shoulders were slouched down in defeat. I felt ashamed of the little leprechaun with this two fists up stitched onto the front of my hoodie. I wasn't living up to that Fighting Irish image.

The Chef took a few seconds to quickly tidy the desk and prepare his notepad and pen. He said to tell me exactly what had happened from the beginning. The beginning of what, I thought to myself. Once there was a big fucking bang!

I was glad I had some humour left inside me despite the circumstances. I recalled the events for him. I spoke in a low, flat tone. Without emotion, I told how I had enough of the Legion, and how I borrowed the VAB to get away from the training manoeuvres at CENZUB. He stopped me at times to get some clarity. There was no clarity in such a mess. I was disillusioned. The whole fucking thing was a sham anyway. I continued describing how I went to see a doctor that night in CENZUB but to no avail. Then I had felt desperate. I prepared myself to leave with "mon VAB."

He kept writing as I spoke clearly and slowly. I got to the point when, "I entered the picturesque city centre of Reims at approximately two a.m. with this 13 tonne Armoured Vehicle, bouncing along the cobblestones." I detected a slight grin from the corner of his mouth, but he controlled it well. I then described how I found, "une bonne petite place pour le garer"- a good little spot to park it.

"Où ca?" he demanded.

"I parked it in front of a little pink boutique, maybe it was a bakery, a patisserie, or a lingerie. I cannot recall exactly."

He continued writing, but then gave in to the smirk hiding behind his stern face. He burst out laughing. To my amusement, he stood up and left the office, all the while laughing and coughing. The ADC stormed into the office with a red face. "C'est quoi ce bordel ici là?" he shouted.

I shrugged my shoulders, "Je ne sais pas, mon Adjudant chef".

After the SCH laughed his guts out and had a quick cigarette outside, he came back in looking relieved. His face was less stern and he looked like someone who had just released a good shit, lighter and more relaxed. He picked up his pen and completed my statement. He then got me to read it and sign it before he left the office.

I waited for a good forty minutes sitting there, wondering when the military police would arrive. I considered that Fort de Nogent in Paris where I first presented myself almost five years previously was the closest Legion base. They surely wouldn't be happy to come all the way here to Beauvais to pick me up. What would happen after that, I pondered.

Eventually the ADC came in and sat down. "Bon... Stefanazzi," he said while exhaling a long sigh. "I called the Legion in Paris and explained the situation. But they told us that they want nothing to do with you. We cannot keep you here either. However, don't waste your time and money trying to fly back to Ireland. It will be the same result for you again. Even if you try to go to Spain or Belgium, you will be stopped at the airports there too."

How ridiculous is my situation, The Legion don't want me back. But I can't fly back to Ireland. What the hell am I supposed to do? I'm stuck here in France.

"How much money do you have?" the ADC said.

"One hundred Euros," I said. But I had about five hundred Euros. He suggested that I should get the TGV back down to Avignon and present myself back at my regiment, the 1REG. If I done this, he hinted, they might consider taking me back in.

He said that I should telephone the local Gendarmerie station in Laudun, just before I arrive at the 1REG gate to let them know I was there. He would be in contact with the local Gendarmerie in Laudun. He no longer needed me there so I was free to go. But he made it clear that I was not to hang around in Paris. I was to go straight back down to the 1REG immediately. He then let me leave.

The ADC and SCH stood at the exit and sparked up a cigarette each. Looking as confused as I did, they wished me, "Bon Courage."

I walked back out into the dark grey afternoon with my dark grey hoodie. I put my hood up. My head was in a mess with thoughts scattered everywhere like torn pages from a book. I bought a ticket and took the same shuttle bus as I had that morning but going in the opposite direction.

Alongside a busload of arriving Irish tourists, I found myself going back into Paris. I saw some sights I had bid farewell to that morning. I got off the bus and walked up the Champs Elysees, approaching twilight. The first kebab shack I stumbled across, I murdered two big cans of 1664. They were ice-cold. I then went on a two-day drinking binge in Paris and I done two lines of cocaine.

I couldn't face the idea of going back down to the 1REG. I was really unsure what to do. I didn't believe what the ADC had said about attempting to fly to Dublin from somewhere outside of France. Maybe I should have gone to Barcelona and try flying from there. I had already made up my mind that I was finished in the Legion. I had accepted my deserter status. But now I was faced with the unthinkable option of crawling back to my regiment with my tail between my legs. I knew the Legion would love to see that. It was all about power and obedience.

I don't know how, but something shifted inside me, on my last night in Paris. Maybe it was the two lines of white stuff that I sniffed up my nose along with the load of whisky and Cola I poured down my neck, but I convinced myself to go back and just finish off the bloody contract.

I not only convinced myself to do it but somehow, I knew

without a doubt, it had to done. It felt like some kind of divine intervention, a sick joke even. Whatever hell they would throw at me, I would take it on the chin for five more months. The universe was telling me that it was my destiny, like a pre-ordained path. I couldn't get off it no matter how hard I tried. The Legion could kill me if they wish. I was dead anyway. But that's if they let me back in of course.

For some reason, I never even considered going back to the Irish embassy in Paris and seeking their assistance to get me back to Ireland. I often wondered if they would have helped me or not. And I didn't even consider going to my Cousins in Bordeaux. Somehow I was convinced that finishing my contract was the only path.

LA CIOTAT

With just enough money for a train ticket to Avignon, and with a thumping hangover, I made my way back down south. I attempted to sober up, but not too much in case I changed my mind. I went back to the 1REG that evening. It had been almost four days since I left the infirmary and jumped the fence.

Arriving at the pedestrian gate of the 1REG, I pressed the buzzer on the intercom. I presented myself and waited for the guard. The SGT on duty came out and told me through the metal bars on the gate that I was not allowed inside the base. He told me to wait outside while he made a phone call.

I waited outside for almost an hour as it grew dark, wondering what possible outcome there could be. I mentally prepared myself to sleep outside the gate if it came to that. My anxiety fuelled imagination conjured up a scenario of me, rolled up in a ball, shivering on the pavement outside, while one of the military police comes out and throws a bucket of water over me. The faceless MP shouts, "Dégagé d'ici clochard de merde."

My day dreaming took a break when I saw one of the military police come out, but no bucket of water. It was the same CCH that had to deal with my shenanigans while I was in isolation. To my surprise he said, "Look Stefanazzi, you can come in and you're going straight in to the prison just like the others, but no more messing around. You got it?"

"Oui Caporal chef," I said obediently. I knew he had probably just spoken on the phone with the CNE, the OPSR. I went inside and joined the few other prisoners in the prison compound. I wasn't put back into solitary, thank God.

The next day, I was escorted by the prison guard to my room in the CCL. I took a shower and got dressed into my formal uniform and Kepi Blanc. I had to present myself in front of the Chef de Corps (CDC) - The Commanding Colonel of the 1REG. My formal uniform was composed of a grey suit with gold-coloured buttons. Attached are insignia and medals in barrette form. The outfit included a beige shirt, green tie, black shoes and Kepi Blanc.

I made no effort to put it on correctly. I just threw it on anyway I could. It had many creases and the tie wasn't straight. I had long lost my pride and I couldn't have cared less about wearing the Kepi Blanc. I was broken, depressed and numb.

I still hung onto a small sparkle of hope that the CDC might say they are kicking me out of the Legion and they were terminating my contract with immediate effect. I would be sent immediately to the 1RE in Aubagne to complete the process.

To what extent did I have to fuck up in the Legion to get kicked out? I used to hear guys say that it was too much hassle for the Legion to terminate a contract. It was easier for them if you just deserted. But I couldn't achieve either. Then I remembered the epiphany like moment I had the other night in Paris. I knew somehow, from a deep unconscious source of wisdom, that I was destined to finish off my time.

As I waited in the corridor to be called into the CDC's office, a SGT came out of a nearby office. He had one of those cushy administrative positions. I didn't like the look of him, a real admin Trou de cou. I knew he was just another scumbag that probably sucked the Colonel's cock. He spoke down to me in a condescending manner and poked his cheesy fingers at my medals. He said in a voice I knew he took pleasure in, "Because of your dishonourable behaviour, you don't deserve to be a Legionnaire. Don't you know, Stefanazzi, that you can no longer wear one of those medals? You have to take that one off.

Then you must get the whole set readjusted at the tailors."

I said nothing and stared blankly at the wall in front of me, holding in a strong urge to reply, "Take the fucking smarties and shove them up your hole."

The ADC in charge of the prisoners called me into the CDC's office. He had already been in there for a good while. I walked inside the large office but I deliberately refused to make eye contact with the COL. I was feeling completely dejected.

I looked up for the first time at the COL's red face when I stopped and turned towards him. About four metres back from his large wooden desk. I gave him a shite salute. My face wore a flat expression. There was no pride whatsoever in my appearance. I felt like a corpse. I remained silent for a period of time when the required formal presentation was expected. There was a long silence to see if I would give it but I remained catatonic and speechless. Finally, the COL said cleverly, "Do you want to go back into the isolation cell?"

With that, I let myself cry but without any embarrassment. I was broken at last. "Non mon Colonel" I managed to say.

"Bon, CPL Stefanazzi…" he began. "Je te condamne à quatre-vingts jours en tôle. Forty days for leaving your post on duty and forty days for taking the VAB. And that's not all. I will see you after those eighty days are complete, for possibly another twenty in return for the structural damage you created to the isolation cell. You will have a small break between the two periods of forty, as I am obliged to allow you out for a few days. Ok Stefanazzi, you will do your punishment that you deserve. After that, you will take any accumulated PLD before your end of contract in August. Maintenant, tu peut disposer."

"Je peux disposer à vos ordres mon Colonel," I said and I saluted a little sharper this time. Despite the long sentence, I was feeling a little better. I left his office as the tears dried on my face. I would do my time in prison and then take my PLD.

No more bullshit. Just put my head down and get on with it, I told myself.

The CDC wanted to make an example out of me within the 1REG so that other Legionnaires wouldn't try the same thing and get off lightly. I understood that but I definitely didn't get off lightly. Even though I spent eighty days in the Legion prison, I was still summonsed to a civilian court in Nimes because the COL had pressed charges against me.

Strangely, the Court date for the Tribunal de Grande Instance in Nimes happened to be the day immediately after my eighty days in the Legion prison were up. I knew nothing about it. I was only told when I was on my second last day in prison.

I finished my prison sentence and the day came to go to court in Nimes. I dressed in my formal uniform. The ADJ Adjoint from the OPSR's office drove me to the courthouse in Nimes.

There was a lawyer there to represent me. She spoke to me briefly before we went into the courtroom. I tried to explain to her in my limited French how I was the victim of an assault and provocation in the Legion in previous years. I told her I was worn out completely and that I felt desperate that night in CENZUB. She appeared not to care and she just scribbled down a few notes.

Inside the courtroom, there were many trials going on. The judge went quickly through each case. Then my case came up, "The Chef de Corps of 1REG vs CPL Stefanazzi." I never got a chance to speak, or was even asked to speak. I just sat there in my formal uniform, my Kepi Blanc clutched in my sweaty palms, feeling betrayed. There was an officer there from the 1REG who represented the CDC. With the stress of it, I broke down crying.

The lawyer representing me gave her defence plea from the few notes she had taken outside. It all lasted less than few minutes. There was no mention of the eighty days which I had just spent in the Legion prison or the time I had spent in the psychiatric ward at the Laveran hospital. When it was over we left the courtroom. Then the lawyer told me that her fees were seven hundred Euros and that I must pay her up front. It was easy money for her. She had a small credit card machine. I paid the fee by card. To make it sound like she had done a great job, she said that I was lucky with the outcome. The judge had only given me a one month sentence, suspended over five years.

With hindsight, I should have represented myself and told the judge about the shit I had been through. It might not have changed the conviction but at least I would have felt better if I had the opportunity of explaining myself. I felt utterly betrayed by the Legion. I felt raped. Maybe my father was right five years ago when he said that I would be raped; raped morally and spiritually.

I finished off my five year contract and that's what I got out of it; a criminal conviction. That was my departure gift from the Legion, never mind PTSD and Schizophrenia.

A few years out of the Legion, I found out that due to collaboration within the European Union, details of that conviction were communicated from the French Police to the Irish Police - An Garda Síochána. It came up when I was getting vetted for a Job. When the conviction was translated from French to English, it sounded worse than the reality of it. On the Garda Síochána records, it read like this, "Abandonment of Post/Duty by Military in Peace Time, Diversion or Dissipation Military Weapon Denier or Object presented During the Service."- Tribunal de Grande Instance, Nîmes, France.

But there was no weapon involved besides the VAB itself. This was a thorn in my side. It was declared by An Garda Síochána every time I got vetted for a job. I was even denied entry into Canada because of the conviction. The Legion likes to boast that they look after their men and that any discipline is kept internal, a strong tradition which they claim to uphold. But this is clearly not the case. They broke this old tradition with me.

When I wrote a letter to An Garda Síochána to query why it has not become a spent conviction, I was told that it would stay on my record for forty years, according to the French authorities. But they got this wrong. Ten years after the conviction, I wrote to the office of The General Prosecutor in Nimes. He returned a letter stating that my record would now be wiped clean as ten years had passed since the conviction. He acknowledged a ten year period was considered rehabilitative. After this, I was conviction free completely. He advised me, although I no longer had any convictions in France, it was still up to me to write to An Garda Síochána again and make sure that they delete this conviction from their records.

It did not make sense for An Garda Síochána to disclose it as the conviction never appeared on my French Police Clearance Certificate. It was only on the French Police internal private records. The Law in France prevents the French Police from disclosing minor offences with less than a two year sentence. However, An Garda Siochána seemed to do as they pleased. They disclosed it every time I got vetted and they disclosed it on my Irish Police Certificate when I attempted to get visas to work overseas.

The whole ordeal caused me a lot of hassle. What's strange was the date that An Garda Síochána had recorded for my conviction. Conveniently for the Legion, it was recorded as being handed down on the day after my contract with the Legion ended. My five years ended on the 26th of August and the conviction and court date was recorded as being on the 27th of August. This was clearly false. I was convicted at the TGI in Nimes on the 26th of June. It seemed that something strange was going on.

This was an attempt by the Legion to clean their hands of

me. Once Again, they didn't want to be seen to break that old Legion tradition of keeping discipline internal. They wanted to uphold this lie. They had no problem once my civilian conviction was recorded on a date after the five years were up. Then I was no longer a serving Legionnaire. This is proven by the following; at the 1RE in Aubagne, when I was leaving at the end of August, I was given my Service Certificate. On this Certificate it states that I had no military incarcerations. But I spent in total just over 220 days in a Legion prison during my five years of service. On that same Certificate and under the section for civilian Convictions, it is marked 'Unknown.' But they knew very well about the conviction handed down in Nimes in June, two months earlier.

The whole military jurisdiction situation was unclear. I remember one time during my Radio and Signals training course at the 4RE, the French Minister for Defence at the time was visiting the 4RE in Castelnaudary. All the prisoners who would usually be out gardening during the day were locked up inside the prison for the whole day out of sight. Apparently, the Legion prison was not supposed to exist.

I began those eighty days in prison - en tôle. I moved around in fear, expecting someone to give me a hard time. But it was prison duty as usual for me. Strangely, I was left alone to do whatever gardening duties assigned to me. Nobody came near me and I didn't get any hassle. The days flowed by. I was trusted to carry out my routine. Changing bed sheets in the morning was followed by cleaning the permanent officer's quarters and the MP's quarters. Then sweeping and gardening for the rest of the day.

The days became weeks. I kept my head down, determined to finish my eighty days. The ADC in charge of the Service Général and in charge of the prisoners seemed to turn a blind eye to me. He even made sure the CCH prison guard gave me some of the easier duties as time went on. Most days I was trusted to go off and work on my own initiative. I was given a list of things to do each day. I would come back at lunchtime and dinnertime. After dinner we were all locked in the prison compound.

But like always you can never get too comfortable in the Legion. There was always one arsehole that would step in and infect everyone else with his miserable existence. This time it was one of those CCHs who liked giving you meaningless jobs. Nothing was ever done to his liking. He was a French CCH, tall, skinny and bitterly sarcastic. At one point when he ordered me to scrape all the gulleys with a hand brush just to annoy me, I refused to and I said, "Why are you giving me this shit for nothing?" Before I could blink, he had his two arms around my neck and he pushed me up against a metal fence, shouting abuse in my face. When he was finished choking me, he just walked off. Roll on those last forty days, I thought.

The days were long and monotonous but at least it was springtime and the weather was improving. The Camerone festival was approaching. Because of this, there was a never ending amount of gardening, painting and polishing to be done.

I tried getting into a healthy routine of running around the base in the evenings. We were allowed to run laps with a guard present. With the other prisoners, we set up some circuit training in the prison courtyard for after our runs. I was exhausted at the end of each day, but in a good way. I slept without any problem. The break from alcohol did me good too. But that didn't last long, even in the legion prison.

The week leading up to Camerone, three of us had to clean out a large hall. The prison guard only came to check on us every half an hour or so. One prisoner was from Newcastle in the UK. He was a right character. It was good to have another Anglophone around. He was the joker in the bunch of prisoners and gave us some great laughs. There was another guy, Cheskov from Russia, whom I got on well with.

That day, the tree of us were sweeping the hall and clearing aside the chairs. There were a few small rooms at the back of the stage. Miller, the clown from Newcastle went wandering around the back of the stage. He was peeking into one of the rooms. Then he came out, his eyes wide open like a child in a sweet shop. "Lads, lads, come here quick, have a look!" he said with excitement.

There was a stash of boxes of red wine in that little room. I'd say a good hundred bottles or more. We made a plan together. We would leave one window slightly open in the hall area before we finished work. We agreed to keep our treasure find, a secret between us. The plan was to try to get some bottles at a further opportunity.

But Miller couldn't wait and got stuck in, necking a whole bottle. At this point, we were nearing the end of the working day. Soon the guard came back, locked the building and took us back to the prison compound. But before the guard had arrived, Miller had already downed a second bottle. The effects were hitting him. He was staggering all over the place, and was buckled by the time we got back to the compound. The guard didn't pick up on this because Miller was always acting the fool. We all had a good laugh in the prison courtyard when the effects really hit him. He lit up six cigarettes at once in his mouth and smoked them before he passed out on his bed.

A few days later it was the weekend and the regiment was practically empty. When we were allowed out of the prison compound in the evening to run laps around the main square of the base, we used that opportunity to move the wine. The guard on duty was very relaxed. He went back to the guard room while we were running. He said that we had forty minutes to run and then he would be back to collect us. He trusted that none of us were going to try jumping the fence or anything like that.

It was evening time on a Saturday. The base was deserted. Cheskov and I went back to the hall where we had left the window open some days before. Miller kept running, so he could be the eyes on the square. He would come and get us immediately if he saw the guard coming back.

Cheskov was a small guy, compact and more agile than me. He got in easily enough through the window without making any noise. From inside, he lifted up the cases of wine to me. "Only red," I said. We took six cases of six bottles. Not to make it too obvious that some were gone, we left about twelve cases still in the room. He climbed out and we closed the window. There was a bushy area of trees nearby. We hid the six cases of wine really well there. With the buzz of a little adrenaline and our mission completed, we ran off and joined the runners before the guard came back.

We were happy with ourselves having pulled it off. Every few days, when the guard was slacking, we would go grab a bottle of wine each and then hide in a quiet spot on the base.

At the far end of the Regiment, there was a ditch that was well sheltered with pine trees and bushes. Sitting there, we had a nice view out through the fence onto the main road. The three of us would chill out there with a bottle of wine each and watch civilians walking past the base. Now and then, a nice French woman would walk past. We would whistle at them. We laughed, knowing they were probably wives of some NCO on the base. Miller would shout, "Suce ma bite," in his Geordie accent. We were in stiches laughing every time. The women would look around but see nothing. We were well camouflaged in our little ditch. We were far from the trenches of WW1.

Cheskov was at the end of his contract too. He had got twenty days for disobedience of some kind. It took a few weeks but we got through those six cases of wine. They were nice.

The first period of forty days went by quickly. It turned out that I finished that period on a Friday morning of an extended bank holiday weekend. I was expecting to get permanence duty or some other duty at the CCL but I didn't. To my surprise, I had the whole weekend off. Rather than just go on the usual piss up in Montpellier for three days, I decided to go and visit my cousins near Bordeaux. They knew nothing about my past few months of madness. I didn't want to bring it up. I just wanted to enjoy their company and forget about the Legion for a few days.

My cousin's parents were retired. They lived in a peaceful village, an hour from Bordeaux. They were happy to see me. They really treated me as family. That weekend, my cousin Emmanuel and his wife also came to stay with his parents. It was great to catch up with him.

I pretended that everything was going well for me in the Legion. My cousin was a SCH in the French regular army. We had met a few times since our coincidental connection in the Ivory Coast. We were chatting away and then out of the blue, he asked me about a story that had been circulating in the French Regular Army. He asked me if I had heard about some Legionnaire who had deserted with a VAB from CENZUB. Apparently the story had gone around like wildfire through all of the French Armed Forces. Before I could even respond, he could read my face. He smiled and said, "As soon as I heard that story, I knew it was my cousin Kévin, un vrai Stefanazzi."

I filled him in on the true story. Like a Chinese whisper, there were so many other alternatives of it.

I had missed Emmanuel's wedding a couple of months back. I apologised for missing it as I really wanted to be there. I explained the whole story to him and how I was in a psychiatric ward in Marseille, while he was getting married in a village in the Pyrenees.

Before I joined the Legion, I never knew of my third cousins in France. It was one of those beyond chance encounters when we met in the Ivory Coast. It was good to have the support of him and his family in France. Those few days break with them gave me the strength to return to the 1REG and start my second period of forty days in prison. The last forty days felt a lot longer than the first, but I knuckled down and kept a low profile. My PLD was on the horizon too.

When I returned to the CCL after that weekend with my cousins, I was told to pack my bag and go straight back to the prison. I was refreshed and motivated to get stuck into forty days of gardening.

Before I had left the CCL for that weekend off base, I had completed a written request for my last PLD. I had thirty days of PLD accumulated. That translated to six weeks of paid leave. I had to take them before the end of my contract in August. The dates all seemed to match up perfectly like everything was unfolding as was meant to be.

I had even requested an overseas PLD to Ireland. I thought there was no way they would grant it, after I had tried to desert. But they did. On returning from PLD, I would only have two weeks of service to complete in the Legion before the five years were up. This would involve one last week in my regiment doing the rounds or my "Circuit de départ." I would be giving back most of my gear and signing off in different offices around the base. Then the very last week I would spend at the 1RE in Aubagne. This would involve completing another Circuit de depart before walking out the gates as a civilian. And that was a moment I was truly looking forward to.

My last forty days in prison went by slowly. I was literally counting down the days until I finished. One day I sat down and on a piece of paper, I added up all the days I had done in the Legion prison during those five years. It came to a total of about two hundred and twenty two days without counting the extra twenty that might be coming. Bu luckily, there had been no further mention of the extra twenty day punishment for damaging the isolation cell door, since I stood in the CDC's office three months back. And I didn't dare ask about it.

One week before my time was up in prison, I got great news from the ADC of the General Service. My six weeks PLD to Ireland had been granted. I was delighted but also in shock that it was approved. But they probably didn't want me to come back from my six weeks leave in Ireland. That way, they could list me as a deserter.

By the time I had finished in prison, I felt I had become part of the Service Général itself. Every day I was to be seen outside sweeping, trimming bushes, weeding, painting rocks, or polishing the large brass regimental signs and plaques. The guard changed every morning. I saw the same SGT's and CPL's come and do guard time and time again. There seemed to be some guys who were often assigned to guard duty. They were probably near the end of their contract too and getting all the extra tasks. One SGT from Romania who I knew from the 1CIE, was on guard duty a lot. When I was on my last few days, he came up to me while I was sweeping outside and said, "Hey Stefanazzi, you're still here! How is that possible?"

"Quatre-vingts jours Sergent," I said. "Quatre-vingts jours."

The time had eventually come for my overseas PLD. It was a dream, come true. I collected my Passport from the OPSR's office. They gave me two passports of mine which they had in their file. In a way, the time spent in prison was good. It meant that I saved up money for three months before going on such a long PLD.

It felt unbelievably good that sunny Friday evening, getting dressed into civy clothes. I left all my camouflaged gear in my locker at the CCL. Never again would I need to put them on. I knew that on my return from PLD, I could remain in sports clothes as it would be my last week in the 1REG and I would be doing my Circuit de départ.

That glorious Friday evening, I walked out across the main square. I was dressed in blue Jeans and a t-shirt. I carried a large rucksack on my back. I smiled to myself as I watched some new prisoners being marched by the guard towards the canteen for their dinner. Life in the Legion never stops. But tonight I'd be having Steak au sauce Roquefort et frites with a good bottle of Red wine, in Montpellier. Walking across the square, I passed a former colleague from my section at the 1CIE. I had served with him for four years. On seeing me he said in a joking manner, "Where are you off to, Stefanazzi?"

"I'm just taking six weeks PLD, that's all," I said and we both laughed. As I walked out the main gate of the 1REG, feeling the hot evening sun on my face, I knew that I was almost there. I didn't fly straight back to Dublin. I needed to unwind.

After another great weekend in Montpellier, I rented a bungalow in the seaside village of La Ciotat for seven days. I would fly to Dublin after that.

The place where I rented the bungalow was called the CHALE. It was a centre owned by the Legion. They rented out accommodation to Legionnaires and their family who were on leave. Not many people knew about it. I had invited my brother and his girlfriend to join me there.

It was July. The weather was hot in La Ciotat. Our days were spent swimming in the sea, lounging around, and having barbeques in the evening with cold bottles of Rosé wine. It was a winding down period for me before returning to Dublin. It was also the start of trying my best to forget about the Legion and focus on my new civilian identity. For years afterwards, I tried in vain to forget about the Legion. But I could not forget it so easily. Despite my denial, it had become part of me.

One of the days while we stayed at the CHALE, a new Legion recruit (EV) was sent over to clean our bungalow accommodation. He was a young chap. As usual, he was dressed in a blue tracksuit which we all got during our initial screening in Aubagne. He appeared nervous and afraid and he was constantly running around the place. He had all his cleaning equipment ready and was eager to get stuck in to the cleaning of the bungalow.

At least he was motivated. I remembered that I was too at that early stage. I let him clean for a while, and then when I found out he was American I told him to stop and take a break. That was enough cleaning. I cracked open two ice cold beers for us. We sat at the kitchen table. I introduced him to my brother and his girlfriend. I told him that I was just finishing up in the Legion. I advised him not to do those five years. I said, "Get out while you can, it's not worth it." Whether he did or not I will never know. Sometimes people just got to find things out on their own. And besides that, there are many others that really enjoy Legion Life. I cannot deny them.

BORDEAUX

When I returned from my six weeks PLD, I went to the office of the OPSR, to return my two passports. This was standard. The military police and the ADJ Adjoint OPSR were surprised to see me. The ADJ asked if I had been back in Ireland during my PLD. I said that I was.

"And you came back?" he said, shaking his head in disbelief. Yes, I could have stayed in Dublin without returning. But that was exactly what they wanted for me, not to return. The alert to stop me at the French border controls had been lifted.

Ironically, I had been desperate to desert about four months prior to that day, when I jumped the fence. But now I had returned from Ireland by my own free will, to finish off the last two weeks of my contract. No one had expected me to come back.

I didn't serve the eighty days in prison for nothing, never mind those five years. Of course I came back to finish those last two weeks and complete my contract till the very last day. I wanted my Service Certificate. I wanted to officially walk out the gates of Aubagne like everyone else.

I also wanted to bring my formal uniform home to Ireland which I did. I didn't know then that one day it would be hanging up in The National Museum of Ireland – Collins Barracks. But more importantly, I had that moment of light in Paris when I realised that not finishing those five years wasn't an option. It was a moment of epiphany which broke down the sense of time. The past present and future all became one and I felt connected to something greater than me.

That last week in the 1REG, I completed my Circuit de départ. I stayed in sports gear. I was left alone to complete it, by going around getting a form stamped in various offices. On my last day, I returned to the OPSR's office to collect my personal items in a file. I got my two passports and a few items that I had surrendered five years before when I presented myself at Fort de Nogent.

There were a set of keys I had forgotten about to the house I left behind in Killester, Dublin. There was no Leatherman pocket tool. It had been given to me by my good friend Martin from the FCA before I joined the Legion. I always wondered if I would get it back. I now knew that the CCH in Paris had taken it for himself.

It was customary that my section organize a little drink that last evening for my departure. But it just felt like a procedure. I went through the motions of saluting and shaking the NCO's hands. The transport section of the CCL was largely composed of people at the end of their contracts. We weren't all so familiar with each other anyway.

That weekend, I left the 1REG for good. I had accumulated a fair amount of stuff during the five years. I gave most of it away. I sold some useful items to new recruits. I dumped other stuff. It was nice to lighten my load but I had still had two large canvas bags to bring back to Ireland with me. It was the start of a minimalistic lifestyle which I have carried on into later life with me. My life at that point consisted of two dark green bags of stuff. And even when I considered the contents of those bags, I realised that I could have done without them.

That weekend, I caught up with a couple of Legionnaire friends in Montpellier, at the Irish Pub we knew so well. It was a proud moment for me. It was great to have a few beers with a good friend of mine from Roscommon who was serving in the 2REI. He was a solid chap and a great soldier.

We had first met at the 4RE in Castelnaudary. He was a new Legionnaire in basic training and I was doing my Radio and signals course. Now, when I was saying farewell to him, he was a CPL with four years of service. He had another year left to do. We had a good few pints in Montpellier over the years. I wished him the best of luck. We agreed to keep in touch and meet for a pint one day back in Ireland. Our friendship was one of the good things that came out of the Legion; Amigos para siempre - Friends for life.

I made my way to the 1RE in Aubagne. I left it until just after midnight on Sunday to arrive. I was still a little drunk after a great weekend in Montpellier with my friends from Roscommon and Wales.

Anyone who was arriving for their Fin de Contrat, had to be in the 1RE at the latest by ten p.m. on the Sunday night. I reckoned, one final little bit of disobedience can't hurt. Or maybe it could, with one last Claque to the head.

I only stayed for three days at the 1RE in Aubagne. They let us go early, on the Wednesday afternoon. About fifteen of us were at the end of our contracts. I met a couple of guys I had done basic training with five years earlier. I hadn't seen them since. It was a nice feeling seeing them again at the end of our contracts. It turned out that most of the sixty two of us who started basic training hadn't made it this far.

Those few days I spent in Aubagne, consisted of doing another Circuit de départ, by getting a form stamped in all the relevant offices. I completed mine during the mornings so I could spend the afternoons at the outdoor swimming pool on the base. It was late August and the weather was great.

Wednesday morning came. I had my Circuit de depart completed. Traditionally, on the last day everyone puts on their formal uniform. Together, a group photo is taken with the CDC. This photo is then included in the back pages of the monthly Legion magazine, Le Képi Blanc. I was looking forward to having my photo in the magazine.

Just as we were all about to get dressed into our uniforms, I was pulled aside. The SGT on duty told me, "CPL Stefanazzi, you can stay in sports clothes and stay in your room. Watch TV if you want. I've been instructed to inform you that you're not going for the group photo with the CDC."

I was disappointed afterwards about it, but at the time I couldn't care less. So I just chilled in my room watching the music channel while the others changed into their suits and went off for their photo with the COL. I missed out and I wasn't included in the group photo for Le Képi Blanc magazine. I had always enjoyed looking at those group photos over the years, to see who was leaving and to see the look in their faces.

After Lunch, I had my last coffee in the Legion. I sat on a bench outside the little shop called the "Foyer du Légionnaire." It felt surreal, to be actually finishing up. I sat there in my shorts and singlet, sipping a little black coffee, in the nice hot sun, trying to believe that this was really the end. In a nearby building, I could hear new recruits being roared at. I went into a daydream:

I remembered back to the time I was there in that building myself with the other Irish guy, Brian, five years previously. At that time, I was sad that he was being let go and even a bit envious. Those of us chosen to stay received our complete uniform and kitbags. I remembered we were standing to attention on the square, dressed in our new combat uniforms. We had all our heads shaven. The others who didn't make our group, like Brian, had their civy clothes back on. We watched, as they were led away in single file towards the exit of the base. They had each gotten some cash for two weeks work. They had all their personal stuff returned. I remember feeling that I wanted to be with them and walk back out through the gates, back to civilian comforts. But my stubbornness wouldn't let me.

The CCH had shouted at us, as we watched the others leave, "Now is your last chance, Qui veut partir civil? Mama, Papa, PlayStation? Just lift your hand and you can leave with those guys right now!" There was a long silence. Nobody moved. I wanted to leave but my arm was frozen. Something stopped me. And now here I was five years later. That same something had got me through.

The sweet black coffee brought me back from my daydream. Here I was on my last day relaxing outside the Foyer, without anybody asking me to do anything. I was finally at ease. I had actually done the impossible. I had finished five years in The French Foreign Legion.

I looked at my watch. It was one fifty p.m. At two p.m. it would be our last assembly. After that, we could collect our papers at the administration office. I sucked up the last drop of coffee. I strolled back to wait for the last Siren call, and the last Rassemblement.

The papers we collected included an important Service Certificate, a list of contact details for the Legion and a Certificat de bonne conduite. I was refused the good conduct certificate. I didn't care. At least I had my Service Certificate. We were now free to go.

Like many anticipated scenarios, walking out the gates of the 1RE in Aubagne was an anti-climax. The Russian guy Cheskov who had been in prison with me, finished his contract on the same day. I wore a Dublin G.A.A. Jersey. I got him to take a photo of me at the gates of the 1RE. I did the same for him. We took one last glimpse back inside the base and then turned our backs and walked away.

We walked to the train station and together we had a beer. He was heading to the Côte D'Azur to look for work in Private Security. We bid each other farewell. Leaving by train in opposite directions, we went to face life after the Legion. Some say that the man leaves the Legion but the Legion never leaves the man. Maybe there is some truth in that.

I had organized that my dad would fly over to Bordeaux that weekend. Because I finished up early in Aubagne, I stayed a few nights in Montpellier until his flight arrived on Saturday. Then we would go and spend a week at my cousin's holiday house in the quiet countryside. This turned out to be a bad idea. I left the Legion for the same reason that I left his company at eighteen years of age. Now, at twenty three years old, I was hoping that things would change. Maybe I could have a better relationship with him. It was supposed to be a week of distressing and possibly even bonding with my father and healing childhood wounds. But it was far from that. We argued from the first day. I soon regretted my deluded idea to bring him over. Nothing had changed. The past cannot change.

I wasn't any mentally stronger for the five years I spent in the Legion either. My mind was a fragile eggshell waiting to crack despite my body being in great shape physically. After the week with my dad was up, I flew to Dublin. He stayed on in France for an extended holiday. He was retired by that stage. I wished my French cousins all the best and I promised to stay in touch with them. I took the TGV train to Paris.

I had some time before my afternoon flight at the Charles de Gaulle airport in Paris. I sat down at a restaurant and enjoyed my favourite French meal, Confit duck leg with fried potatoes and salad. I washed it down with a good glass of red wine. I followed it up with a cheese plate and another glass of red before a crème brûlée and espresso to finish.

I relaxed at the airport and waited for time to pass. I then went to a disabled toilet cubicle to change clothes. I changed into my legion formal uniform and put my Kepi Blanc on for the last time.

I went through border control and found a bar near to the boarding gate. I sat there and placed my Kepi on the marble bar top. I sipped a beer and allowed myself to enjoy the odd glance from other Irish passengers who were also waiting on that same flight to Dublin. On boarding the Aerlingus flight, an air hostess curiously asked me what the uniform was. I modestly, but proudly replied, "The French Foreign Legion. I have just finished five years there."

I was proud of myself for getting through those five years. I was proud that, although I was broken in the legion, I had discovered some part of myself that couldn't be pinned down. It was a part of me that remained elusive, mysterious and unknown. This had allowed me to escape, somewhat, the brainwashing in the Legion. More importantly, it proved that, I might not ever buy into the expectations and beliefs of any group or society. I couldn't sell my soul or commit myself to any ideology however certain it might appear, if my own complete identity was uncertain.

My next adventure after the Legion was one of self-discovery or self-searching. This was an internal Journey or rather an attempt to see the internal on the external and fuse the two together. However, I wasn't aware of this as I was sitting on that Aerlingus flight back to Dublin sipping on a can of Beer. The truth was slowly revealed to me, just as life unfolds, along one path.

EAST

AFTER THE LEGION

"There is one body and one spirit,
Just as you were called to one hope when you were called"

Ephesians 4:4

"Indeed we belong to Allah,
And indeed to him we will return"

Surah Al-Baqarah 2:156

"With words, priests and poets make into many
The hidden reality which is but One."

The Rig Veda no. 3579

IRELAND

My account of those five years reflects a bitter distaste and bad experience of the Legion. Over the years when I have been asked, "Do you regret joining?" the easy response has been to say, that I have no regrets. I think however, that what I wanted to say is that I have actually accepted it as part of my life.

Even though we know that the past cannot be changed, we are not forced into having no regrets. But sometimes it seems that way. We believe that it is pointless to regret, as nothing can be done about the past anyway. But regrets can come and go like the tide. Regrets can be healing. There are times that I did regret joining and I did regret the suffering that my stubbornness not to desert brought upon me. How can I learn something if I don't allow myself to have regrets?

Even though I would say that overall I was unhappy in the Legion, I still became very much used to the way of life and thinking within its ranks. I was brainwashed but in a more unconscious way. Years later, when on some unexpected occasions, the thoughts of going back to re-join grab hold of my conscious attention, my confidence gets a beating. On these increasingly rare occasions I would think to myself, what the hell am I considering going back there? Usually these thoughts would surface when I feel a little lost, or when I am without direction in my life. They are part of a process, a healing process.

I always wanted a family I could count on. I felt that my biological family and my Legion family both failed me. I realised that I was alone after all with or without a family. This hard truth forced me to face myself and look deep within. It also forced me to accept my lineage and my ancestors. I began to feel that they were still alive in me somehow. This simple but difficult truth can transform loneliness into a loving solitude.

But the feeling of loneliness can also trigger a psychotic break, a breaking down of our individual reality to realise that we don't exist as an individual. I don't exist but God and all my ancestors in me do. In fact, only God exists, in an infinite amount of forms we call our world, along with the beings in it.

It's often denied that we are really alone in the world. I didn't need my family as much as I once believed. I could survive without a family. I began placing more importance on friendships too. I gained more self-respect and I gave more consideration to the people I wanted around me. I chose carefully who my friends were. It even made me more open to the possibility of starting a new family, one of my own choosing.

They say that we don't choose our family but I disagree. Of course, family can be wonderful and it can keep us grounded. On one level it's all we have. But it can also be another distraction, an excuse for us to hide from ourselves, to limit ourselves and settle for less than our potential offers. It can also be a source of blame and a reason for our diminished responsibility. We can never reach self-transcendence while clinging to family roles.

RATHFARNHAM

Less than a month out of the Legion, I found myself as a full time student in Trinity College Dublin doing a degree in Engineering. Really, I was still lost. I had free education through the public education system and because I had sat a good leaving Certificate exam when I was eighteen. But I was back living with my Mam and younger brother in their new home. My parents had already separated. The transition from Legion Life to this life was too quick, too soon. I didn't really know what I wanted to do. Again I got lost in a cloud of family dynamics.

While studying, I would daydream about going abroad and finding work in a private security firm like so many ex Legionnaires did. But I knew deep down that if I was unhappy in the Legion I would be unhappy in that kind of work too. I also realised that I was doing engineering somewhat from my father's influence. I wasn't enjoying it. So I dropped out of Trinity College after six months. I really needed to start listening to my heart, to find my inner voice. My real journey was only beginning. And it wasn't a journey with a gun and backpack or with books and calculators. It was journey into my heart, back to my lost soul.

I began doing any odd jobs I could find. I worked in a laundry and then as a barman. I did some labouring and some gardening work. I moved out of my mams and into rented accommodation with other people. Eventually I enrolled on a sports and fitness course. I completed it, getting my Certificate while still working as a barman with a recruitment agency. I was sharing a house with people in Rathfarnham. Even though I enjoyed the area of Health and fitness, I couldn't see myself working full time in a Gym. Every job seemed boring after the Legion. I knew that I would hate working in a Gym very quickly. I couldn't stay long at any job. It was time for a new adventure.

I applied for a Working Holiday Visa to Australia. I had been out of the Legion for two years but I was unable to settle in Ireland. I booked a flight to Australia and went into the unknown. Civilian life was a piece of cake compared to the Legion, or so I fooled myself to believe. I was almost a year in Queensland, Australia, when my mind began to unravel.

From this point on my story starts to take a turn away from the rational as I begin to loose grip on reality. I will tell of my experiences while crossing the unknown line between sanity and insanity. Craziness and madness are common terms used in place of psychosis but are often misleading. The following chapters are comprised mainly of a collection of memories over a two year period during which I had reoccurring psychosis. But first let us get some perspective on the idea of 'mental illness' before we look at my psychotic breakthroughs.

GAIA

I believe that there is much value in describing psychosis itself. It is too easy to avoid this and simply use the terms hallucinations and delusions without going any further into their subjective description. Psychosis is often overlooked as illogical and the substance of it considered irrelevant. But I believe there is great healing capacity in looking head on at the actual experience and the content of the delusions. We should not brush this life changing experience under the carpet and a Piano; brand name schizophrenia, placed on top. If we do this, the realness and hidden truth of the mystical experience will turn to wood worm and destroy that piano, slowly but surely.

My decision to write about my autonomous recovery was founded on the fact that I needed to expose my whole life story in order to put my psychosis into a context. And for this to happen, I needed to get my hands dirty. This meant exposing parts of me that I did not like. In other words, I had no choice but to embrace my Shadow Self.

Over a two year period I had been diagnosed on different occasions with Schizophrenia, Bipolar disorder type 1, and Schizoaffective disorder by different psychiatrists in Ireland Australia and Bulgaria. Schizophrenia was the most used label.

Once I had healed myself, I discharged myself from the mental health services. I got a copy of my whole medical record from the Department of Health (HSE) in Ireland; a huge mass of paperwork. It is clear from my file that the opinion of about seven different psychiatrists in Ireland, Australia and Bulgaria is that I had treatment resistant Schizophrenia. They had me drugged up like a balloon. I looked like the Michelin man and I spoke like a scared child as a result of the powerful antipsychotic drugs. It is important to understand now that this definition of "treatment" ignores or denies the Spiritual Whole.

Where once a diagnosis of Schizophrenia was considered a life sentence, thankfully it is slowly beginning to be understood by some people as a purely psychological and spiritual condition that can not only go into remission but can heal. It can become an illness of the past. In fact the illness of Schizophrenia only exists in the socially conditioned Self, in the mind of a person who has become a by-product of their environment and social norms. It is this same environment which is founded not on love but on fear.

I personally believe that the cure is in recovery but that Real Recovery is in the cure. What do I mean? I mean that recovery must remain completely subjective. Power and dignity must at all times remain with the person who is struggling.

The critically important thing is to understand that it is not only mentally ill patients who are in recovery. Every single human being on this earth is in recovery, recovery from the delusion that we find ourselves in. There is not one of us who has an exemption, not even Jesus Christ.

This realisation breaks down the divide between patient and clinician. But we do anything to deny this. We work harder, get a better salary, get married, have kids and recreate the same cycle of ignorance over and over again. I find it sometimes hilarious, because those people who we label as 'mentally ill' actually have a head start on the road to recovery. Their potential enlightening experiences blind others who just don't understand. Their so called "Madness" threatens our everyday fear based rationality.

I am not a believer in Lifelong Recovery yet I do respect this belief held by many. But it saddens me. I think a better name for that approach is Lifelong Denial. I mean denial of a possible enlightening experience, denial of a possible connection with the Universe. I myself have said that I am no longer in recovery, not even that I am recovered, but that I have recovered. But there is an error in using the word "Recovery." Ultimately there is nothing to recover. For me I could say that Schizophrenia is in the past tense, like a broken arm. It remains in the world of forms. You see, it's all about how we word these things or how each individual puts words to their own story. This is my story and my truth.

Not once in those two years of Western medical "treatment" was I asked how my experiences in the French Foreign Legion were. In fact there were times when I was extremely psychotic and I was expecting the Foreign Legion to come and extract me from a high dependency psychiatric ward. My claim to having served five years in the Legion was even considered delusional. Nurses and doctors laughed at me and at my delusion that I was once a soldier in The French Foreign Legion.

Any form of hierarchy only exaggerates and worsens the outcome for mentally ill patients. Why? Well, we just have to look at traditional societies around the whole world with thousands and thousands of years of tradition behind them. Seers, mediums, shamans, witchdoctors, healers, priests, tohungas, druids, are all terms for those important people who held a respected position in their tribe. They understood the spiritual nature of our existence. They were not a piece of shit, or treated as one. Often, a psychotic break was their initiation; the birth of a healer, the wounded healer.

In our modern culture, stigma and discrimination around mental health issues still exist and probably always will unless there is an acceptance that Jesus Christ was mentally ill. But this alone is not enough. More importantly, the Stigma will continue to exist until we accept that it is not merely a medical illness but a trauma based psychological and spiritual experience. It is the mud in which the lotus flower can grow. It is the suffering before enlightenment. Nirvana is the state in which we can manoeuvre safely within the realm of psychosis embracing the power of its non-duality. This requires training and strength. To deny thy self is to deny the mind. For discrimination to go away, psychosis must no longer be viewed as an illness. Only then can the societal and self-inflicted wounds of Stigmata heal.

Some people put themselves through great physical pain to test their perseverance. They swim cycle and run an incredible distance in order to be crowned Ironman. I say fair play to them. But I don't see any more rationality in that path than the path of mental perseverance.

I would like to see a day when people who come through and cross the finish line of the complete mind body and soul battle with Schizophrenia, crowned an even higher title. Maybe we could call it Goldman? What I'm getting at here, is that the person who has achieved this great feat is actually stronger and better for it than they were before. Unfortunately, the opposite view of being mentally weak and vulnerable is the basis for stigma and discrimination. The greatest sports person is nothing without a strong mind. But the strongest mind does not need his or her physical body because the strongest mind understands death and rebirth.

Although my acceptance of being ill for a period of time helped my recovery, my self-stigmatising had been damaging for my own personal growth. I use the idea of 'self-stigma' to describe the period when I began to believe in the lie of a lifelong illness. If the future remains unwritten, how could I possibly know it would be life-long?

We think we know because we are reduced to a statistic, reduced to our own limited perception of a categorised self in a world of other selves. But there is always the possibility of complete recovery. This is very difficult to accept, especially when everyone around you tells you otherwise. And the other thing to note is that what is being recovered was missing before the breakdown. Well, it seemed to be missing.

By going into the other realm, we are in fact recovering our true self. This requires a spiritual death and rebirth. This is why every soul on this earth, is in recovery.

Many people are searching for God without realising that they themselves are in the way. Instead of "finding God" I suggest "loosing your mind!" We need to make space for God.

Cognitive dissonance was a cause of daily psychological stress in the Legion. I could have either deserted or bought into their Ideal System. I didn't manage the last option of desertion and so I had to put up with the stress of not buying into their ideology.

Finding myself in other institutions; the mental health system and the institution of the Irish family, it proved more difficult to escape those environmental prisons. So my mind chose the other option to gain relief from the festering psychological stress. I gave in. I attempted to add another new part to my cognition by accepting the possibility that I was really just a sick patient. Maybe there are higher authorities out there who know more than I do. I became a pawn and a patient. I was forced towards that outcome. In doing so, I gave away my vital force.

But this was absurd, because there are no higher authorities beyond ourselves. When you really really really get that, then you don't need to read on!

But like a scared child, we go on pretending that there are higher authorities. And when this remains the case, yes, there's probably no chance of recovery.

So called "Experts" were telling me that I would never recover, that I had a physical illness with obvious abnormal brain chemistry. These same people were explaining to me the symptoms of something they had no direct experience of. I mean common guys! Really?

They were describing a realm they had not yet seen. They said my disorder was as physical as diabetes. I thought that I knew very little of mental illness, having zero education in school about it. It was very tempting at this point to surrender power and become a lifelong patient in the mental health system, perhaps a comfortable existence even. But so dangerously comfortable that it seemed it would be like a slow giving up. A slow assisted suicide I would dare say.

I began making friends who had similar psychotic experiences during the two years I was in the mental health system. But as I was getting better, their mind made hopeless outlook on life was very sad. Even sadder was their broken spirit as they believed in the lie that they were being told. Very few of them were recovering as I was. They were living very limited lives, terrified of coming off their medications. They could not see that their spirit was unbreakable, unconquerable.

This common spirit is the foundation of humanity; it is our common sense; our common divine self. It's the most obvious thing in the world yet we cling to our false identity. But our false identity is not bad, it's just false, that's all. It is a necessary falseness. We cannot deny our false identity and become God completely, that is the biggest delusion; that is the fall of Lucifer or the human sacrifice of a deluded Jew, which was the crucifixion. They are both the same thing, only expressed in different ways.

Our common sense lies in a childish curiosity, an eternal enthusiasm about the mystery of our existence. Be yourself and be God by being both your true and false self as one. There is no wrong expression of God. That is the hardest thing to accept yet the one that will bring the only real peace of mind. That is the game of life; the divine play of forms. The image or idea you create in your head of Gods nature is as false as your own identity. God is simply the potential that encompasses all possibilities of being. You are but one expression of that potential, one of the many forms of God. When you realise that, your falseness turns to truth and you become God. Jesus was only one of probably thousands of people to realise this.

It is a mind-blowing realisation that delivers you from time. Thus we can understand how we use terms like "Christ consciousness" and "The second coming" to describe our own awakenings. But denying our false self is the same as becoming God incarnate, and that is pure insanity in a world we deem to be sane.

Unfortunately, I didn't have all this knowledge going into my first round of Psychosis. I was pretty certain that I was separate from God. And I was pretty certain that my false self was not false.

For a time, I was no different than any other mental health patients. Like them, I buckled and gave in. I believed that yes, this was the end of a normal life for me. I even believed that I had a lifelong veritable illness. This easy route was really a temptation. Maybe I could be a baby again, suckle on my mummies titties. What a sad and pathetic existence. I bought into the lie and I took the bait.

Doctors, nurses and family members continuously reminded me, "Kevin, you're not well" and "Kevin, you have an Illness." Ironically, any low self-esteem and depression which arouse from this left me more vulnerable to continuous psychotic breaks. It was a vicious downwards cycle without an end in sight. For some reason God was attempting to push through the veil and awaken in me, but I was afraid, I was not ready, I was in denial.

I had gained a huge amount of weight and I slept fourteen hours a day. Instead of accepting that the meds had dangerously affected my metabolism, I was told that it was solely down to my diet. Bullshit!

But even with that easy path of giving up, there would always be more suffering. I knew that I had a choice. I chose Grace. I took the keys off Saint Peter and I freed myself once again.

As the Fog of medication wore off, and I got my vitality back, I began to notice something insidious too. I kept seeing secondary physical illnesses such as diabetes, obesity, epilepsy, sleep apnoea, Parkinson's disease, heart disease, fatty liver disease, the list goes on, developing among others who had none of these before their "treatment" for a mental illness. This was horrifying to see.

The meds were, in a non-direct way, knocking twenty or even thirty years off their lives. Sadly, they couldn't or didn't want to see that the meds were causing the secondary illnesses that were killing them. The medication, in my opinion was knocking the whole homeostasis of the human body out of kilter. They were expected to do sport and exercise but how could you when the meds sapped all of your energy, coordination, concentration, and motivation? When they left you feeling physically retarded, when they increased your feeling of hunger and left you with a constant dry mouth. I went through this myself until I took back the reigns of my own life.

I was probably close to developing diabetes and Tardive dyskinesia, before I rebelled and freed myself. I was already experiencing rapid uncontrollable jerking and muscle twitches. I often spilled a cup of anything I held. I felt myself sticking out my tongue and lip smacking uncontrollably to relieve the tension brought on by the antipsychotic drugs. I felt retarded but unable to do anything about it.

An important symptom of schizophrenia is strange behaviour. Ironically, the medication induced a dreamlike state in me and a sensation of being slightly drunk. The medication produced this sensation and thus, enabled me to continue with my disinhibited and inappropriate behaviours. This was very unhelpful. Because of their numbing effect, the meds facilitated my odd behaviour. This in turn, led to a vicious cycle of hospital admissions. This is the irony and destructiveness that the medications can produce. But on the contrary, all the socially abnormal behaviour that I displayed was being explained as a symptom of Schizophrenia. The fact that the meds facilitated this was denied by all those around me.

I couldn't sit still. The restlessness was torture. It was impossible to go to the Cinema as I'd leave after five minutes. I was told this was my illness, but it was clearly the medication. I couldn't read newspapers or books even though my eyesight was perfect. Again, this was put down to my so called illness. I could barely walk up a flight of stairs without being utterly exhausted. Again, this was lack of exercise!

Luckily for me, I did have on my side, age, physical strength and probably and most importantly a stubborn character that questions everybody's authority. A tonne of resilience built up through my service in the Foreign Legion definitely helped. And so, I left the mental health system by my own accord and I walked alone in the dark.

It was like completing an Ironman blindfolded backwards through the Amazon jungle. All I can say is that it was definitely worth it! But I couldn't have done it without myself; my True Self; my Golden man.

I felt mentally stronger than before I had, let's say, that temporary mental illness. From crossing the finish line of the Schizophrenia Ultramarathon Challenge, life has changed, life is different. Bu there is one essential component to point out at this stage. It is truly madness if we return to our old worldview and mainstream way of living that we had clung to before our mental breakdown.

Our old social conditioned selves and the society in which we live puts pressure on us to do so. Instead, we must accept and integrate our experience as a spiritual death and rebirth. The person before is no longer in existence. The Schizophrenic dies way before his physical death. He/she must learn to live with that.

We are expected to resume our blind existence in a logical global delusion. If we do this, we risk ignoring the powerful experience and the beautiful struggle that we went through. We risk ignoring the liberating potential of the Mystical Experience. This ignorance is very dangerous. There will always be an endless amount of suffering if we attempt to resurrect our old damaged self.

Even if you want, we can look at an alternative perspective; the Christian alternative. For the sake of it, let's give that beautiful and wise maniac Jesus Christ a say. He was a sage, a rebel and a ruler. He claimed to be in this world but not of it. He was right. But he was still trying to accept his new spiritual rebirth.

Because of his former boring existence, dead end job as a carpenter and living with his mum, he had a mental breakdown. No big deal. He became a rebel and a pain in the ass to the order of society. Big deal.

Struggling with psychosis and in an attempt to deny his boring, materialistic reality, he becomes lost and addicted to his own mania. Who could blame him? Such a powerful euphoric experience, it is completely subjective in nature. It can be pure bliss. His followers who were most likely feeling lost and disillusioned in their own lives encouraged him on his path of self-destruction. It's likely that they too had their own little bipolar episodes. But who was he really? I don't know. I never met the chap. Even if I did, we wouldn't be able to speak the same language. Did he even exist? I don't know. It doesn't matter. More importantly, do you exist?

Thank you for your madness Jesus the Nazarene King of the Jews. Once he realised his divinity, he went through his own spiritual death. He went off and preached to the people. In many ways he left Jesus the Carpenter behind and became a new person; God incarnate. But it was a mistake to leave his false self behind. In fact it just went into a deeper disguise, an excellent camouflage. Unfortunately his ego was still very much with him but hidden to his conscious, inflated self.

He thought he had left the old unawakened Jesus behind and was to begin his ministry as God made man. The opposite is true, and he clung on to his old self. He focused too much on his physical existence. His psychosis made him believe that he could physically cure people and perform miracles. His spiritual death was not fully complete. He drew too much attention to himself and because of that he was soon tortured and crucified. He wanted others to experience what he did. He tried desperately, sometimes utterly frustrated and impatient, to express this through words; an impossible feat.

It sounds as if I'm speaking in negative terms about him. I'm not. Do I pity him? No. Do I look up to Him? No. Do I love him? No. Do I hate him? No. Am I the second coming of him? No. But at the same time I could answer yes to all these questions.

We however, are more fortunate. We have the opportunity to come out the other side instead of dying during a psychosis. That is the only reason his death was not in vain. Apparently he did say, and to his credit that "Greater things you will do." But really there is nothing greater or lesser we can do. Everything we need is inside of us. Jesus knew that but many could not fully get it.

I believe that when God is fully and truly awakened in human form, he will have nothing to say. But when he is in the process of awakening, he will have lots to say, he can't stop talking.

So for us, the "Mentally ill" of this world and for our own experience of going off the rails, we must look back and decide on how we are going to view our experiences. Let's say we see our psychosis as purely negative and we wish it never reoccurs. Instead of being touched by grace, it then becomes an experience in vain. We return to an unsatisfying, underachieving, frustrated life. Probably we will then continue to be at risk of relapse. This fits perfectly with the mainstream medical model of a chronic disorder and prognosis.

Another option for us is to take the Christian path. In doing so, you will place Jesus Christ above yourself. This is equally risky. In both of these options, you will condemn yourself to a life as a scared and obedient adult child. What's the alternative? Mmmmm, let me think. Maybe, try listening to your heart!

My deepest self cannot allow me to describe myself by any category such as a certain religion, atheist or even agnostic. Once I choose one of these words, I once again enter into the realm of naming spices and become lost in the smells of the world.

So I choose to remain as an unknown consciousness, something which exists in nothing. I can't even say whether that is a choice or not. If someone seriously and genuinely asked me who am I, I would reply honestly that I don't know. I could say that I am God but there's no point in saying that. There's no value in that statement. It would be both uncomfortable for me and for them. Probably a better answer is to reply, "I am the same as you are." That might sow the seed that only they can water.

Let us look for a moment at the rational and medical model which has been widely accepted in understanding Schizophrenia. Medicine is based on statistics. That model will never support a cure.

Recovery without a cure is an empty word. It offers false hopelessness. It supports the lie of our materialistic world. It also supports the idea of a chronic disorder. Psychiatry has hijacked and redefined the word "Recovery" in order to suit their profession. We, the "sick ones" have lost our mind and now we need to recover it. How stupid is that?

The funny thing about this whole argument is that underneath so called mental illness is actually important knowledge, knowledge that our whole global way of life is going in the wrong direction. Arguing only pushes this knowledge further away into the fog of our world. This is where it becomes almost comical. You could even laugh. Because ironically it doesn't matter, the wrong direction is the right direction too. Whether psychiatry is growing in strength or if it is on the way out, it doesn't matter. The revolution is from within the individual, always has and always will be. However unconscious the psychotic person may be, offering them a recovering life in a sick world is absolutely ridiculous.

Unfortunately for many, the only proof of my own cure is the fact that I am medication free for many years and living a meaningful and satisfying life. Is it free of boredom and insecurities? Of course it's not.

I do believe there is a cure but I cannot say what it is. It's something that words cannot describe. At the same time, this autobiography is a huge effort in doing so.

Many people claim to be recovered but still take long term medication. Many will also claim there is no cure. I acknowledge such beliefs. I can only tell my story.

Sometimes, I really don't know why I have recovered. Sometimes it doesn't even matter. Whether someone is taking meds or not, that's not my concern. I'm looking at the whole picture; the Spiritual which is often hidden in the Physical. I'm looking at the search for meaning rather than the search for happiness. The search stops when we arrive home. The search stops when we realise we don't have to survive. Planet Earth is our home. Gaia is in our hearts.

Although the issues in the following account of my mental breakdown are very personal and difficult to share, I do so with a better level of self-acceptance and confidence developed during recovery. Not entirely depending on outside approval, I fear less people's judgements as I grow closer to respecting and accepting myself. I am certain that if I had prior knowledge and education around schizophrenia, it would have altered my experience and interpretation of it, or perhaps even prevented it from developing.

On the other hand, if I had not experienced it first-hand, I do not believe that my imagination could ever provide me with the same level of understanding.

Primarily, I would hope that those with similar experiences would benefit from this account. I do hope that it offers some people hope of a complete recovery. By sharing my story, I would also like to believe that it may help safeguard those who are susceptible to psychotic breaks, from harmful situations. When I say harmful situations, I mean inwardly and outwardly.

At the very bottom of the deepest psychotic experience, we do not lose our sense of right and wrong. I am greatly saddened when crime and schizophrenia are linked in the media.

THE HOWTH ROAD

Let us go back to my early childhood again and this time, to a petrol station on the Howth Road in Killester. This is one memory which I feel is important to my story.

I was about four years old. I recall being in the backseat of my father's car with my older brother. My father pulled in at this roadside service station. My father went inside the shop. Shortly after, I opened the back passenger door. I exited the car. Then I saw that another car was about to reverse park alongside us. Being He-man, a normal childish delusion, I decided that I would not allow this other car to approach. Having the strength of the universe, I stood firm with outstretched arms, confident that the car would not proceed past my halting palms.

I was small enough that the driver obviously could not see me in his rear-view mirror. The car reversed over me. I found myself lying flat on my back looking at the underside of this parked car, confused as to why my super powers had failed me.

Some other time before or after this incident, I was in my buggy. He-man was replaced by Spiderman. I improvised to create a web like mask using the string net from a bag of oranges. I wore it around my head for the best part of a Spanish summer holiday. I was Spiderman. Again, this was just normal childish behaviour.

On yet another occasion, a few years later, I remember playing with my older brother and our cousin in our back garden. This time I was older, maybe seven years of age. The game was called Madman. One of us must act as the Madman and chase the other two, who would hide from this crazy man. Of course I was always designated as the Madman as I was the youngest. They said that I acted it out the best. My older brother and cousin got a great laugh as I chased them around the garden. Funnily enough, years later I would enter into true madness.

Two years out of the Legion and while readjusting to civilian life, mental illness crept up on me and caught me off guard. It became a two year struggle with madness. Psychosis pulled down reality from before me. In doing so, it pulled down my identity. It left me naked and standing at the crossroads of life. The future had only one path, yet there were many paths to choose from.

What psychosis does to the person is it completely dissolves the feeling of "Free will." This can be blissful. But at the same time it can be utterly confusing for the uninitiated.

For the person in psychosis, the following line makes complete sense: "THY WILL BE DONE ON EARTH AS IT IS IN HEAVEN." This becomes their living reality.

Honestly, I cannot think of a greater life changing experience.

BULGARIA

Psychosis could be defined as losing touch with reality. I prefer to view it as a struggle. It is a struggle to integrate our divine essence into our human form. This struggle to evolve was never on my education curriculum growing up in Ireland or in my community. It was a struggle I had to face myself and heal myself.

From an outside eye, the description of psychosis may not make much sense. However, for the person in the psychosis there can be the feeling that all things make sense.

Connections and associations are made between things which would not ordinarily be made. The world becomes a web in every possible way. The seemingly random nature of our world falls away. A hidden sacredness and wonder is revealed. Everything means every other thing. This immense secret seems to be a beauty beyond our mind. How could it possibly have remained hidden from our view for so long?

But sadly, it becomes a fleeting misery when our confused and paranoid mind tries to grasp it. Therefore, the following descriptions of psychosis may be confusing and difficult to read. I understand that it may be difficult to distinguish reality from what is not real for you; the reader.

I will tell the story as if the content of my delusions were real in order to avoid continuously repeating that there is a level of insanity present during a psychotic episode.

Before I left Ireland to begin my new adventure Australia, I went on a holiday to Bulgaria. I was excited. I had everything prepared back in Dublin for my Working Holiday Visa trip to

Australia. I had considered staying in Australia if it worked out over there.

I still had enough savings from the Legion. The past two years of working odd jobs helped to give me a good start in Australia with lots of work experience in different roles. I was determined to get some kind of work quickly once I arrived in Australia anyway. But now I could just relax and enjoy a few well-earned weeks in the sun, in Bulgaria.

While on holidays in Bulgaria, I found myself alone a lot of the time; story of my life. I had become used to this way of being.

I began making mental connections with things which would ordinarily seem unconnected. To kill time, I attempted to learn the Cyrillic alphabet and some basics of the Bulgarian language. I had a notepad and pencil. I also scribbled down some random place names which seemed interesting.

I wrote down ANDROMEDA, a name of a hotel that I walked past. I played with those letters and then I spelled them backwards. To my amusement, I interpreted ADEMORDNA as "Adam or DNA." I felt there was some hidden meaning here about the biblical Adam and DNA in science. I had tapped into some underlying flow in our everyday existence.

The idea of 'Science versus Religion' was already going through my head. Ideas had being emerging on this theme since reading the two Dan Brown novels during my last year in the Legion; The Da Vinci Code and Angels and Demons. I was excited that I was now on a path to discovering some magnificent truth or revelation. I didn't want to lose this new found enthusiasm. I wanted to keep these fantasies going. They helped me avoid my loneliness.

As the days went by in Bulgaria, everyday experiences and encounters appeared to have deeper, hidden meanings. By interpreting these meanings, it led to paranoid and self-obsessed behaviour. At one point I shared out a pack of playing cards. Each card I gave to different members of staff at my hotel. I gave one to the manager, the receptionist, the barman, and each of the cleaners. I kept the 'King of hearts' for myself. This was the beginning of what I did not see at the time as grandiose delusional thinking. But unconsciously my need for love was manifesting itself in such odd behaviour. Love was missing in my life.

There was no stability in my past Legion life. While there, I could not maintain any relationship with a girl. Or at least I used that as an excuse. I denied my deep need for intimacy.

One night soon after distributing my cards as secret signs, I was in a bar for karaoke night. The lyrics of songs felt more meaningful than usual. On hearing UB40s song Kingston Town, I began thinking songs and television broad casting where somehow directed towards me. I continued to function despite these early signs of psychosis and some odd behaviour of mine.

Lack of structure in my life, too much free time and excessive alcohol consumption didn't help the situation either. The holiday to Bulgaria ended. I didn't think much of those strange happenings. But I did realise that I was drinking too much alcohol around that time. Alcohol was helping me prolong these inhibited states of early psychosis.

I had made a commitment to myself that while I was in Australia. I would abstain for as long as possible to see how long I could go without drinking. I hadn't forgotten my promise to God back in the isolation cell of the 1REG, two years before.

ROCKHAMPTON

Soon after that holiday to Bulgaria, I left for Australia. I gave up alcohol for the first four months while there. The first job I got in Australia was working on a Cotton and Cattle property in Queensland. It was a vast and isolated farm, and a four hour drive inland from the coastal city of Rockhampton.

By Christmas, I had become good friends with the farm manager. My work on the farm had just finished up by then as the cotton seed had been planted. I was invited by the farm manager Douglas back to his home in Rockhampton to spend it with his family. That Christmas spent with them was a nice occasion. I have remained in touch with them ever since leaving Australia. They were a friendly couple with two kids. There was a real family feel to the home environment. They were a Christian family and we went to church on Christmas morning. I was unsure of my religious views at that time. I never really gave it much thought.

Douglas' brother Liam also joined us for the Christmas dinner but not for church as he wasn't a believer. One of the kids made a bet with Liam, that he couldn't make a Christmas pudding. To prove that he could, he gave us great amusement, by staying up late on Christmas Eve making that pudding.

As Christmas occurs during summer in Australia, it was very hot in Rockhampton. We all spent St. Stephens' day at the beach with friends of the family. It was a fun day. We played some soccer on the beach. That evening, I thanked them for their kindness and I returned to my own life. When I had finished up my work on the farm just before Christmas, I had bought myself a car. And I found a room to rent in a house in Rockhampton.

Like I had planned, I decided that I would use my new life in Australia as an attempt to stop drinking alcohol and live a sober existence. It was now four months into my Working Holiday Visa and I still hadn't taken a drink. But I was becoming bored with myself in the evening times and I longed to go out for some cold beers. So I did. Soon after, I started dating a girl and I also got a new job at a water park in town. But both the relationship and the job only lasted a couple of months before I moved north to the city of Mackay. There I took up a job offer in the coal mines.

It was tough work but it paid well. An Australian ex-legionnaire I knew had been the link for me to get the job. It was the same Aussie chap that joined me and the other lads on the trip to La Jonquera about five years previously, on one of our weekends off in the Legion. I was somewhat reluctant to take this job in the mines as I felt it was indirectly linked to the Legion. The lifestyle of mining certainly reminded me of Legion life; work hard play hard.

A few months into the coal mining job, I went back to visit my friends in Rockhampton during my four days off. I was working a four days on and four days off continuous roster. The periods of four days in work alternated between four consecutive twelve hour day shifts and four twelve hour night shifts. I was becoming sleep deprived and unwell during my four days off work. I was also sad and lonely after having finished what was a short relationship with a nice girl.

DENHAM STREET

At this point, it was about eight months on from the early warning signs of madness in Bulgaria, which for me were unknown. But this time, my mind really cracked.

I found myself being escorted by Australian police and paramedics to hospital where I would spend two nights in a psychiatric ward. This was my first hospital admission in Australia for a psychotic break.

I was sleep deprived. I had just come off a number of night shifts at the coal mine. I was finding it hard to change my sleep routine. I was getting back in touch with that hidden realm of secrets which I had caught a glimpse of in Bulgaria. Along with this, I was facing a major identity crisis; I was questioning my own sexuality.

This was extremely difficult to deal with. I couldn't bring myself to discuss it with anybody. I was worried what my friends in Rockhampton would think as they were very Christian. I thought they would judge me and my doubts around my sexuality. So I rang my sister back in Ireland and cried. She was the only one who could possibly understand me. "I think I'm bisexual," I confessed to her. She was very reassuring.

This is what happened just before my admission to hospital. After another sleepless night at a hotel in Rockhampton, spent listening to a CD of Bob Dylan's greatest hits, I drove to my friend's house in Rockhampton, hoping to tell them something about my bisexuality.

They were surprised to see me at five a.m. They were having breakfast before going to work. I had a gold covered bible in my hand. I asked my friend Douglas to read us a section from Job 14 at his kitchen table. I had opened the bible randomly on that page during my sleepless night before, at the Hotel. I found it to be speaking directly about me.

I cried as he read Job 14 carefully. Showing compassion, he put his hand on my shoulder. I couldn't communicate my distress to him, except for a load of confusing babble that came from my mouth. I couldn't bring myself to say that I thought I was bisexual. I left them with a CD as a gift; Whitney Houston's Greatest Hits.

Douglas and his wife looked concerned. They wished me all the best as I left. I drove away. There was nothing they could have done. What was coming was coming. The mental breakdown was necessary to achieve a breakthrough.

Further up the road, I pulled my car over. I rang my manager at the mines. There was no answer so I left a voicemail, saying that I was quitting the job because the world was ending soon. Dawn was breaking. It was about six a.m. Thirty minutes later, at Sunrise, the police and paramedics found me at a busy roundabout on Denham Street.

As I was driving to the roundabout, I had four directions to choose from. But my car was stopped right up on the middle of this grassy roundabout, surrounded with flowers and shrubs. While I was driving and approaching that roundabout, I felt completely lost. I did not know what direction to take. Instead, I drove right up onto it.

Working as an assistant driller in the coal mines was hard work. Despite the good money, it reminded me of life in the Legion, a work hard play hard lifestyle. I couldn't live that lifestyle any longer. I was breaking down.

The engine of my car was off, the handbrake was on, and the doors wide open. I had Aboriginal didgeridoo music playing at full volume. I was standing on the roof of my car facing the

Sun as it rose over a nearby Caltex petrol station. I made some mental connection with the Sun and the Caltex logo of a star. People looked out from their car windows in disbelief. I was bare-chested with my t-shirt tied around my face covering my mouth and nose. I had emptied a black plastic flower pot and it was now placed over my head protecting me from the Suns first rays to hit. They would melt my head.

I saluted the sun. I remember feeling a powerful sense that I had complete understanding of our existence on earth but that all others were living in a blind illusion. Like robots, everyone was going around the place, either walking or in their cars. They were trapped in a hypnotic dream. I was watching the world from outside of it. I had snapped out of our everyday little prison that we call reality. I saw absolute truth. I was in heaven and everyone else, in hell. This feeling was unlike no other I have ever experienced. I stood there on the roof of my car watching others go about their blind existence. My head then caught the first sun rays that sprayed like golden water from the horizon. I was born.

"Come down off the car," two police officers said calmly. I obeyed and went along with them. I tried my best to explain to them and the paramedics about my enlightened state but it was pointless, they just couldn't get it.

Afterwards, at the hospital, I explained to the psychiatrist the meaning of what I had spelled with black permanent marker across my left forearm. I had written, "Je Croix." It was a pun between the French word for "Believe" and the English word "Cross." A smaller black circle acted as a full stop after "Je Croix." But this black point wasn't done in marker. It was a real tattoo. It was in the same spot where some people claim Jesus Christ received a nail through his wrist. I had it done without realising its significance or meaning, a couple of days prior to this. Impulsively without any planning, I had stopped at a tattoo artist and got the small black circle done without knowing why. The relevance and meaning of that small tattoo only came to me in my psychosis.

I was also trying to explain to her, the psychiatrist on duty, that DOG is GOD and vice versa. She acknowledged that she had a dog, a golden retriever, and I smiled. I was the Golden retriever. I was unable to communicate my feelings or express adequately what I had experienced. Nothing I said could equal the awakened state which I felt I was in. Every word that came of my rambling mouth kept missing the mark. Language couldn't touch it.

After having slept it off in the psychiatric ward for two nights, the psychosis faded. I didn't think much of it. They released me. The police had brought my car to the hospital parking area when I was admitted.

I drove back to Mackay, where I was living. I got a call that same afternoon from a priest of St. Patrick's church in Mackay. I was surprised by the phone call. Then I remembered that I had put my name down in a large notebook at the back of the church to do a reading. But that was a few weeks before and I had already forgotten about it.

I was now feeling nervous as I had never done a reading before. I agreed with his request that I would come to the church that evening a little early to rehearse before the evening service.

It happened to be Holy Thursday. My reading was from the book of Exodus about preparing the Passover meal. There was a part in it where I read "I am the Lord." I looked up at the congregation as I said this. In that instance, it hit me. I held back a tonne of emotion. I managed to finish the reading. I was the Lord. This was the beginning of my reoccurring delusion of being God.

I never knew about grandiose delusions as a feature of

schizophrenia. I had no education on such symptoms. The realisation of being God results in a flood of emotion and tears. It's both beautiful and powerful. It's also madness. But it's very real. God, Love and Madness are real. They are all one.

BRISBANE

With my sleep back in order, I regretted trying to quit my job at the mines. I phoned my boss again. After explaining to him that I had been sleep deprived and apologizing for the voicemail, he said "No worries mate." He then sent me for a quick medical. I got the all clear to return to work.

I continued working in the coal mines and I continued to become sleep deprived. I could see connections between things which I interpreted as more than just coincidence. I found hidden messages in newspapers, car registration numbers, people's names, television and radio. The sacredness and intertwining of everything was laid before my eyes. Everything and every single event was a microcosm of the universe. Everything was a metaphor for a greater reality. Everything had its place. All was beautifully in balance. Every little detail of our existence moved with clockwork and perfect timing. It was magical to witness this. I mean, absolutely everything was connected in time and space. It was literally mind-blowing.

But being able to accept that coincidence was just coincidence and no more, was a major part of the initial recovery procedure. I later learned to accept that the irrational thinking and searching that goes with sleep deprivation was the trigger for psychosis.

At that point in time, it was a necessary denial of Grace. I wasn't ready for it. Denying it kept me balanced until I could really get to grips with the life changing effect of psychosis. I wasn't ready to embrace the infinite, it was too quick to soon.

It's one thing to say we believe in Oneness but it's another thing to manoeuvre in its reality. With direct experience of the sacredness hidden in our everyday existence, belief is no longer necessary. Psychosis is pure Oneness. The unprepared mind can't handle it. The mind needs to be tamed.

Who does the taming? Only you can answer that.

Until the self is dissolved, the psychosis will continue to cause fear and paranoia. But this realisation came further down the road. In the early days, it was extremely difficult for me to deny the otherworld. The special feeling of that hidden realm was exciting. I was unwilling to let go of these so called coincidences because they were making my life interesting.

The thought of being on some special path was extremely motivating. It was certainly a distraction from the mundane, unfulfilling work that I was performing in the coal mines. The attraction of being caught up in these so called mysterious coincidences was a mechanism for escaping a life which seemed to be without direction.

I later knew (probably two years later) that interpreting these coincidences for more than what they were could lead to preoccupation, sleep deprivation and eventually a psychosis, a hospital admission or worse. To avoid that, I taught myself to pursue my hobbies and interests, identify and develop my talents and find meaningful and rewarding work. But creativity must never be supressed. The coincidences would always be there but I didn't have to understand them.

If I was unable to develop my potential and if I felt held back by barriers created either socially or personally, I risked once again becoming deluded and psychotic. But living a life too careful and too comfortable out of fear was also a risk. This is where the label and the stigma of a mental disorder can do more harm than good. We limit ourselves and avoid risks. In doing so, we disable ourselves.

Strange as it may sound, but it was very depressing to slowly realise that I was not God incarnate, as I imagined Jesus to be.

I had to realise that, in order to get my feet back on the ground. I had to park aside all my spiritual questions and focus only on the material, at least for some time.

This slow coming out of my psychotic mania was initially very sad after having believed my messiah complex to be absolutely true. I had an unshakable belief that I was God made man. It was so obvious and so clear to me. There was also the immense euphoria that came with that knowing. I would dare say that it was pure bliss of a level greater than the highest of orgasms; like golden petrol alight in the veins; a hundred times better than adrenaline.

During that lonely sleepless night, back while staying at a hotel in Rockhampton, I got great meaning out of the bible verse Job 14 - "Man who is born of woman is of few days and full of trouble..." I had opened the bible randomly on that page, looking for a sign. But something gave that verse even more significance. A few days later another coincidence disturbed my rational mind. I had been released from hospital. I had just finished my reading at the church. I was relaxing at home that night. While watching TV, I was stunned when I heard the same Job 14 verse. It was being read briefly in a scene from a movie called I'm not there about Bob Dylan's life. The scene in the film involves Bob Dylan looking at a statue of the crucifixion while that quote from Job 14 is being read aloud. This was too odd to be a coincidence.

My mind began racing again during my four days off from the mines. I visited the local library and I looked up all kinds of things. But there was something very deep and frightening that I had to dig up from my soul. I could no longer ignore it. My deluded disinhibited state of mind allowed it to surface.

The psychosis allowed me to deal with something that was troubling me for many years. In this way, you could say that the psychosis allowed for deep healing to occur. Psychosis has a healing capacity, a healing potential, but only if approached in the right way.

One day, I allowed psychosis to provide me with a subjectively personal meaning for Job 14. I realised that the name JOB from the bible contained the letters JB, the initials for pop star Justin Bieber. The letter O in between represented the Sun. I was the Son of God and the Sun of God. I was in love with Justin Bieber. I became a fanatic. My psychosis facilitated this. I bought his CDs. I listened repeatedly to them in my car, thinking that the lyrics were directed uniquely at me. To deal with the unease of these feelings, I bought a case of beer called James Boag from Tasmania. It had the same initials as JB. I was embarrassed. I was the Sun but I was also JC, Jesus Christ. JC was in love with JB. I was cracking up, but I liked it. Psychosis was therapy.

I stumbled across a book called The Sun of gOd by Gregory Sams (2009). The idea that the Sun is a conscious living being is one of the oldest of all time. But it was shut down by religion and then by science. I thought it was a coincidence that I had been given a similar name as the author, Gregory Sams. In the Legion, I was LEG Gregory Sims.

I liked the Psalms in the Bible. I also liked the story of Samson, his riddles and metaphorical story about defeating the Lion. His own hair was long like that of a Lions. His name meant Sun child or Man of the Sun. I was born on a Sunday. I was born on the feast day of Saint Blaise. Blaiser is a French term for stuttering. Blaise is an ancient name for one who stutters. As a child, I was brought to church to have my throat blessed with candles on my birthday, in an effort to cure my stutter.

My middle name was James, Séamus in Irish. It is also an international name existing in many languages and cultures across the world. James sounds like Shams, the Arabic word for The Sun. It seemed that there was any number of similarities and connections to be made. I was beginning to see behind the Veil. But I wasn't ready to see it just yet. It was too much for me to handle. I had no peer support or guidance. I didn't know that "I" was not my mind.

I did believe that the Sun was conscious and the origin of all life on Earth. But I also felt that the Sun wanted to become human so that it could express itself. The Sun first became plants and then animals. Throughout the ages, the Sun had attempted to take on a conscious human form. But many had missed the mark. The Buddha and Jesus were both attempts by the Sun to transform into flesh and speak through a mouthpiece. They had almost succeeded but fell a little short of the full embodied Sun.

All religions were founded on a mystical experience. They all began with an individual who had direct witness of their divinity; the awakening consciousness of the Sun in them. From that beginning, religions grew into diversions from this universal truth. They became a failed attempt to define and rationalise the mystery of God, the mystery of the Sun. In doing so, they only created the Split.

I was now ready to become the Sun, not a God, but the actual star in our solar system that gives us life, fully expressed in human form. The life force of the Sun is a macrocosm of our bodily microcosm. So if I was the Sun, what about other suns in other Solar systems? Well, I was those suns too. Every sun was like a cell in my body. This was a beautiful psychosis. But it was also an escape from dealing with the fact that I was in love with Justin Bieber. Or maybe it was a way to allow myself to love him.

This deep obsession with Justin Bieber had started after I watched a television programme on him. I was captured by his strong faith in Jesus and by his beauty. I became infatuated with him. I went to the cinema to see his movie. It had just been released. I went three times to see the same movie. I was attracted to a seventeen year old Justin Bieber. I felt that was very wrong. I sat there crying in the cinema. I cried at my lost youth.

On that same television programme about Justin Bieber which sparked my interest in him, there was another report about crocodiles. In that report, there was an Australian man who had two of his fingers on his left hand eaten by a crocodile. This was significant to me as I had been experiencing pain due to an old injury and dislocated finger on the same hand. The same two fingers were bothering me. It was severely affecting my work at the mines and was the cause of chronic pain up into my left arm. The days leading up to seeing that television programme, I played with the idea of amputating those same two fingers by placing them in the drill rig and having them chopped clean off. The thought of doing that was disturbing. I was getting closer to the next major psychotic break. Somehow I was still just about functioning.

I was a Belieber and a Believer. I knew that the letters b and v were pronounced the same in Spanish. I felt uncomfortable with this obsession towards Justin Bieber. It became a dark secret of mine. But it was the necessary spark to doubt my sexuality and dig up Walter the Softy I had buried all those years back. I was out of control now and I gave in to the obsession. I booked a ticket to the Justin Bieber concert in Brisbane. He was on his world tour. I spent a load of money to fly there, for the concert ticket and to stay at a hotel for two nights. But I no longer cared about money. I began having delusions that Justin Bieber and I were somehow connected. I flew to Brisbane.

On the aeroplane, I took my seat next to the window. Then a boy and his mum came and sat on the two seats next to me. The boy had a deformed left hand with two missing fingers. They were the exact same two fingers that the man in the

TV programme had eaten by a croc and the same two that I had considered amputating in the mines. This couldn't be a coincidence. All these were signs that I was on a special path but I couldn't handle it. I couldn't understand this path.

In Brisbane, I drank at an Irish bar before the Justin Bieber concert to calm my nerves. I wore a white top hat and a purple t-shirt. Purple was the colour of Jesus Christ when they mocked him and dressed him in a purple robe. It was also the favourite colour of Justin Bieber. The white top hat I wore was similar to my Kepi Blanc but that never crossed my mind.

During my first hospital admission in Rockhampton, I had seen a drawing of a white dove on the noticeboard. I asked the nurse to photocopy it for me. She did. I kept that copy of it. The dove was a sign of the Holy Spirit. Now in my hotel in Brisbane before the concert, I copied that dove onto the top flat part of my hat with a black permanent marker. Nobody could see the dove unless I took the hat off or they were standing above me. My plan was that during the concert I would throw the hat like a Frisbee. It would land on the stage. Justin Bieber would see the dove on the white hat and pick it up. This would connect us. Of course this never happened. My seat was high up in the arena far away from the stage.

As the effect of the few beers wore off, I stood there feeling out of place, pathetic and embarrassed wearing my white top hat and purple shirt, surrounded by loads of screaming teenage girls. Despite my mild psychosis, I felt like a creep. I knew some of the parents there were looking at me and thinking the same. I returned to my hotel that night feeling like a failure. I returned to Mackay the next day and I went back to work at the mines. I tried to forget about Justin Bieber.

I was still holding onto the mystical path. I desperately needed the fantasy of my psychosis. I wasn't ready to face my lonely and dead end existence. Other occurrences such as a total lunar eclipse were adding to my growing delusions until one specific moment where I firmly believed that I was definitely Jesus Christ, without a shadow of a doubt. It was the only answer I could find to explain what I was going through.

On one of my days off work, I began noticing crown symbols in different places. That same night I went to a nightclub. The entrance stamp was also a crown. The doorman stamped it on my right wrist. Inside the club, the bouncers had a large golden crown on the back of their t-shirts. They knew I was Jesus. They were protecting me from the evil influence in the club. I was completely sober and not drinking any alcohol.

The next day I had the fading crown stamp on my wrist tattooed over with real ink. I never went back to the mines after that. I rang and explained to my boss by phone that I was leaving the work for good this time because I was on a spiritual path. But I was living in some fantastical Armageddon situation and mentally ill.

During those last few weeks working at the mines, I was becoming more and more psychotic. My co-worker's names were both biblical names; Matthew and Daniel. They were both angels in disguise as New Zealand Maoris. They were covered with tattoos. They joked with me by calling me Moses. They came to work in the underground coalmine but they had recently joined our team for a secret divine reason.

I began to believe that our coalmine was actually hell. They were there to get me out so I could fulfil my prophecy of the second coming and begin my ministry. This was a big secret and they were careful in showing me subtle signs of it. But in fact it was beyond their understanding as they were half blind to the truth. They were instruments of God but did not have access to the divine plan. They were half man half angel. So I kept quiet about it. It was as if the divine plan was unfolding but no one could see their place in it, except for me. I was both the creator and the subject.

During my very last night shift in the underground mine, the water hoses I had to work with on the drill rig became snakes. I was wrestling with them. I could feel my ancestral spirits from Ireland and further afield, all around me. I was exhausted and I needed a break. Soon we stopped for Crib. We stopped to eat our meals.

On my insulated Crib box, I had written the initials C.M.F.R. in permanent marker. Those initials stood for the Irish Language, Céad Míle fáilte Romhat. I then remembered an Irish song that I sung in school and at mass service as an altar boy growing up, "Céad míle fáilte romhat a Íosa" - A Hundred Thousand Welcomes to you Jesus. I began humming the song gently as I opened my Crib box. Then a blast of light hit me from Daniels headlamp.

I realised straight away why I had written C.M.F.R. unconsciously on my lunchbox. I had written it to myself and that I was Jesus. I opened my Crib box and ate my last midnight snack, one of many last suppers. We took a short rest and then back to the drill rig to finish our drilling for the night. We finished up our work around five a.m. Then we prepared to return to the surface.

As the three of us drove out and up to the light of a new day, I knew the mines would collapse behind me. I was born in hell but made of diamonds. My two Maori warrior angels were taking me out. They knew I had a divine mission to fulfil but they remained silent about it. I never returned to that underground hell.

MACKAY

Mackay comes from the Irish: Mac Aoidh - Son of Aoidh. The Celtic name Aoidh means Fire or Fiery one. Mac Aoidh could be translated as Son of the Sun. Aoidh was also the Celtic God of the underworld. Psychosis is the underworld. Aoidh was able to roam and dwell in the darkness of psychosis and understand that realm. It is that parallel dimension which we are so terrified of but which our soul longs for. Jesus called it the Kingdom of Heaven. The Irish Celts, we call it *Tír na nÓg*.

All the pagan animistic festivals of dressing up in animal outfits was a celebration and attempt to invoke this otherworldly sense; to bring light, to find love and strength in times of fear and darkness. But we have all become so stuck in our conditioned illusion of self.

The psychotic state offers us complete disinhibition. It is the breaking down of this delusion that we are a separate contained consciousness. It is the portal to the land of eternal youth. It is the greatest truth behind the greatest lie.

The ancient knowledge and direct access to the divine for the Irish people had been covered up over hundreds of years, over generations and generations. Eire, our sacred land is female. The arrival of Christianity, a corruption of the Christ's real message, began an attempt to put out the eternal flame of wisdom of our ancestors. The Shamrock was introduced to hide and to limit God to three beings and cut off those outside the elite from any possible deserving of their destiny. But the Golden harp was ours and it played music for all to hear, big or small, the poor and the rich, the strong and the weak, men, women and children. The music of Heaven was our welcome to all.

Green was introduced as our national colour to keep us grounded in our earthly reality, prisoners on our own land. But the truth could not be hidden. Royal Blue was our national colour, the colour of the sky from where we came. We are divine beings in earthly bodies.

I understood it all. It was in my blood, in my DNA. All that ancient wisdom was being revealed to me from my unconscious ancestral spirit. Paganism was no mystery. Christianity demonised paganism when in fact Jesus was but a Pagan shaman.

I felt my ancestral roots spreading back through time from Eire across the globe, touching every culture. The Berber nomads of Africa knew who they were. Dressed in blue robes, the Irish named them An Cine Gorm – The blue people; our African cousins. The Irish word for knife is Scian, the Arabic is Sakin. No more needs to be said.

Driving back from the mines towards Mackay that morning, I asked my Maori guardians to let me off in a small town. I bid them farewell. I got in contact with an Irish priest in this town. I called in to his house beside the church. I introduced myself as a fellow Irishman. He offered me a bottle of Guinness but I requested a cup of tea. He had lived for many years in Australia. I told him that I had a huge secret I needed to get off my chest. I knew he wasn't ready for it but I told him anyway. I said that I knew in my heart that I was the Christ.

After his initial shock, he handed me some Mass cards to look at as he went off to make a phone call from another room. I thought he was calling the Vatican on a secret line. The Mass cards had photos of people who had passed away. I went through each card looking at the photos. I blessed each photo of the deceased and sent each person to heaven by doing so.

After our chat, the priest gave me a lift back to my home in

Mackay. On the way, I explained to him that the Mitsubishi logo on his car was a sign of the trinity just like the shamrock. He didn't get it. He wasn't ready for my second coming. He told me to rest and that he would be in touch soon. But I couldn't sleep.

I called into a nearby neighbour who was a Jehovah witness. He was originally from Albania. We had a good talk about the bible. I left him with a few riddles to think about.

Some days later I phoned that same Irish priest. He said that he was in the outback with the aboriginal community. On hearing this, I knew he was working with the aboriginal seers. He was trying to convert them. But they were the ones with greater wisdom that Catholicism. He could actually learn from them. If that priest was willing to let go, loose his mind and enter the Dreamtime, the Christ would awaken in him. But he was terrified of Jesus Christ. The whole of Christianity is but will never admit that. The Pope would be the last to kneel before Jesus Christ; the ultimate Doubting Thomas.

The aboriginal elders and shamans who the Irish priest was with were secretly discussing signs in nature that supported my claim of being God. I told him that he had being tricked by the church. He must now listen to the aborigines. Their Dreamtime was the Irish *Tír na nÓg*.

He sounded angry on the phone so I knew he was distracted and being led astray. The Catholic Church was wrong after all. That nice old priest, that poor fella, he could have been a clever fella.

I understood the frustration Jesus had to deal with while trying to get through to such people. They just couldn't hear or didn't want to hear our revelation. I was psychotic, yes, but I knew the truth, the same truth that Jesus knew and was tortured for trying to explain. The Cosmic Christ can awaken in any being, in any form. It can come in the form of the Solar

Christ, a Sun deity. The spirit of Christ was around before the life of Jesus and after his life. It can awaken in whoever is ready to receive it. Our physical body is but a vessel for the divine.

Over the next few days, my psychosis got to the point of what I recall as misinterpretations of reality. What they are is actually the breaking down of our everyday reality, our default way of being. Our basic mode is regulated by the bossy fearful voice in our heads that limits us and keeps us in check. It persuades us every day of who we are. As the years go by this lie becomes more and more engraved in our worldview. We dare not question it. Some argue that it protects us and keeps us alive. It does but it also keeps us as a slave. It doesn't like new paths or new ways of seeing the world. So you could say that the only true freedom is freedom from ourselves, freedom from this mould. The second best thing is to treat our false self with kindness, to accept it but know that it's really just a scared and vulnerable child.

Behind it lies our True Self. Our doubt and our denial rob us of our divine right. That is the cause of madness. We are ready only when we are ready. And even when we are ready, God will take on the form in us which is the reflection of our own stage of evolution.

When cracks appear in our hardwiring, these are sometimes incorrectly called hallucinations or malfunctions of the brain. But actually it is an attempt to evolve out of our prison, to self-realise and to self-transcend. But the Adjudant Chef who has been with us since we were babies runs a very tight ship. The question is; Are we brave enough to love him and leave him? Are we ready to walk in the light, in our own light?

I left the mines for good. Then when I was driving through Mackay, I saw who I believed was my co-worker Thomas from the mines. He was following my car everywhere I went. He was in a state of complete shock and his face was white as a ghost. He had lost control of his body. He was taken over and possessed. He was now Doubting Thomas once again. He wanted with all his being to believe but he just couldn't. In a hypnotic trance, he was following my car around the city. I slowed down. I saw his face in my rear-view mirror when I looked. I pulled my car over to the side of the road. I watched him, as he drove past me in a state of complete fear and denial. The doubt would always remain in him until his inner deity awakens. Doubting Thomas could only accept the Christ when he accepted Jesus Christ as an equal being to him.

Colours of cars carried different meanings. White meant angels, black for demons and red for danger. A registration number plate of a car containing 999 was a good symbol. One white car with this number on its number plate drove alongside me as a shield. The traffic got heavy so I parked my car in a public park, the Botanic Gardens.

I went and sat under a tree for some time. I could feel the birds and nature vibrating around me. I was part of the whole. I understood the Buddha. I needed nothing anymore. Abundance was everywhere. I walked around begging, as I now knew the world would provide for my needs. One guy gave me five dollars and I bought a sandwich. I knew that the mines were collapsing since I left. The world was coming to an end. Traffic would be at a standstill.

Then my Euphoria transformed as my mind tried to understand it. I grew frightened that the devil was after me. I saw a guy with the Omega sign tattooed on his wrist. He was half gay. An omen, I thought. I asked him what it stood for and he said he was an electrician.

I walked the streets towards St. Patrick's Church in Mackay. I then saw a fresh but dead robin on my path, on the way there. I touched its breast, still warm. It was twilight. I went straight into evening Mass. As I was early, I ran into the sacristy. I asked the priest to bless me and he did. The mass was just about to begin. He told me to go and sit near to the altar for the service. But I sat towards the back of the church.

During the mass, I heard the doors banging and rattling loudly in the wind outside. A storm had begun. I thought evil spirits were trying to get inside the church. Then I heard a baby crying in the church. I thought it was trapped in the confession box by an evil spirit. But the crying of the baby came from the Souls of babies which were killed back in Ireland during the last century; an unforgivable sin. They were trying to contact me. I looked around and couldn't see any baby to be seen.

I took on their pain. I became very upset. I raised my white pamphlet high above my head as a sign of peace to the congregation. The wickedness was in them and not outside the church. I decided to forgive them for murdering those babies. But they couldn't see what I could see. They were all blind. I was terrified. I started crying. Then from behind, an old woman put her cold hand on my shoulder. I put my hand on hers. My body froze solid with fear. She was a ghost from another world. I was paralysed. Then she told me to stick out my tongue. It felt like my tongue was the only part of my body that I could move. I was literally frozen with fear. I stuck out my tongue from my stone body, as tears rolled down my face. My left arm was still stuck up in the air with the white pamphlet unable to move. She sprinkled holy salt on my tongue. I snapped out of the paralysis. My whole body relaxed. It was all over. I felt better. I felt like sleeping.

After the mass ended, I remained seated in the pew. The priest sent the altar servers to me. They came and sat next to me as the church emptied. I had a talk with the altar servers. They were grown men. I was talking in tongues, babbling. I went on and on trying to explain myself in what must have sounded like gibberish. They told me that the Holy Spirit was talking through me and this encouraged me even more. It also made sense because it didn't feel like it was me who was talking. They invited me back to the sacristy again. The holy salt woman was there too, along with the priest and a few others. I now knew that she was real. I asked for guidance and where I should go. I was just told to go were the light is.

I took this literally as I went out into the night. The storm was gone. It was dead calm and dark. I was alone and terrified but ready for it. I looked for the light, forgetting that I was the light.

I hung around under street lights away from the darkness. Eventually, I went to a McDonalds that stayed open until midnight. I stayed there for some time. I had discovered some time before that the name McDonald in the Irish Language was Mac Domhnail. This could be translated to Son of World Ruler. This was a hidden sign for the house of Christ. I would be safe there. The golden arches used in their logo symbolised two arches; one to heaven and one to hell. A small gap under the middle pillar allowed for movement between the two. I ordered two Filet-O-Fish burgers. I was the fish and the filet and I was eating myself. The O was the Sun and it was also my mouth. Our true nature is one of consumption. Why do we deny that?

Hallucinations took the form of projected mental ideas and preoccupations. The staff in McDonalds looked like transvestites, a hybrid mix of male and female. I kept smelling dog shit on my shoes all the time. I checked continuously but there was nothing there. Anal sex smelt like shit. It disgusted me. There had been a terrible stench of dead bodies in Indonesia after the tsunami when I was in the Legion. I looked at the staff of transsexuals and wondered if I was still safe in McDonalds, the hidden house of God. I was still uncomfortable with my feminine side. This fear was a projection of my own unresolved trauma. I reminded myself that I was God and my house was everywhere. I left with a new found courage. Once again, I renewed myself. I was the light in the darkness.

I grew restless and bored at my house in Mackay. I left and booked into an expensive hotel in central Mackay. My friends from Ireland were secretly gathering in this hotel for a special convention to acknowledge my Kingdom Come. I saw different pop stars as I walked around the city. I saw Justin Bieber in a front garden of a house. He was sitting there wearing sunglasses. He smiled at me.

I walked past Michael Jackson on the street. I heard voices of spirits in the trees. I spoke with the bushes. Then I saw U.S. military agents patrolling around in under cover cars. I pretended I didn't know they were on to me. I heard references to me on the radio and even while I played CDs in my Walkman.

A bizarre experience occurred while I was a passenger in a taxi. I saw from the corner of my eye, the driver turned her head towards me and made a strange sound of vibrating her tongue on her lips very fast. It sounded something like "lebulebulebulebulebu"! This was weird and distressing. It was definitely not her voice and not even human. She was possessed by an alien. As my psychosis escalated, I was tuned in to a higher frequency than our senses usually receive. My senses could receive a longer range of waves. I had a sixth sense. The alien wanted to communicate with me by using her body. The aliens world was parallel to ours but out of the field of our everyday perception.

Although I was a passenger in that taxi, I was driving the car with my mind, my breath and my eyes. Separateness had crumbled down once again. She was a very thin woman. She looked weak after her brief possession. I gave her a Mars chocolate bar when I paid and left, telling her to eat more and stay strong. That alien was a Martian from the dark side of

Mars - Ombra di Marte.

I was growing more and more confused. I was spending a lot of money on hotels and taxis. I was constantly on the move. I had my golden covered Bible which I carried around with me in my right hand and I walked the streets of Mackay. But I decided that my Ministry would be different. I no longer opened the Bible. It must remain closed forever. I was annoyed that it was written by man in my name, in the name of God. How dare they do that? How ignorant are they to think they are the only conscious species?

My hand had now sealed the Bible shut forever and covered it in gold. It was a book of lies. Gold was their disease because they could never own it. I walked past the same St. Patrick's Catholic Church. I no longer had any respect for them after realising that Jesus was actually a false messiah. In fact, I was no longer Jesus. I had risen above that title in outer space. I was purely God in the highest. I was the Sun, made man, the source of life on earth, the brightest gold of all. I was like the Greek God Apollo or The Egyptian God Ra. They were all the same thing anyway, just another manifestation of my essence. I was an alien. I was it. This is it. The Sun was my satellite. The Sun was also one of my incarnations. I was God the Father, the formless, the creator of forms.

I felt at one with the Sun in the sky whose rays belted down on earth. I was convinced that I was the Sun walking around in human form. The Sun, the source of all light and life in our solar system had at last become personified into human form. It made sense. After billions of years of evolution, the Sun had eventually succeeded to project its one being into human form, so it could have a voice. The golden boy, I was born on a Sunday. Everything was of my doing. I had made the Gold covering on the Bible I carried with me.

Lying on my King-size bed in my expensive hotel room,

I was watching the music channel on the TV. I then saw the same Gold Bible that I had briefly in a music video of the song "Good Feeling" by Flo Rida.

My third eye had burst open. My heavenly kingdom was laid before me. I was outside of time and space. I was everything. I left my hotel and continued walking the streets. Everything behind me and out of my field of vision turned to solid gold. I wore a yellow baseball cap with the words GOOD AS GOLD printed across the front of it. That was an advertisement for the beer called Four X Gold. But I was the fourth Cross missing on the hill of Calvary. Jesus was the Son, I was the Father.

I walked past St. Patrick's church again. It was mid-afternoon. A car pulled up at the side of the church. I saw that it was the same Asian priest who had blessed me, a few days before in the sacristy. He exited from his car along with another older grey haired man. This older man, a retired bishop, appeared white with fright when he saw me approaching. He was stunned.

But I came before them not with anger but feeling sorry for them. I raised the Gold Bible in the air with my right hand and I said "It's Okay guys, I'm here now, your work is over." I was deadly serious.

They stood there speechless. I read in their faces, that the one thing they had devoted their life to; their hope in the return of Christ was the one thing they feared the most. When faced with their Saviour right before them, they were frozen into a state of complete denial. I left them in their pitiful state.

I continued on aimlessly, but still on a quest, around the centre of Mackay. I became annoyed at the blindness of everyone else. How could I get through to these people and explain all the wisdom I had? I got impatient. I flung the Bible to the ground which I knew was written from the hand of man, not from God. I no longer needed it.

I stood there, breathing heavily, on the pavement of the main street. I felt as if I was controlling the wind and blowing the palm trees in the centre of town. I remembered Jesus' anger in the marketplace of the temple. But I wasn't Jesus. I looked up. Across the road, three men on motorbikes dressed entirely in black with black helmets, looked towards me, accelerated heavily and sped off. They were there as demons and could sense me, the power of the Sun. I didn't know what to do.

I walked across a zebra crossing and stopped halfway. I turned and looked at the golden coloured car that had stopped to let me pass. I went and sat on the bonnet of that car. I had painted it gold even before I saw it. The driver shouted out the window. Horns began beeping. With my head between my hands, I looked down at the ground. This world was blind. How could they not see me in the sky? Two things then happened simultaneously. A dark Aboriginal boy ran up and handed me my Gold Bible just at the exact moment that two police officers grabbed my arms and led me back onto the pavement.

Holding the Bible firmly shut, I explained to one of the officers calmly that I was the Sun who gave birth to him. His name badge read BERTSOL. But like everyone else, he was blind. They brought me to the police station.

In the police station, everyone was frozen like statues in a trance. Two officers were crying as they couldn't move. Two others were possessed by aliens and walked around without any sense. But they were in control. I became very confused when I could not leave. Then they put me in a cell. The aliens were in command and the other police officers were terrified.

There was ongoing debate amongst them. Some wanted to let me leave and others did not. I tried to read their secret signals but they were lost in this world that I had created. I should never have flicked that switch, the big bang, and created this existential mess.

Soon, a mental health worker came to interview me. He was

a morph of doubting Thomas, my co-worker at the mines. I was then accompanied to his car and they admitted me to hospital nearby.

That second admission in Australia lasted about four weeks. On being released, I was advised to take care of myself as each time the psychosis happens it can get deeper and more difficult to recover. Again I ignored this advice as I didn't know what was happening. I didn't know which world was the real one. Had I known then what I know now I would have been able to integrate the two worlds, because there is only one. All our living and all our dead are right here right now in the Kingdom of Heaven. But there are other beings here too, outside of space-time. Ultimately we are One Being. Fear is born with separation, the split, original sin, the creation of Hell.

It would only take me another few weeks out of hospital for the seemingly meaningful delusions to take hold and push me once again into another deep psychosis. This third time, I would go very deep and I would spend about nine weeks in hospital. Most of that time, I was in the high dependency unit. I was very heavily sedated. A flight was arranged between hospital social workers and my family in Ireland. I returned home to Ireland as a result.

Preceding this last admission in Mackay and my return to Ireland, the same theme to my psychosis of being God continued.

The English Queen was trying to stop me from fulfilling my destiny as the true King of the world. I was once again staying in an expensive hotel in the centre of Mackay. Ireland was going to be the new Israel, the real Promised Land. Dublin was Dubh Linn or Black Pool. I was the light of the Sun, born in this darkness.

I had suffered with a stammer in my childhood. The bullying and frustration that went with it was no longer in vain. Having recently watched the film, The Kings Speech, about King George VI and his stammer, I knew that I was the true King of the World. Its release around that time was no coincidence. My Maori angels had called me Moses. Moses had a stammer too.

I bought The Mirror magazine showing the wedding of Prince William and Kate Middleton. Even that was a distraction by global elites. It was part of a conspiracy to cover up my solar divinity and my reign on earth. But still, and despite all of that, I must remain unseen to the people.

When, during my Manic phase and I had made my way to the hotel, I booked into room 303. I had all the alcohol removed from the room by staff. I now decided that as King, I must lead by example and live a healthy lifestyle. The promise I had made to God in the Legion was actually a promise to myself. I had gotten out of that isolation cell from my own pool of eternal power.

That hotel had a conference room where I believed a feast was happening later that evening to celebrate my arrival. I helped people set up the banquet area. I introduced myself to one of the men who was arranging the room. His name was William, a morph of Prince William. I thanked them for their work. I told them I would see them later. I let them continue and I left. There was a conspiracy to ruin that evening.

Later that evening, I believed a Red Dragon was sent to destroy my plans. It was inside that conference room in which a secret gathering was occurring. I was about to face The Dragon. I was scared to death. I left my bedroom and I went towards the conference room. My blood was hot and my palms sweaty. All the adrenaline on this earth would not help me. I was going face to face with death, the biggest battle of my life.

I approached the closed double doors of the Conference room. My heart was racing and I was utterly terrified. I paused a second, almost backing down. Then I went for it. I pushed open the doors and entered to find an empty room in complete darkness. The dragon was in me. I was the source of my own fear.

I returned to my bedroom and slept. The next day came. I believed the TV and radio in my bedroom were bugged. Secret agents were in the next room monitoring my every move. I sat on a chair on my balcony with a white towel draped over the rail to symbolize peace to the world. I was being broadcast live, all over the world on TV. I was being filmed by satellite. There were other cameras hidden in parked cars nearby. I looked down and saw a line of cars drive by the hotel. It was a procession of people who had come to get a glimpse of the Sun incarnate.

A World War was brewing with Asia rising up against the West. The chair I was sitting on would soon become a large throne in the Hotel. I felt a huge ray of heat and power coming from my neck extending behind me like a Lions mane. In the ray of heat behind my head, descending from the Sun, spirits and dead people flocked towards me and melted into my back. In this same gigantic aura or halo around my head but out of my field of vision, there were winged angels and demons battling in the sky. I felt little twinges of their battles on my neck.

As the world was slowly crumbling, all beings would be absorbed into me and turn to solid gold covering my back. It was the big crunch, the opposite of the Big Bang. Everything was being sucked back into me. All that would eventually remain of the universe was a gigantic living statue at the end of all time and space. I was the core of this Golden statue. It would take the form of my being but without any mind. It would be pure consciousness, the end of original sin. It would be both the source of light and water; an open mouth from which a river gushed and beaming sunlight shining forth from its eyes. Time ticked to a complete stop. I remained as this being forever.

As my strange behaviour alerted hotel staff later that day,

I was asked to leave. I left the hotel and walked the streets. I stayed in another hotel.

I purchased a two metre long hollow wooden crocodile at an antiques store. I kept it in my room to protect me from evil spirits. I felt the presence in my room of spirits of those who had passed away. I felt my grandparents with me. Michael Jackson was there too. He took the form of St. Michael, the Archangel. As I went in and out of sleep, the wooden crocodile came alive in my room and I wrestled with it.

During the next day I believed I could shape change into different animals. I hid in bushes. I could telepathically turn the traffic lights from red to green. In a park I could feel ducks at a pond being drawn towards me. I felt ancient Celtic spirits travelling across the oceans through the air to communicate with me. I ruffled plants and trees with my hands and whispered to them. I could somehow communicate with secret pagan worshippers back in Ireland through the plants.

A mental health social worker from the hospital came to my hotel. He happened to be Irish. When I opened the door of my hotel room and saw him wearing a white shirt, I interpreted this as meaning that he was an angel. I also believed that he was not physically there. This was a projection of himself from a meeting in the hospital. I visualised in my mind, the doctors sitting together in this meeting with the realisation that I was indeed God. When he asked would I accompany him to hospital, I informed him that I was taking care of everything and that I had many people to meet. As I exited the hotel and walked down the road, I noticed two police vehicles following me. The social worker had called them. I was handcuffed, put in the hold and brought to hospital.

In hospital I was put into the high dependency ward. I covered myself in white bed sheets and waited for a helicopter to come and take me to a secret location in the U.S. or the

Vatican. There, I would to meet with world leaders to discuss the future of the new world. But there was nothing I would do or change about the world as it was I who had created this mess. My identity would remain hidden to the public. As God, I would live on earth but I could never be revealed to the people. Nobody came to get me.

My conviction of being God was unshakable for a long time. It took weeks before I slowly came out of that psychosis. It was a slow and gradual process. Delusions lingered much longer than any hallucinations. I thought about the nature of God. How could they prove that someone is not God if we don't have a consensus on the definition of that word? Who is anyone to say that another person is not God?

During that long admission to hospital, a local priest came to visit me. I had requested to talk with him. We sat outside in the garden area, on a wooden bench. I told him of how I was convinced that I was God or Jesus but I was confused about what I was supposed to do. He told me that this was not possible as Jesus had died two thousand years earlier. That made sense. Then he paused. On seeing my disappointment, he said that if I really was the Christ, then my work begins right there inside the hospital and not outside of it. Although he meant well, such advice only encouraged my delusional beliefs to continue.

I considered that if I was a reincarnation of Jesus, then there would be other reincarnations of him too. This meant that there would be the reincarnation of the Christ consciousness in other human bodies. But my body was the only one I needed to focus on. So what was this reincarnations message in this physical body of this Irishman, to the world? Well, it was obvious:

Hell is right here on Earth. We are living it every day. Heaven is camouflaged in nature, in us, but it is now ready to emerge. Heaven has been disguised brilliantly by the evil word of Schizophrenia or Madness. Insanity as we know it is actually the 'Truth.' Wow. That must be the best camouflage of all time. How obvious yet how well designed it is. My number one fallen angel had done a great job in preparing and developing this Enfer sur la Terre. Well done Prince Lucifer.

Hell and Satan are nothing more than the everyday illusion we call 'Reality' and the powers that try to protect this unsustainable lie. But the reign of Satan and Demonic forces controlling our minds and driving the material rationality over the Earth is now losing steam. It was a necessary era. But now it is time for a new era.

Every being that once lived on this earth is arising with all the ancient knowledge through the living people of today. The oldest and most ancient cultures of the world were right all along. The Truth is found in Nature and is Nature. The Christ or the Salmon of Knowledge is now been born into the Aquarius Era.

My second coming was simply this message to the world; Love is Madness, God is Mad.

Whether people come to realise who they really are either through developing schizophrenia or through the use of sacred entheogens doesn't matter. Psychoactive mushrooms, plants, frogs and cacti across the globe are divine beings, protecting the truth, guarding it throughout the satanic era. The force of nature of God was waiting until the force of Man and Machine finally surrendered. The earth is a woman. The realisation comes without an intermediary. My second coming is this message to the world, to save all living people and their ancestors who are still alive in them, from this Hell we are all in. I am not an intermediary but a catalyst, an instantaneous spark.

But for now I must go along with the system; play the game; be a mental patient. My time will come. Our time will come when the time is ready. My consciousness is outside of time anyway.

After many weeks of much sleeping and heavy sedation, I was encouraged by the nurses to walk a little outside. Each day I walked a bit more. I remember the huge effort required to walk the half kilometre perimeter of the hospital. I needed to sit down every so often on a bench to rest. I had no energy. I felt completely drained. I remember how it could take me ages to lift myself out of bed. Shifting my position from lying down to sitting was a huge effort. I had a deep pain in my back around my kidneys. One time, I simply couldn't lift myself from the bed due to the sedation. It felt like paralysis. I was afraid. I pressed the alarm and called a nurse to help me. I put out my hands and she pulled me up to a sitting position. I felt one hundred years old.

As I slowly regained some energy, the nursing staff continued to encourage me to go on trips into the city centre of Mackay by bus. In the beginning, I was being locked up to control my behaviour. Now it was the opposite. I was being urged to start moving again. Really, they were all very nice. They made plans for me like going to visit a museum or a trip to the cinema or a coffee shop. It was like my behaviour needed to be kept in the range of what is socially acceptable, not too fast and not too slow; the goldilocks zone. But it was this same range of obedient living, which in my highest states had been revealed to me, to be nothing but a pathetic existence. This is our everyday blind reality, our everyday lie. No wonder so many people feel lost in our world.

I remember on my first outing alone from the hospital, I was shuffling around the town. I could barely lift each foot. I was hunched over with a stiff neck and rigid arms. Sometimes I would become aware that my tongue was sticking out. I was surprised that I wasn't embarrassed. I was too numb to feel. I would pull my tongue back inside.

Even swallowing was a strained conscious effort. If I didn't do it regularly, drool would dribble from my mouth. As people walked by me on the footpath, I felt slow, weak and vulnerable. Even being aware of this weird sensation, it was not something that I could shake off. This was the effects of the heavy dose of antipsychotic medication. It felt like a form of semi-paralysis; a forced attempt to believe that I was a chronically ill person. I could have easily bought into that. But I knew the truth was arising globally and unstoppable. So I happily shuffled along the footpath like an old man.

Years after when I see people walking like this, I know immediately that they are likely on heavy antipsychotic medication. Even a few years later and free of all medication, I could still feel a slight rigidity and slowness around my whole body as if my nervous system was still readjusting to the powerful involuntary effect of being dosed with those powerful pharmaceutical drugs. They were man-made drugs used to uphold a man-made lie. I don't like this expression and I am reluctant to use it but I know what it feels like to be a 'Vegetable.' I was once a plant before my evolution to human form.

PERTH

On returning to Ireland after this third hospital admission in Australia, I slowly began to understand what had happened. I felt a crushing disappointment. I still had an extra year extension left on my Working Holiday Visa. Before I cracked up, I had the opportunity to get sponsored in the company I worked with at the mines and get residency in Australia. The job was boring but the money was good.

I was only home in Dublin three weeks when I made an impulsive decision. I bought a ticket to fly back to Australia, hoping to find new work in the mines but in Western Australia. I denied my mystical experiences. I wanted to jump back into the material world.

After only two days in the city of Perth, I became very anxious. I was sitting on a park bench and staring blankly ahead. I was feeling agitated. I felt it difficult to breathe. I could not relax. The effort to find accommodation and a job seemed too huge. My old Legionnaire confidence had fallen away, revealing a confused and lost little boy. I was having a mild panic attack.

I realised then and there that the Australian dream was over for me. I didn't have the strength and determination to continue. It would probably take me at least one year to recover from such a serious round of psychotic breaks. But in truth it ended up taking me a good three years to get my vitality back. In fact, I would recover as a new and better person. It was pointless to return to the old broken one.

Sitting on that park bench and feeling agitated, I was not even three days back in Australia. I was still getting over the

Jetlag too. I went back to my hostel. Other travellers were on a buzz. They seemed upbeat, happy and energetic. I sipped at a beer in the bar next door, envious of their enthusiasm about life. My head was stuck between two worlds trying to process the last three months of madness. I couldn't do this anymore. I gave up. I booked a flight departing to Ireland for the next day. It would take me years to understand that the two worlds can co-exist.

It was a total waste of money flying from Dublin to Perth and back again within four days. At the very least, I had walked along the Swan River. I had seen a black swan, native to Western Australia. I also learnt about my impulsiveness.

I was determined to get my life back on track but I wasn't ready yet. I wasn't sure if it ever really was on track. There was too much stuff to mentally sort out and process. I had only recently seen the Movie, The Black Swan in Ireland. Psychosis is a feature in the movie and I understood exactly the experience of the central character. Here I was standing in Perth looking at a black swan for the first time. I took this as having some deeper meaning but I couldn't figure out what that meaning was. I couldn't completely deny my former delusions. There must be some truth to them. My heart told me so, but my mind didn't like it.

The delusions of grandeur still lingered. They tried to get my attention but there was something else too. There was something pulling me to acknowledge my limited interpretation of them, just in the same way that the conscious rational mind is futile in interpreting dreams. I had a deep sense; a deep knowing even, that there was something very true and very right hidden beyond their irrationality. I was confused. I was torn between believing either I was mentally ill or in tune with the synchronised Universe. The truth was a combination of the two, harmony.

I began my rehabilitation in Ireland by attending a day hospital, a mental health day centre and various support groups. I gave up alcohol. I went to Alcoholics Anonymous meetings. I believed that I was an alcoholic and I found some relief in accepting this. It was a definite answer. I worked on my physical fitness although it proved difficult after gaining so much weight from the medication. I felt tired and lethargic. Only two years earlier, I had run the Dublin City Marathon in a time of three and a half hours. Now, even running one mile felt impossible.

SUNNY BEACH

As I gradually recovered, I was feeling positive again about life. Counselling had helped me with this. I gained a new perspective on life. I had continued to take medication since I left Australia. It was now about a year since my return to Ireland. I felt that I was ready for a small holiday. I booked a holiday to Bulgaria for two weeks. I was sober for almost a year by then. My physical fitness was good. I felt strong and confident again. I had achieved year of recovery and left madness behind me. My mind convinced me that the sickness was gone but in fact that was only a denial of its mystical nature.

During my holiday to Sunny Beach, I was enjoying meeting new people and visiting different places. Life was interesting again and even without alcohol, it was promising. One day while I was swimming at the pool, I felt a twinge in my neck. The next day when I woke up I had what felt like a trapped nerve from my neck down into my left arm. It was very painful. The next two nights, my sleep became affected because of this.

Before this trip to Bulgaria I had my first homosexual experience. As part of my rehabilitation, I decided that I needed to face this part of myself that I had supressed for so long. This was not an easy thing for me to do. But it was something I knew that I had to explore. I met a guy in Dublin who was very feminine in appearance. I was attracted to him. The socially conditioned part of me, that whispered in my ear that it was wrong and evil, only increased this sexual attraction. His nickname was King. That coincidence no longer surprised me. I knew it was happening for a reason. I considered myself bisexual at that point. The relationship was short lived. For me, it was a sexual exploration.

I had decided to explore that territory which I was afraid of but intrigued about for so long. It turned out that it wasn't what my fantasies had led me to believe. I was still pleased with myself for having experimented and letting myself live out that other side of me.

Now in Bulgaria, I was ready to turn my attention back to girls. My need for sexual intimacy with girls was high. But I had developed a complex feeling of being undeserving of it. It was a negative taboo engraved into my psyche. I found it hard to approach girls. I needed sexual liberty with them but I couldn't get it.

Because of a crick in my neck and lack of sleep in Bulgaria, I began slipping into delusional thinking without realising or admitting it to myself. I carried with me the guidebook of Alcoholics Anonymous (AA), which refers often to God. It's like the bible of the AA. The whole idea of God described in the book was making more and more sense to me. I was highlighting parts of the book with a luminous marker and I was feeling euphoric. Everything was clicking into place. I had it all figured out.

One day I went on a guided tour of a seaside village where the relics of St. John the Baptist are claimed to be kept. But I had to pull out of the tour due to the crick in my neck and a pain that shot down into my arm. The pain became intolerable while visiting a monastery during the tour. I excused myself from the group and took a taxi back to my hotel. I began thinking that the pain in my arm and going to visit the relics were connected.

Later that day, I visited a different swimming pool at the resort. I asked a guy sitting next to me at the pool, for the time. It turned out that he was from Jerusalem. This could not be by chance. I started entertaining the idea again that I was Jesus.

Then an idea just came to me. The pain down my arm was the same pain that I had while hanging on the cross during the crucifixion two thousand years ago.

Over the last year, since I had returned from Australia, I had denied the mystical nature of my experiences. This denial would only lead to further relapses. That day in Bulgaria, I couldn't see that a huge relapse was brewing.

I had gone to a local doctor, the previous day, to get some pain relief. I was given a steroid injection in the shoulder and some painkillers to take. The doctor and his wife were both very friendly and very religious. He invited me for lunch in a nearby restaurant.

As we were sitting outside, I felt there was something important about my position at the table and under a beautiful tree. It was just the two of us having lunch. The fact that he was seated to my right meant that I was God the Father. Nobody sits to the left of me. As we ate, he began telling me about Petra in Jordan where he was from. He told me about the Red Sea. I didn't know why but he urged me to visit these places.

Later, I felt that I had to visit these places as part of my divine work on earth. Maybe the steroid injection and the Solpadine he had given me aggravated my psychotic thinking. I gradually became psychotic over the next few days.

I ended up being arrested by police and brought to a cell in the police station. Much of the psychosis remains in my memory.

Unconscious knowledge was revealed to me. The pain in my left arm was a reminder of how I was left hanging by one arm during the crucifixion, when I took the form of Jesus, two thousand years ago. While I was on the cross, my right arm was chopped clean off at the forearm by a guard. This was the same wooden arm of Capitaine Danjou that was taken by the Mexicans in the Legion Bataille de Camerone.

When I was in the form of Jesus, in captivity just before my crucifixion, I shouted out declaring my hand to be the right hand of God. At that time, I was a false messiah. I was confused about the nature of my divinity. But now I was back on earth, not as the second coming of Jesus but as God the Father, called down from the spirit of the Sun by humanity. I was not the wrongly interpreted God the Father from the Bible. I was the Sun of our solar system made human. Using the body of Kevin, I was the voice of the Sun itself. I was the living conscious awareness of the Sun which had eventually awoken in somebody. The human body was just a host.

Everything up till now was a test. My life until now was an unconscious initiation. Now my ministry could begin. I chose Bulgaria as the place to begin it. The Pliska Rosette contained an ancient symbol - IYI. The older civilisations of Bulgaria understood the Solar Divinity and the possibility of the Power of the Sun descending down into human form.

KOSHARITSA

My psychotic holiday in Bulgaria got even crazier. During my renewed revelation, I walked into the church in the village of Kosharitsa. I remembered who I really was, once again. It was near the hotel where I was staying.

The church was empty. I sat quietly in a pew. Above the altar was the symbol of a triangle inscribed within a circle. I had only got a tattoo of this same symbol, on my leg, just the previous day. It was the same symbol used by Alcoholics Anonymous as their logo. On seeing this symbol above the altar, I was overwhelmed with emotion. I realised beyond doubt that I was God made man. For a whole year, I had done everything to deny this. I cried in the church as I felt the love of God take over my body.

But it felt a huge burden to take on this responsibility of being God. I was alone in this world and in this small church. My task was immense. Everyone was in darkness. And I knew that it would be impossible to get through to these blind humans again. I had already tried it in Australia, and I had tried it in Galilee.

I wiped my tears away. I turned my head around. I had seen an elderly woman dressed in black in the little office at the back of the church. Now she had disappeared.

I got up and walked out of the church. But just as I arrived at the door, something uncontrollable hit me. My body was taken over and I got an urge to do something. For some reason unknown to me, I went up the stairs of the belfry. I climbed up and out through a trapdoor in the ceiling.

I stood at the top of the tower. I rang the church bells

loudly. I had an amazing view, over the whole village and the surrounding plains, down towards Sunny Beach and the Black Sea. It was an announcement to the world, of the coming of my presence here on earth. Locals were shocked. They looked up, from down below on the road outside the church. They shouted up. They pleaded with me to come down. I left the church and continued on my way down the road and towards the busy resort of Sunny Beach.

I arrived at the beach. While swimming in the sea, I swam down deep and collected a plastic buoy. I put in my shorts. I heard a baby crying while I was deep under the water. Then I pretended to be drowning. Two lifeguards came out to my assistance. As they walked me out of the water and onto the land, I felt I had just been born again. The buoy stuffed into my shorts was a symbol of my rebirth. I dropped it on the sand. This was my birth as the SunKing.

I covered my face with my two hands as I walked past people on the beach. I was a child new to this world which I had never seen before. I thanked the lifeguards and I left. As I walked on, I pointed at people with one hand while my other hand still covered my face. With a flick of my finger towards the sky, I gave each person their final judgement and allowed them into heaven. I sent nobody down to hell but I still felt angry at their blindness. As I pointed at each person, I could see the terror and helplessness in their unconscious eyes. I felt sorry for them. It was my fault for starting all this.

As I walked around the resort of Sunny Beach, I felt and moved like a robot. As I looked around me, I was painting the world into existence as I perceived it. I made movements with my hands as if I was painting the world around me. Everywhere that I looked, I was creating all things. I was time and I was everything. It felt exhilarating.

My trousers were torn at the sides. I walked around barefoot and topless. Sand covered much of my torso. I passed a tattoo artist who had a large smiling sun tattooed on his back. I had talked with him the previous day but without knowing he had such a tattoo. He had his T-shirt on, then. This was just another proof that I was the sun. The signs were everywhere to be seen.

In the centre of Sunny Beach, outside a McDonald's restaurant, there was a small flower garden. I walked through this flower patch and opened up a manhole. It was concealed amongst the plants and flowers. I got down inside the manhole and into the filth. I was at head level with the ground. I flung whatever rubbish there was inside out onto the flowers. There were empty containers, pipes and pieces of wood covered in mud and dirt. I was raising hell on earth.

Inside the manhole, I found a long old heavy wooden stick with a rounded end. I used it as my staff. I climbed up onto the patch of grass and flowers. I patrolled around on the flowers, shouting at people not to come onto my garden. A small crowd had formed and people were asking if I was okay. Some were concerned and others just laughed. I made no eye contact with them. I looked down at the ground as I walked around in the flowers. I said loudly at them, "Stay out of my garden." This was The Garden of Eden which I had chosen. They were not allowed onto it. I gave them their chance once. They screwed it up. There not getting another chance.

I proceeded to a nearby hotel called the Kuban. When I looked high up at the name of the hotel, I knew the letters in KUBAN were a code for KEVIN. I walked up the polished marble steps and towards the reception, leaving a trail of mud on the white tiled floor. I told the reception staff confidently that a room was awaiting me there. It had already been secretly reserved for me. The room was "404" I demanded. I insisted that it was already reserved and that "all was arranged for me!"

The number 404 was linked to what I believed was a spiritual awakening or epiphany. I had experienced it on the 4th of April while in Mackay in Australia, the previous year.

The hotel receptionist was confused. The security guards came over. They escorted me out of the hotel down the same marble steps again. The police were already waiting outside for me. I was shot in the head and killed instantly. I breathed new life into my carcass again and my eyes opened. I found myself lying on the ground and they handcuffed me. Because I was immortal, I rose from the dead. I stood up and was taken to the police station. They put me in a holding cell.

I stripped naked. I believed that the world was ending outside. I was invisible. I was like a black hole. I was sucking the whole world back into the void. Time grew slower and slower. It was the opposite of the Big Bang. Special religious people were being notified of my detention. Soon a procession of people would pass by my cell to witness the new born King.

I was screaming and making the first rules about the new world. The first rule was: Everyone has the right to water. I was the Aquarius, the water bearer.

The next day, I was taken in a police car back to my hotel in Kosharitsa. On the way back, I thought that I was being brought up into the hills, to be shot and butchered into pieces. The world was terrified of its God. It was not ready to have one. We arrived at the hotel complex.

When I was taken out of the police car and the handcuffs removed, I ran for my life. I ran barefoot across the fields. The police and hotel management people called after me but I kept going. I saw camouflaged snipers and local hunters hiding in the bushes. I ran dodging their bullets and shots. But nobody actually pursued me across the fields, nor any shots fired. It was all in my head.

The Sun was going down. I was out in the scrubby wasteland. By blinking my eyes, I could go back in time to the middle ages, back to the time of dinosaurs and to the beginning of the Earth. Each blink was a thousand years or whatever I programmed each blink to be. The plan was that, as night fell and the sun set, I would kneel down and the whole earth would be consumed into my back. The world would end. I waited. It grew dark and nothing happened.

Then I realised that the local gypsies were werewolves. I was the God who could at last undo this curse of theirs. I saw them moving in the distance and spying on me. I was being followed by the gypsy community in the area. They were discussing my presence and they accepted me as a God. At this point, I was being bitten by ants all over. My feet were cut and sore from the dry scrubland. I became very confused. I limped all the way back to the hotel slowly. I could feel the spirits of dead gypsies in the trees around me. I crept into my room. I slept for a couple of hours.

In the early morning I rose before dawn and left. I walked through fields of sunflowers. Their heads were bowed down. As I walked through the fields, the sunflower heads rose and moved to face me. I had my left arm bent at the elbow, the same side as I had the pain on. My left hand was held at the same level as my left ear. My wrist swivelled around. This was as a missile launcher. I was now at war with different countries that weren't ready to accept my divinity.

Soldiers and tanks were all hidden among the fields of sunflowers. I was being shot by all sorts of gunfire but I was immortal. My movements were in sync with my breathing. I made different strange sounds as I moved like I was a machine. I heard the Foreign Legion all around me. I heard the voices of the lads from my section at the 1REG. They were sent to exterminate me, an order from the French President. I felt blood dripping from my right hand. My body was in shreds with the heavy gunfire. But every time I drew a breath or blinked, I could heal my wounds instantly. As I walked, I made a triangular shape above my head drawing energy from the Sun to recharge my special weapon. I sucked in this energy. I was the Alpha but not the Omega. The letter A was a sign for the pyramids. I was an Egyptian God. My left arm carried a weapon, the Alpha weapon. It was the ultimate of all weapons, greater than any nuclear bomb ever made. I won that battle.

I made my way to a compound on the outskirts of town. It was surrounded with railings. A car was in there which I believed was put there for my use. I tried but I could not open it. In the surrounding buildings, I believed U.S. Special Forces were spying on me. My every move was being tracked by satellite. Then a man came along with his large dog. He demanded that I leave the area. I believed he was Adam, the first human. I felt I could communicate with his dog through a sixth sense. Then the police arrived and spoke with Adam. They were forceful and brutal while arresting me. I got a few belts of their batons. Again I found myself back in a cell at the same police station. I was lucky not to have been attacked by the dog.

It was very confusing to me why I was not being accepted as God among these people. What must I to do to convince them? In my cell, I was summoning up special delta bombs. I was destroying nations one by one and making the world smaller and smaller. To achieve this, I was using the small square tiles on the wall like a keyboard. The cell was my command centre. I was God but they thought that I was from an Egyptian alien race. I formulated instructions about the future running of this world. The world was terrified that I would have ultimate power. They were not ready to let me lead. This was the reason for keeping me in the cell.

Then I realised that because I was the source of all light, everything outside the cell was in darkness. People were all becoming lost in the darkness. They were slowly dying while suffocating from the Suns increasing heat. As I was the Sun, I needed to keep moving to produce oxygen for the earth. While I was kept stationary, the Sun could not move. It would then overheat and destroy the world. Military forces from around the world were coming to get me out. They now understood that I needed to roam the Earth. They knew that I had to be free and allowed to keep moving. If they didn't get there in time the whole world would suffocate from lack of oxygen.

The US marines, the Royal marines and the Irish Ranger Wing were coming but they were not able to get through to the cell. I heard fighting outside the police station, shouting and distant gunfire. This was it. I was being rescued. Eventually the order would be given in France and the Foreign Legion would come and get me out of the cell. I would then receive an apology on my release for their failed attempt at my assassination.

But there were clashing orders between the Vatican and the French Government. Many at the Vatican thought I was the Antichrist and I could not be released. I knew because of their false belief, I could be in this cell for thousands of years. I would only come out when the human race had long become extinct. The police building would decay over millennia. Then only small animals would inhabit the hot earth. All buildings would crumble and I would walk out of the cell. But they didn't know this, so I needed to try get out before that happened. Even though I was immortal, I didn't want to wait so long.

I felt that I could shape change into a fly or insect and crawl out of the cell. I entangled my arms and legs in the bars. I closed my eyes. I felt myself becoming part of the metal. Because I was the Sun and the basis of all elements, I could melt through the bars very slowly. While I was melting into the bars, the policeman on duty crept up silently along the corridor. With all his force, he belted me on the arms and legs with his baton. It was extremely sore. Later that day, I was brought out and showered down a couple of times. I suppose they believed that I was high on drugs of some sort but I was not. I was high on natural drugs.

The next day, I was released from the police station. Back at my hotel, an ambulance came with a police escort. They took me to a psychiatric hospital in the nearby city of Burgas.

BURGAS

I spent six weeks at the Ivan Temkov Hospital in Burgas, before I was well enough to fly back to Dublin. The conditions were terrible but I got used to them. The first couple of weeks while I was acutely psychotic, I was in a locked room. I then shared another locked room with another patient, a Muslim guy from Sweden. I think his psychotic break was drug related because he recovered quicker than I did. He was Allah and I was God. Funnily, we accepted each other and became friends even.

One day we began writing all over the walls. Then I smashed the window by throwing a small heavy bedside locker at the glass. It wasn't long before a bunch of nurses and security came stampeding into the room. They used leather restraining belts to strap us both to our beds for the next two days. It was my fault. Allah cursed and shouted at me for smashing the window. I pissed in my hand and flicked my piss at him in order to bless and baptize him. He spat back at me. We were completely bonkers.

They took off the restraining belts. They separated us. We both got our own rooms, two Kings equally powerful. The Swede seemed to recover quickly and he was released from the hospital soon after that. I got worse however and the straps went back on.

They kept me strapped to my bed. I screamed and shouted in vain for hours on end until I lost my voice. A nurse would come in twice a day and give me an injection in the back side. Because they injected me in the same area, over and over again, it became very raw and painful. I grew to hate the sound of the key in the door when I knew the nurse was coming with a syringe.

Being strapped to the bed, which had a waterproof mattress cover, I was left lying in a pool of my own urine for long periods. But I was only strapped around my waist. My hands were free. I could just about sit up on the bed. But when I did this the straps would tighten and cut into me. I got itchy bed sores all around my buttocks and on my back. It was dire. I was so furious at one stage with the situation that I just took a shit while lying there strapped to the bed. I grabbed the warm faeces in my right hand and reaching backwards, I smudged it into a large cross on the wall behind my bed. I made a shit Christian symbol.

While lying strapped to the bed, I became more and more desperate. Just like in the prison cell in the 1REG, an innovative idea came to me.

I realised that if I could remove the waterproof cover, the urine would then soak through the foam mattress. Slowly and meticulously, I managed to unzip the mattress cover. Twisting and turning, I pulled it off and threw it across the room. I was happy with this little achievement. The urine dripped out through the foam mattress onto the tiled floor below. Next I began to tear little pieces from the foam mattress. I kept at this. Eventually I had torn up the whole mattress. Pieces of foam lay scattered around the floor. But I was now lying on a rusty layer of thin metal bars and I was still strapped to the bed frame with those leather belts.

It must have looked like a horribly twisted BDSM scenario. I was naked with shit on my hands, strapped to a rusty metal bed. There was a large cross, painted in shit, on the wall behind. There was a pool of piss on the ground and bits of foam mattress scattered everywhere. The walls were covered in scribbles from psychotic patients. The bed was immovable and bolted to the ground. I lay back on the metal bars looking behind me, towards the upside-down cross. I felt as if I was going through an experience like the crucifixion.

With the mattress removed, the leather straps around my waist had loosened slightly. I twisted and turned until I was lying across the width of the bed. I had one foot touching the floor. My other leg was bent up and kneeling on the metal bars. The metal bars cut into my knee. The straps were cutting into my waist which was now red raw. There was no going back. I was desperate. But a force outside of me had taken over my body just like in the prison cell of the 1REG. I took hold of the leather strap and began rubbing it on one of the rusty bars. I stopped and looked. To my amazement I had made a very slight incision into the thick leather strap. With this, I got a surge of strength and hope. I rubbed and rubbed furiously the thick straps for a long time, until they broke. I freed myself and walked around the room. I wondered had anyone ever get out of those straps like me before. Harry Houdini, beat that! But maybe it was Harry's soul in me, and not me. Thanks Harry!

My sense of achievement and satisfaction didn't last long. A bunch of security guards and nurses came in with new straps, a new mattress, and a big needle! They strapped me up really tight by the ankles wrists and waist. I could barely breathe. It was one of the worst feelings I have ever had. It forced me to surrender.

Eventually the straps were released when I promised the doctor that I would behave. As my condition gradually improved, I was even brought on little guarded walks outside on the hospital grounds. The air was fresher now. The first golden leaves of autumn were scattered around the place. Then one day, when the head Psychiatrist asked me during a review if I thought I was still God, I replied "Of course not" even though I still thought I was. He ordered the nurses to move me up to the next floor which was an open ward. The idea of an open ward seemed like paradise. He knew I had suffered enough.

A few hours later, I was settling in to my new bedroom on that relaxed open ward. I was brought some clothes from lost property to wear. I took off my hospital pyjamas, took a hot shower and changed into these clothes. I was surprised by the gold coloured shirt they had chosen for me. I knew that the head psychiatrist had chosen it on purpose, from the stock of lost property. I was God but I had to keep it a secret from now on. He knew it too. This was their way of telling me to keep it a secret. The gold shirt had a small logo on the pocket showing a man lifting the world on his shoulders.

During my last two weeks at the Ivan Temkov Hospital in Burgas, I was showing signs of recovery. I was given more freedom by the nursing staff. I would walk outside in the nearby sea gardens and along the beach. I would pick up odd bits of paper and find hidden meanings in ordinary things. I began learning more of the Cyrillic alphabet to pass time. I learned basic Bulgarian from the other patients who I became friendly with. I noticed the head psychiatrist leave the hospital in the evenings, to go home. He drove a very nice white Jeep with the digits 666 on the registration plate. This was another clear sign that he recognised the Devil in his work. Psychosis can become a real Hell. But for those who are able to separate from their fearful mind and embrace Love, it can be the same doorway into Heaven.

Looking back on my psychotic breaks, I have identified a common factor. There had been an intense attraction to a girl which acted as a trigger. In Bulgaria, a barmaid whom I had an intense obsessive attraction towards became part of my psychosis.

One day, in the midst of psychosis, I was looking out from the balcony of my hotel room. I saw her laid out in a white wedding dress in the back of a white car. There were white roses around her black hair. She was dead. It was her funeral. It all seemed very confusing. I ran down the stairs and out of the hotel to where the car was. But it turned out that the car was just full of paper cups and catering items. She wasn't laid out inside. Fear is the root of an unpleasant psychosis. This is a good example of how my hallucinations have been. This is their true nature. They are projections of supressed fears and our unconscious mind. They are simply misinterpretations of reality by a vivid imagination. Love is madness. Madness is real.

FAIRVIEW

Arriving back in Dublin from Bulgaria, I spent one week in a psychiatric hospital for a review. I hid my delusions and paranoid thoughts well. I was released but only on the condition that I stay with my mother. What a typical Irish scenario.

I became unwell soon afterwards. During some sleepless nights and while out wandering the streets, I became psychotic. The Police - An Garda Síochána, picked me up late at night. I thought my phone was hacked and I was being tracked by satellite. Not for the first time, the world was coming to an end. The Gardaí brought me to the Emergency department of Beaumont hospital. I left as soon as they were gone. I became more sleep deprived and more psychotic over the next few days. I was eventually admitted involuntarily by the Gardaí into a psychiatric hospital in Fairview. I spent about eight weeks inside.

Many times, they locked me in the seclusion room. When I was in the main ward, I would keep pressing the fire alarm. The nurses would come, tackle me to the ground and drag me back into the seclusion room every time I done this. They used the excuse that I was violent but that was a lie. I was just pressing the firm alarm. They couldn't manage that.

I thought that nurses where religious people in disguise coming in to hospital to test me and see if I was indeed God. But these religious people could never accept me or even understand my divinity. Jesus was their God and nobody else could ever be equal to him in their mind. The Catholics had destroyed Jesus's original teaching. They kicked him upstairs and made him a God so nobody else could achieve that. Then they planted this seed of pure evil, their precious lie, around the world. Ireland was a fertile ground to grow this poisonous weed.

They say that St. Patrick chased the snakes out of Ireland. In fact, he only introduced a greater evil. This is why Irish people drink so much on St. Patrick's Day. The Shamrock is actually a sign for Satan. They are not celebrating the arrival of Christianity. They are drowning their sorrows about the disconnection from their animistic roots. Their archaic souls are calling them from deep within. But they will never admit that to you or even to themselves.

While inside the seclusion room, I believed they would cement me inside. Large trucks and machinery would arrive. They would cover the room in layers of bricks and mortar. The only solution they had was to hide me forever. Because I was immortal, I could not be destroyed. Because of this delusion, the padded seclusion room was terrifying for me. The world could not accept me as God and this was the only way to hide me away. This was a frightening experience. I begged them to release me. The padded seclusion room blew cold air from the ceiling. The only option I had was to curl up in a ball on the plastic mattress, cover myself with blankets and sleep.

This hospital admission in Ireland was my rock bottom. It felt very long. I felt mistreated. Even in the poorer conditions of Bulgaria, there was still more respect in their approach.

I was now getting very irritable and frustrated. There was no need to keep me in for so long. I was almost becoming aggressive with the staff who I felt were treating me unfairly. I was losing all hope and I was desperate to get out. I had never been violent towards anyone before during my psychosis but I felt they were abusing their power by keep throwing me into seclusion because I pressed the firm alarm. That definitely wasn't a valid excuse to put me in seclusion. It was surely a form of abuse. They got the dosage of medication wrong too. The agitation caused from the medication was extremely irritating. It meant I was tapping my feet and rocking while I was sat. I made humming sounds. I literally could not sit still for any amount of time. This intense anxiety and unease from the medical side effects was torture. I was lip-smacking, rubbing my hands on the walls and pacing the corridors. Their treatment was driving me insane!

In an attempt to help me relax, an Occupational Therapist gave me different sensory items to feel and squeeze and help release the tension. Eventually, a brave nurse took some responsibility. She allowed me to run laps on a small grass field outside, trusting me that I wouldn't flee. It is small acts like this from responsible people, which make all the difference.

I played along with the psychiatrists. I gave them what they wanted to hear. Then one day, my status was changed from involuntary patient to voluntary patient. I was still slightly psychotic even though I hid it well. I decided to leave the hospital.

My parents were just as controlling as the hospital staff on the outside of the hospital. They bought into the lie that I had lifelong Schizophrenia. They were embarrassed by my socially awkward behaviour. This is the main reason why people are admitted; not because they are violent or dangerous, but because their behaviour is unacceptable to an inhibited fearful society.

I was only out of the hospital a few hours when my father did something awful. Because of my socially embarrassing behaviour, he tried to handcuff me with chains that he carried with him. We were in a supermarket car park when he tried this stunt. He failed to put me in his chains. Then he rang the Gardaí. The Gardaí came and arrested me nearby. Because I was the "Sick person," they thought I had made up that story about the chains my father carried. My father hid the chains when they arrived.

The Gardaí brought me back to the hospital in Fairview. They said to the staff incorrectly that I was the one being aggressive. I was admitted involuntarily for another four weeks.

Thankfully that was my last ever admission in a mental hospital. That was six years ago. That was the end of my two year struggle with Psychosis. Psychosis was actually my minds way of healing past trauma from my childhood and my service in the Legion. But it was also my Soul trying to call me home. Psychosis has the potential to heal a person very deeply if it is allowed to be played out. By containing it and denying it, we risk destroying the person and creating demons of them.

Even though I was still deluded during that last admission, somehow I knew that I had to get out. I was supposed to be in 'Care' but it certainly didn't feel that way. I had to get out, both of the Mental Health system and away from a dysfunctional family. The Psychiatrist who was in charge of my case was from West Africa. He was a very religious person. He never really wanted to listen to what I had to say. He wasn't very helpful. He didn't like me and I didn't like him. Exaggerating that I was an aggressive patient, he put a transfer request in for me to be admitted to St. Brendan's Hospital for long term treatment. The referral order was denied. The real reason for him to try and get rid of me was never mentioned. Only I knew it.

In my bedroom, I kept a phone directory called the Goldenpages. I had a view of the car park from my bedroom window. One afternoon I saw my Psychiatrist arrive in his car. He parked it. I scribbled down the registration number, model and make of his car on a piece of paper. I took my mobile phone and flicked through the Goldenpages. I found a number for a car removal company. I rang the number and in a confident voice I requested a collection,

"Hello there, yeah, I have a car that needs to be taken away.

Yeah… it's a Nissan Primera, 96D-11404, green….Yeah…. Ok look I'm very busy, Can you get someone out today? Ok great thanks, yeah, ask for Aoidh Mackay, Bye Bye."

The towing company came that afternoon to collect the Psychiatrist's car. I had a good laugh when the nurses had to explain to the towing company that this was a mental hospital. Nobody knew who Aoidh Mackay was. They guessed it was me. The nurses were very angry at me and told me off. They came to my room and insulted me. Shortly after this, I heard they were attempting to transfer me to St. Brendan's hospital.

This was bad news. I knew of the reputation of St. Brendan's. I kept my head down and stopped interacting with any of the staff. I had to be very careful. They were now looking for any excuse. Any little thing I done that they didn't like, and they would use it against me. I kept to myself. I denied that I was God. I was constantly asked and quizzed about it. I felt my dignity was not being upheld. I didn't like their condescending manner. I gave the impression that I was getting well and I told them I had given up my stubborn delusions. I stayed quiet and reserved, not wanting to draw any attention to myself. The whole system was designed to control, to bully, and to punish.

When I got a copy of my whole medical file, many years later, under the Freedom of Information Act, I saw a load of inaccuracies and exaggerations recorded about me. The reason for my isolation was always aggressive behaviour instead of just pressing the fire alarm. It was recorded that I was having visual hallucinations of a ginger cat inside my room. This was completely inaccurate. There was really a ginger cat that would walk past my bedroom window. The window went down to floor level. The nurses used to laugh when I mentioned the cat. Then one day, one of them entered my room just as the cat walked past the window. "Oh there really is a ginger cat," the nurse said in surprise. They also laughed and regarded my claim of once being a French Foreign Legionnaire as a delusion. They only believed it when my family confirmed it as the truth.

Thankfully I was released with the help of The Mental Health Commission, who revoked my admission order, following a tribunal. Without them, who knows how I would have ended up; possibly in St. Brendan's Hospital and receiving forced ECT. I might never have recovered at all. Thank God it didn't go that way. That was my last hospital admission. It was my rock bottom. Did I learn anything? Yes.

I realised once again, that only I could help myself. The sad truth about the whole thing was that I was completely alone again. My family had taken the side of the Mental Health System. They would never look at me in the same way again. Anything I would say or do would be looked at with a level of scrutiny and scepticism. My credibility and dignity was torn out of me. Without my consent, their agreed consensus and labelling of me as someone with Schizophrenia was a violation of my integrity as a human being and an attack on my character. Who gives them the right to say I had schizophrenia? I never agreed to that.

Maybe I should have stayed in the Legion after all. But now I had an important choice to make. Despite the anger I was feeling, my choice did not involve blame. I must rise above that. I could have kept myself chained up with my own chains or I could free myself. I knew without a doubt what the answer was. In the words of William Ernest Henley (1888), "I am The Captain of my soul."

WEST

AFTER SCHIZOPHRENIA

"The Schizophrenic is drowning in the same waters,
In which The Mystic swims with delight."

Joseph Campbell (1904-1987)

CLAREHALL

The last Christmas which I spent with my family, I had invited a girlfriend over. My mother and two brothers were present. It was the first ever Christmas that I had a girlfriend home. The situation was alien to me. It turned out to be a disaster. I felt suffocated by being there. I just wanted to spend the day with my girlfriend. I had no interest to be there with my mother and older brother. But I was a prisoner to societal norms. I felt that maybe we could be a happy family just like in American Christmas movies. I had to let on that all was good when it wasn't

In the morning, we went to Clontarf to do the traditional Christmas swim in the icy cold sea. That tradition was only for mad Irish people. Only I and my girlfriend were brave enough to get in.

Later on, back at the house, we all sat down for Christmas dinner. I became bored and uneasy as the day progressed. As my girlfriend chatted with my older brother, I became disturbed inside. I found it hard to believe that I would be jealous of my own brother. I realised how little fate I had in him as a person. I felt ashamed and disgusted at my own insecurity.

But I was also annoyed at myself for not being able to maintain a conversation due to a debilitating stammer. It had been a problem for all of my life. What annoyed me more about it was that it forced me to listen to people's bullshit all the time as I didn't have the fluency to fill in gaps. I had a lot to say but I often just gave up trying, not wanting to sound like a stuttering cockroach. My stammer has led me to avoid groups of people in my life. I can chat with someone one on one but groups provide a real struggle.

Dinner was over. I prepared the Christmas pudding. This was my favourite part of Christmas. I heated half a cup of Irish whiskey in the microwave and poured it over the pudding. Everyone shut up for a while. I turned off all the lights. A blue ring of fire burnt around the pudding in the dark room with the little sounds of raisins crackling and crisping up. It was the only good part of the day. I savoured that moment in the dark when everyone was quiet and we just gazed at the ring of blue flame burning around the pudding. I always wanted that moment to last forever. I didn't have to listen to peoples shit and I didn't have to stutter.

Once desert was finished, my mother insisted she would go and find the Clarinet. Both I and my older brother were in a marching band called the Artane Boys Band when we were young. We had both played the Clarinet. It was now stored away in the attic. I hadn't played it since I was fifteen years old.

Inside of me, I felt rage building up when she brought the Clarinet to the Christmas table. I remembered how I never wanted to be in that band. I remembered my fearful and anxious adolescence. During all those years of doing stuff to please my parents, I always felt lost. I never knew who I was. If someone asked me what I liked to do, I couldn't give a truthful response. I begged her not to take out that Clarinet but she did anyway. I was furious but I kept my fury locked up inside. I was very close to grabbing the bloody Clarinet and smashing it off the kitchen table. The only good thing that came out of the Artane Boys Band was the opportunity to meet U2 and participate in their music video, "The Sweetest Thing."

What a shit Christmas. I felt like a miserable child. I could no longer stand their company. Next when they decided to watch some movies on the television, I retreated to my bedroom early. I felt awful and confused. I was not really sure what was happening in my head. My girlfriend came up to my bedroom and she spent the night there with me.

Charlene was from the USA and had only been in Dublin for about six months. We had met during a surfing trip to the west of Ireland just two months before. It was the first relationship I had had since my breakdown over a year before. I was still in recovery and I was vulnerable. The relationship became intimate quickly. She was at the centre of my uneventful life. I was unemployed and living in my mother's house. I had given up alcohol and was attending weekly meetings with the AA. In the place of alcohol, she became my new addiction.

I had about eighteen months of sobriety around this time. I didn't want to admit it to myself but I had begun to obsess about her. My life was becoming miserable. I thought about her every moment of the day. I was jealous and insecure without knowing why. I had a huge fear of rejection. My imagination was pestering away at me. I would get disturbing visual thoughts of her having sex with other men in different sexual positions. My mind was self-destructing. Even though these intrusive thoughts disturbed me, in a weird way I entertained them. I wanted to feel the pain and anger that they aroused in me. But there was another possibility that I did my best to deny. Maybe it was a real fantasy of mine to see my girlfriend having sex with other men. This disturbed me. I might actually enjoy such a scenario. But I wouldn't allow myself to own such a fantasy. I denied these thoughts. My head was a mess. Pain provided meaning to my life. It was as if pain was all I've ever known. I couldn't permit myself to feel real joy, real love. Pain and pleasure were inseparable.

I couldn't get enough of her body. All the sex we had was never enough. I tied her up but that only fed the fire inside of me. I craved her like a drug. I could eat her whole body if she was one giant candy doll so much was my weakness for her. I didn't understand that this love, lust or passion, whatever it was, belonged to me. It was mine, with or without her. I didn't allow myself to own it. I felt undeserving of it.

I became suspicious and paranoid. She could sense it when I asked her where she was and who she was with, each time we spoke over the phone. Early in the New Year, I couldn't hide my insecurities. She broke up with me. We attempted to be friends for some months after but I was only kidding myself. My obsession took over and became unbearable. When I reached two years sobriety from alcohol, I thought "what use is a sober life if I can't have a bloody relationship with a woman without becoming an obsessive creep?" I gave in and bought a bottle of red wine.

I sat crossed legged in a park with the bottle between my legs. It was a screw cap bottle but I couldn't open it. There was still a battle on in my mind. For half an hour, I tormented myself whether or not to open that bottle. Then I got up, left the bottle lying there on the grass and walked away. I thanked the righteous half of myself for saving me. But I had only walked for two minutes when the other half of me said "A two year prison sentence for what? Just drink the fucking bottle."

I ran back to the park, sat down where I had left it, spun the bottle cap open and guzzled down the dark red liquid. With all those strong flavours I had forgotten, my veins warmed and I smelt defeat. I put my earphones in and played sad love songs on YouTube. I wallowed in my sorrow. Before long I returned to the nearby store for a second bottle. I got smashed drunk.

CHRISTCHURCH

Eventually I had to face the fact that my relationship with certain family members was not good. I was no longer tied by the restraints of societal norms and expectations. I had to separate from them to protect and sustain my mental wellbeing. I had a good relationship with my younger brother and my older sister. I decided that I would keep them in my life. I still kept a connection with my roots.

I knew I could no longer live with my mother. If I did, I would have another psychotic relapse and further hospital admissions. I would become a chronic and hopeless Schizophrenic, living in a co-dependent relationship with her. I knew these obsessions that I was experiencing with different girls were connected somehow to my relationship with my mother, tied up in complex child psychology. This realisation was another turning point in my life. I had to severe the umbilical cord myself. Holding on to a dysfunctional attachment that I formed with my mother during my infancy would mean another psychotic relapse.

Our childhood happens once. We don't get a second chance. Clinical experts would say that children never detach from their parents, but I was never properly attached to begin with. The whole idea of someone as an "Adult Child" was a dysfunctional one. How can an Adult be a Child at the same time? It's true; we all came from the same place, our mother's womb. There is no denying this. But some of us were also brought up to believe that God was our true Father and his incarnation, Jesus Christ, was a baby born of a virgin. What a load of horseshit. The real question I was now faced with was "Do I want become a man, true to myself, or remain trapped as a scared child, a slave to my birth family, to society and to religion?"

I left to join the Foreign Legion at eighteen years old. I should have never returned to my parents afterwards. I needed my own place to live and my own independence. I could continue blaming my parents and make a list of all the things I perceived they done wrongly. But that wasn't the answer. Instead of hating or blaming, I needed to focus on myself and take responsibility for my life. By choosing estrangement from them, I could begin the real work of soul revival and figuring out who the hell I was. Part of me was them. I could not deny that. There was no escaping that fact. But there was a deeper essence to my being, calling me from the depths of the unconscious. It was this part of me that is common across all living things. It is not dependent on our lineage. Carl Jung called it the Collective unconscious.

By spending time alone in nature, I could strip back all the roles I had performed in my life up until that point...

Son, Brother, Uncle, Godson, Godfather, Friend, Grandson, Cousin, Third Cousin, Student, Graduate, Soldier, Boyfriend, Employee, Tourist, Teammate, Caporal, Comrade, Patient, Believer, Non-believer, Maniac, Irish, European, Caucasian, Atheist, Agnostic, Buddhist, Catholic, a Dub, Alcoholic, Bisexual, Gay, Straight, Sex Addict, Schizo, Voluntary worker, Chef, The Devil, Jesus Christ, Legionnaire Gregory Sims, Me, Myself and I, a highly sensitive person. Aoidh Mac Aoidh. Each one of these had its own identity.

As I walked alone, among forests, mountains, or on a secluded beach, I could sense that all of these were only half-truths. If I kept playing roles within a dysfunctional family and a dysfunctional world, I would probably relapse into another psychosis. I would play out my prognosis of Schizophrenia which they had all promised me with certainty. Submerged in nature, I began to realise that psychosis was not an illness.

Psychosis was a gift, a calling to wake the fuck up. Schizophrenia was the result of denying this calling. But I was full of fake guilt and confusion. I had to realise my own power. I had to take responsibility for my own life. I had to accept that the delusion of being "God" might really have some truth to it.

I left my mother's house. I declared myself homeless, sleeping rough in Dublin City Centre. Soon I was placed in an emergency hostel run by the St. Vincent de Paul Charity. I stayed there for three months. I was determined now and I felt strong. Survival mode kicked in again. I knuckled down and I looked after myself, No.1.

I got a part time job in a coffee shop. I went running in the phoenix park three times a week. I went to the swimming pool and swam hard. I used the city centre as my gym, doing pull-ups wherever I could find a horizontal bar, scaffoldings or playgrounds, followed by push-ups, sit-ups and squats. I was exhausted at the end of each day. I went to free meditation classes. Luckily, I had my own small room at the St. Vincent de Paul shelter where I could retreat to. I worked hard in the coffee shop. With my appetite and metabolism back to its best, I ate like a horse without gaining weight. I was on fire.

Despite my homeless status, my strength and confidence came back to me. I even allowed myself to drink a few beers now and then. I was disciplined. I felt like a Legionnaire again, but this time it was different. I was doing all this for me alone. I had given up serving others, except for Cappuccinos and flat whites! I had given up believing others, being responsible for others. My black and white view of the world was torn down. It no longer held me prisoner. This was my life and I was taking it back. I saved up some money from my job. I went for a small holiday abroad, for a week.

On my return, I was told that my bed was closed at the shelter.

I was not allowed back in. Homeless people don't have the right to a holiday, was the message I got. I was angry but even more determined. Again I started sleeping rough around the city. It was the summer time. The milder weather helped the situation. Some nights I would get a one night bed here and there. I had to call a Freephone number for the homeless division every day. If there was a free bed someplace, I would be told what shelter to go to.

None of the hostels were as good as the St. Vincent de Paul one I had first stayed in. I no longer got an individual room. I shared with others. Some places had six to a room. One place was an old pub with about thirty people, all sleeping in the same large area. Some of the shelters were terrible and some were Ok. The indirect message I kept getting from the services was that I was being put into these worse hostels because I left the St. Vincent de Paul shelter to go away for a week's holiday. I had to play ball with them and conform to the services or they would punish me by putting me in the worse hostels. It was all about control and obedience, not much different than the Legion really. But it was a piece of cake. I relished the challenge. Bring it on bitches!

I was no longer on medication for over a year at that point. The homeless services were aware of my diagnosis of Schizophrenia. In their eyes, I had no right to come off the meds. One day, I was given an appointment with the mental health team for homeless people in Dublin City. I met with the Psychiatrist. I explained and pleaded with him that due to my condition, could they please assist me in getting an individual room in one of the homeless hostels. I was very sleep deprived at that point. But I may as well have been talking to the wall. He just gave me a slip of paper for antipsychotic medication. I left the office and threw his prescription in the rubbish bin. I slept rough that night.

Another time, I met with the same Psychiatrist. I told him again that I was desperate. I needed my own individual room and not medication. "We can't help you with that," was his response. "But we can help you with some medication to make you better. You are sick." He even smiled at my ridiculous idea, that Schizophrenia was very much a social and psychological disorder. But in his narrow view, it was purely medical. For him, in his deluded mind, Schizophrenia was as physical as cancer or diabetes. Again, he just handed me another slip of paper for Olanzapine, an antipsychotic drug. This time I didn't take the slip of paper.

I left that piece of paper on his table in front of him. I had been sleeping rough the night before. I was really exhausted from not being able to get a good sleep. I realised, not for the first time in my life that I had to help myself. Before I left his office, I asserted myself. I told him firmly that I want nothing further to do with the Mental Health Services. I told him that they were not to contact me anymore.

I continued getting phone calls and voicemails for some weeks after that. Another Psychiatrist who was in contact with my mother threatened to have me admitted involuntarily to hospital. Eventually they did stop but only after I phoned them and left a voice message. I requested that they stop harassing me.

I continued sleeping rough or getting a one night bed when I could. One afternoon, I was feeling pretty hopeless about my situation. I couldn't get an individual room anywhere no matter how hard I pleaded with the services. I was moved from hostel to hostel. I was sleeping rough in between when there were no beds. Nothing seemed to be improving.

One afternoon, I called into an old hostel near Smithfield, called the Morning star hostel. I was hoping that I could get in there. But there was no place for me. A nice friendly old man I met there suggested that I could go into their chapel and say a prayer. I was sceptical. I no longer believed in God and I was losing belief in myself. I was feeling hopeless. Why the feck not? I thought. He handed me a small medal called the Miraculous Medal, hanging on a thin blue string. What harm could it do? I thought. I thanked him. I went inside. I sat alone, amongst the silence and sanctuary of the chapel. I can't remember praying. I remember just sitting there for some time. I put the medal around my neck and I walked out back into the concrete jungle. Who bloody knows? I thought to myself.

I found out later that the hostel was run by Legionnaires of another order, The Legion of Mary. That happened on a Wednesday afternoon in September. Two days later, on the Friday morning, I was sitting in another silent sanctuary. This time I was sitting in my own studio apartment beside the Phoenix Park. I was in shock. It was a miracle.

I put the kettle on in my tiny, but cosy furnished apartment, to disturb the unbelievable silence. I looked at the set of keys, still clutched in my hand. I remembered the landlord's words from half an hour before, "Enjoy your new home, Kevin. I'm sure it's a lot nicer than the homeless hostels."

Things happened quickly in those two days since sitting in the Chapel. I had viewed the apartment on Thursday. On Friday morning, I got the call from the landlord offering me the tenancy. The department of Social Welfare paid the deposit and first month's rent, to get me off the streets and off their homeless list. Everything had fallen into place. It certainly felt like a miracle. That was Friday, the eleventh of September, the day I got my own place. It was a bad day for some as I remembered the twin tower disaster. But it was a good day for me.

Around that same time, as I moved off the streets and into my own little sanctuary, a new sculpture had just arrived in

Dublin city centre. Cast in bronze, it depicted a frail homeless Jesus wrapped in rags and lying on a park bench. The sculpture was erected in the gardens of Christchurch Cathedral across the road from the St. Vincent de Paul Shelter. Despite the possible fuel for delusional thinking, I just smiled to myself and shrugged it off. I didn't want to be Jesus anymore. I just wanted to be myself.

Recovery was real. Maybe just maybe, God was too. But I was tired of defining or trying to rationalise the nature of God. I let God be a mystery. I had that weekend to settle in to my new apartment. The following Monday morning, I was starting an honours degree in Social Care.

By perfect chance, The Dublin Institute of Technology (DIT) was only a fifteen minute walk from my new home. Only one week previously, I had been sleeping rough around the city. Now, on this bright autumn morning, I walked into the DIT's new campus which had just opened in Grangegorman. As I was walking in, I noticed two mental health patients who were heavily medicated. They sat with their rigid necks and bloated bodies, sucking on cigarettes, outside a new Mental Health facility that replaced the former St. Brendan's Hospital. It reminded me of times past.

Only two years prior to this, during my last hospital admission for Schizophrenia, I was told that I would be transferred to St. Brendan's Hospital for a long term admission. I could have been sitting right beside them, sucking desperately on coffin nails, trying to forever forget, my true nature.

Now here I was, walking past those high ominous walls of the former Richmond Lunatic Asylum / St. Brendan's hospital. I wasn't a patient. That large site was now home to the Dublin Institute of Technology. It was the first year that it opened. I was one of the very first students from the DIT to study there. Had I been born in a previous generation of Irish society, the outcome may have been much different, with lobotomy or shock treatment a real probability for me.

As I settled into my studies, I even joined the local St. Brendan's Gaelic football team, a team that was originally made up of nurses and doctors from the hospital.

Before I started my Degree course at the DIT, I looked back over the previous years of my life. I reflected. My recovery had initially involved a period of what I call living logically. Metaphysical and spiritual concerns were parked up and I concentrated on practical stuff. I focused on getting myself physically well, getting my concentration back, and socialising. I got part time work too which was a great help in challenging my capacity to work in a stimulating environment. I continued working in the coffee shop while studying. I needed to get back into our normal and expected pace of life. My brain had slowed down too much and I needed to shift it up a gear. My studies would continue to help me with this. Only Love was missing in my life.

One day while I was working at the coffee shop, I was reminded of a conditioned inner unease arising from being attacked in the Legion years earlier. On one particular busy day, the supervisor had grabbed my arm forcefully to get me to speed up or do something else that she needed. I was now capable of asserting myself. Immediately, I asked to talk with her aside. I explained that I understood her concerns as it was a busy day. But I said that I was very uncomfortable with what she had done. It was unacceptable. I could not stand anyone touching me in that manner. It was progress for me, being able to control my anger and learning to be assertive with people. Before this, I always thought that I had only two options; suck it up or explode.

There was another similar incident years before that one, during a fitness course. It was before my mental breakdown.

I was a student at the time. A lecturer on a badly organised fitness course had done the same thing, grabbing my arm. It caught me completely off guard. I didn't react too well, only being a couple of years out of the Legion. I was filled with an automatic rage and fear. I strongly pushed his arm away and shouting in a loud aggressive voice, I declared "No hands, No hands!" He definitely got the message but I was uncomfortably full of adrenaline for some time afterwards. I was ready to unleash the beast if he tried anything. That was before my psychotic breakdown in Australia. In many ways, I could see that my Schizophrenia was a form of PTSD from the beating and bullying I endured in the Legion.

There were lots of Macho men and bravado in the mines, where I worked in Australia. I suppressed my unease with that environment. I was in denial about being surrounded by idiots. I forced myself to put up with their bullshit and fake "manliness." Since then, I have learned to avoid strong male personalities as much as possible as a coping mechanism. I realised that this was a type of avoidant behaviour but I still allowed myself this. Then by recognising it, accepting it and then addressing it through psychotherapy, I could deal with it. If it was ignored or denied, I might not be able to react appropriately in future situations that would most likely arise. It's almost impossible to completely avoid Macho male behaviour. As each year passed, I felt more assure of my recovery. I had learnt self-control. I had learned to be assertive with both men and women. Bullying can be very subtle in its nature. Often the bully is not even aware of their own behaviour. After all, the bully is nothing but a coward.

Completing my Honours degree in Social Care, helped me understand the concept of disability and mental illness as a social construct. This further empowered me to take back control over my life. I often wondered whether I was mentally disabled during my recovery process. Was there a specific point when I had recovered? I think that when I truly understood that the future remains unwritten, was when I was well past any likelihood of relapse. The future is a product of our imagination, creation and beliefs, in the present. The future is a limitless possibility. During contemplation on the term "Disability," I came up with the following tongue twister:

"Being able to be disabled is the ability to disable disabilities ability to able abilities while trying to enable a naval table wheelchair access without legs. For when the sea rises and swells, we in wells, stick crutches and crosses with many cables."

It first appears to be nonsense. But it was once again pointing me towards the futility of words to capture our reality, the eternal paradox of life. I knew that psychosis was madness to our rational worldview. Our mind fails every time in its attempt to express the Oneness that we all feel separated from. The truth of our existence is beyond words. I understood, without the need for words, what is meant when it is said that "Silence is the language of God." The other language is babble.

SERRA DA MALCATA

Christmas became a time of year, when I would go abroad. I needed to avoid the commercial and religious build-up to it in Dublin City. It was on the radio and television and everywhere I looked. I didn't want to spend it there. I wanted to be on my own or at least if I was with others of my own choosing, to be in control of it. It was no longer a time of celebration for me. I tried not to become bitter at this time of year but I no longer gave it much significance in my life. Sometimes hate and bitterness did creep in and that was ok too.

The Christian celebration for me was dull anyway. It reminded me of my own former delusions of grandeur. When I had eventually pulled myself out of the huge ego inflated delusion that I was God, in the literal sense of a defined and limited being inside my limited body, the Christmas story of Jesus of Nazareth was even more difficult to swallow. I couldn't allow myself to be a lesser being than him. The birth of the Messiah Jesus in a stable was just a story I had grown up with. I was conditioned to believe it without question. But now it posed difficulty for my ego to handle. He was no more perfect than anyone else.

Fair enough, I had returned to a normal material existence free of psychosis but I could no longer accept or entertain the idea that some chap other than me could be King of Kings, God made Man. I was jealous of Jesus. Why does he get all the Glory? Christmas became a time to avoid. With the Christmas songs and advertising bombarding and intruding on my senses, the only option was to get away for a couple of weeks. But

I couldn't entirely escape Christmas. It was just one of those things to accept as part of western culture.

I had survived a year of homelessness. I had settled into living independently in my small flat. I was attending my Degree course at the D.I.T. Christmas was coming and there would be a long break from lectures. No way was I going to spend Christmas in Dublin. I no longer had a duty to spend it with my biological family or my Legion family.

I searched the internet for volunteering opportunities. I was familiar with the WOOFING agreement. In exchange for a few hours of work each day on an organic farm, bed and board would be provided. Many countries had a list of hosts offering this type of volunteer agreement. I found an advert from a small farm nestled away in the mountains of north east Portugal, a secluded spot. The farmer needed help with his olive harvest and his herd of wild mountain goats. I made contact with him and I agreed to come and help out for two weeks over the Christmas period.

The organic farm in the Serra da Malcata Natural Reserve was far from civilization. The living conditions were rough. Life there was very basic. The ancient stone houses had no windows. The smoke from the fire inside went up and out through the gaps between tiles on the roof. The animals would wander into the house. There was a cauldron of soup constantly over the fire. It was topped up each day with vegetables from the garden. The volunteers work alternated from harvesting black olives from the two hundred year old olive trees or shepherding the goats into the mountains from early morning until sunset.

There were no phone lines, no internet and no TV. There was plenty of time to think and plenty of time to be bored. Christmas day came. I wandered with the goats up into the hills and forests. It was a world away from the Christmas I hated back in Dublin.

Christmas day on the farm was modest and low-key. It felt like any other day except for the nice meal we had. There was no build up or anti-climax that comes with Christmas in mainstream society. The farmer made a traditional Portuguese dinner. Simple but delicious, it was boiled Salt Cod with cabbage, potatoes and eggs, all cooked in his own freshly pressed olive oil, black pepper and garlic. All the ingredients besides the Fish were from the farm. The farmer really valued the help we offered him. He repaid us with this beautiful Christmas day meal.

I brought a Christmas pudding from Ireland which I purchased in a supermarket. I shared it with the farmer and the other volunteers at the farm. I heated it up and we had it with some fresh goat's milk. It was nice to have the company of the other three volunteers.

The farmer had left the city life behind some years back to manage this old farm. It had belonged to his grandfather who had passed away. His friends and family couldn't understand why he chose this way of life. I also struggled to imagine if I would enjoy such an existence. I used the excuse of boredom to keep me in fear of this alternative way of living. By denying the beauty that could be found in a simpler existence, I remained trapped in city life, addicted to its relentless hustle and bustle which I also detested.

For the two weeks I was there, it was very cold during the night. We slept on old mattresses and woollen blankets. The days got warmer by around noon. Even though it was winter, the afternoon sun had a welcoming strength to it. There were no hot showers. I washed myself in the icy cold water of the crystal clear river that ran through the land.

The farmer lived in a separate house away from the volunteers. I guessed that he had more comforts there and surely running hot water to take a shower. He also had a girl to share his life with. The farmer had a Portuguese girlfriend who lived with him. She worked on the farm too. She had once come as a volunteer and decided to stay there with him. She too, left the city life behind. She had dark hair, dark eyes and sallow skin, a typical Portuguese brunette but taller than average. She was really beautiful. I watched her each day working on the farm. I racked my brain trying to comprehend why she would want such a life. As the days passed, she became the focus of more than just some of my thoughts.

Each time I saw her, she became even more beautiful. With her hands dirty from gardening or milking the goats, she became a deep desire inside of me. I tried to distract myself but nothing worked. Sometimes we talked when we made bread together or when we milked the goats in the morning. I remained aloof in my approach. Lots of volunteers had come and go so I was just another passer-by for all she cared. I felt wrong inside knowing she was the farmer's girl. I felt guilty about the desire I felt for her. I had no right to her. Then one day I picked a bunch of mushrooms on the hills and brought them to her asking if we could cook them. She was annoyed. She said that I shouldn't take anything from nature if I don't know how to use it. I didn't know which mushrooms were edible. She was right of course. But I was hoping that she would know everything. She was turning into a Goddess in my eyes. I threw the mushrooms away and I felt pathetic. I wanted her. I needed her.

My imagination took over. My daydreaming fantasies of her warm naked body against mine drove a deep fire of desire in the core of my being. I was losing control, a familiar feeling. I reminded myself that I had felt it before. The only comfort I got out of this knowledge was that I knew I could not control my mind and this desire. I let go of trying to control it. I knew that it was not only her whom I felt this way towards. There were others before her and there would be others after her.

She was the object of my desire but the desire was internal. It was not external. Despite the guilt, this was my desire. I owned it. I needed to accept it or it would eat me alive. I gave in to my fantasies and I allowed them to take me over. I remained polite and nice to her but I never expressed my desire. It was mine, not hers. I didn't want a potentially very awkward situation developing with the farmer who I liked and respected. He was a decent bloke. It wouldn't go down well if I made moves on his girlfriend.

One day I was helping her make bread. While we were kneading bread in the kitchen area, she took off and hung up her coat. She wore that same coat, day in and day out. I saw her up close. Those smooth brown arms and her beautiful neck were more real than in my fantasies. I could have stayed there kneading bread with her forever.

She thanked me for helping with the bread. She left the windowless stone building to bake the breads in the outdoor oven. I was now alone in the kitchen. My eyes fell upon her coat hanging up close to me. The pink inside cushioning of the coat was exposed, the same part that hugged her body every day. I can't recall ever feeling jealous of a coat. Impulse driven, taken over by desire, I walked up to it. Smothering my face in the warm pink inside cushioning, I inhaled her scent deeply and helplessly, fuelling my fire of desire to become one with her. The next day as I walked the mountain forests alone with the herd of goats, the thoughts of me and her together, naked, entangled and embracing, took my breath away. It drove the fire insane. It was too much.

No, I didn't fuck a goat! Jesus Christ!

But standing behind a tree, I milked and relieved myself by extinguishing that fire of desire temporarily, afraid of where it might take me. "Two more days, hold it together for fuck sake," I whispered to myself. My time would be up volunteering at the farm. I could get back to Lisbon and have a piss-up, maybe even visit a brothel again.

I left the farm and returned to Lisbon where I stayed in a backpacker's hostel. New Year's Eve came. I went out with other random hostel dwellers. I got very drunk. I tried to forget her. Soon I would but it took a while. I knew there would be more girls in the future that would arouse further immense desire in me but I couldn't feel that truth at that time. In the moment, there is only ever one. Logic and reality are not the same.

And so with that trip to Portugal, I had avoided Christmas. I would continue to do so. The next Christmas I would fly to Morocco. At least there in central Morocco, there would be less women and alcohol to distract me from the stillness and peace I was seeking. This turned out to be true to some extent except for the alcohol part.

IMINTANOUTE

This Christmas holiday break, I spent in a small village just outside Imintanoute, at the foot of the Atlas Mountains in Morocco. I stayed at a Cultural centre which provided guests with a unique experience of Berber culture. It was a large building made from clay, in the traditional manner. There were individual bedrooms which were simple, comfortable and silent. There was a large courtyard in the centre of the building. Guests from many different countries came to stay. It was a very peaceful and relaxing stay for me. Christmas day came. It could have been any other day. It was nothing special. I welcomed its ordinariness. It was exactly what I was looking for.

I spent a large amount of time sitting in silence in the garden courtyard. Sometimes at night I would sit outside. I would let my mind wonder, dissolve, vanish and come back again, as I sat beside a clear sky full of stars.

There was no signal on my cell phone and no Wi-Fi. There were little distractions. I only used my phone as a camera and as an alarm clock in the morning. Initially, during the first three days, I was anxious. My mind would bother me saying, "This is boring, there is nothing to do here." I had to weather this anxiety. I knew that peace would come. Gradually the restlessness faded and I spent three weeks there, living a simple existence. When my mind was quietened, peace then revealed itself. It had always been there, just hidden in the background. Most visitors only stayed on average two or three days at this Cultural Centre. I needed three days to get over the withdrawals of a busy mind. Sometimes other travellers might ask me how I could stay for so long in the same place and not see more of Morocco. I heard myself saying in reply that I wanted nothing more than to be at peace. I had no need or desire to see every corner of Morocco. The landscape of tranquillity which I was after was an inner one. At that time, it was true.

It was a culture shock, returning to Dublin, to a busy city life full of distractions. But I had something to remind me of my time there. It was a small piece of cow hide. I attached it with a piece of string to my rucksack when it was time to leave Morocco. There was a story behind it.

On that trip, I was once again reminded of my inner urge to travel. I began to understand what it was that I was looking for, each time I did travel. It wasn't so much about getting away as I once thought. Travelling for me was a means of accessing the unknown. The people I meet, the places and the experiences I come across are all unknown prior to my departure.

The more new experiences I acquired, the more I felt that I had truly recovered from a mental illness. It helped me acknowledge the unknown part of my inner world. For me, travel was an essential part of my recovery from schizophrenia. It also helped me realise that there was a lot more to schizophrenia that just mental illness.

Besides that, I was beginning to understand that the real Journey is the inner one. I had travelled a lot. Once I was in a new country and submersed in a new culture, I no longer felt the urge to see everything or keep moving around trying to visually soak up the sights. I was content with seeing little of it. Being immersed in a new culture was enough. I could travel to every corner of the earth and every country but what was the value of that if I can't go inside and to the core of myself, which is the universe anyway?

Every time I returned home from a trip abroad, I grew closer to believing that I no longer had an illness called schizophrenia.

Without denying the period of my life that I had struggled through, involving many hospitalisations, I could let it go and accept it as part of my life. It was similar to other periods of my Life such as the five years in the Legion and my anxious childhood. Those three periods were a crescendo of suffering. But the period of so called mental illness was also unique because it was not materialistic. It was spiritual and emotional in nature. It would turn out to be a crucially important period of my life. It was the breaking down of my delusional everyday existence. It was my calling. I had a chance to answer that call or ignore it. Ignoring it would surely mean further illness. Answering it would allow integration; integration of the illusion with the truth, the material with the spiritual. Answering it would allow wholeness. Answering it would allow this book to write itself. Answering it wasn't an option. I was being called home. And I was the one doing the calling, the real I.

As I began to understand the extent to which the unknown and the uncertain make up my life, it became ok to fear death but not ok to fear the unknown. The unknown was to be respected and embraced. As a soldier, I had been conditioned not to fear death. Not fearing death goes against nature. I had also accepted that it was ok to kill others with my weapon. I was prepared to do so, but I never did.

For a soldier, there is little room for the unknown. For a soldier, the heart is aching for love but it is covered with armour. Love becomes the enemy, the unconquerable enemy. Some ex-soldiers take their own lives because this becomes too much to bear; this denial of Love.

During my time in that Moroccan village, around the winter solstice, I was invited to go with the Berber guide into the mountains to a remote village. Every year, many people gathered in that village to celebrate and pay their respects to a Holy woman, a sort of Saint or Shaman in their Berber culture.

She had long passed away. There was a shrine in the village, devoted to her. Every year, there was a celebration of her life.

As we drove into the village full with people, I saw the cow they had been talking about. Its eyes met mine as I looked out the open window of our truck. I saw the reflection of my own fear in its eyes. I liked the feeling of compassion that I noticed inside of me. But there was also a feeling of gratitude that its life would be given up for us. It was a healthy looking white cow being led up into the village. Soon it would be sacrificed in memory of the holy woman. The following day, hundreds of people who came from far and wide would eat of the cow in a huge communal meal.

The guide introduced me to his friends as we waited for the slaughter to happen. We were early so we decided to have lunch. We found a place in the shade of trees down by the crystal clear and fast flowing mountain stream. There was a fresh breeze blowing down the valley from the mountains. We gathered fire wood and made a fire.

Two of the lads carried all the necessary ingredients for our lunch. Carefully, a metal Tagine pot was taken out from a backpack along with all the ingredients to make a Tagine. Chicken, potatoes, carrots, peas, squash, peppers, spices, salt and olive oil were all carefully prepared and layered into the pot with hands that had done so countless times before. It simmered for close to an hour as we stood around chatting. When it was ready, the six of us sat on stumps of wood in a circle around the Tagine. Fresh Bread was shared out around the circle. We all got stuck in. By this time, I was used to tearing off little bits of bread and using it to dip and pluck into the mass of food. It had become a daily ritual. A knife and fork even felt foreign to me.

As we soaked up every last drop of juice with our bread, there was noise and commotion coming from the village centre. "Let's go quick," the guide gasped. Two of us followed him running up the hill to where a large crowd had gathered. The others stayed there by the river, perhaps not wanting to witness the bloody scene that was about to unfold.

We arrived at the gathering. My heart was beating rapidly and I was choking with exhaustion and gagging for air, having sprinted two hundred metres up the hill from the river.

By only a few seconds, we had missed the two way swift movement of a huge knife which opened the cow's neck. We pushed through the crowd. We stood directly above the cow. The sandy earth was soaked in splashes of dark blood. The blood on the cows white hide appeared redder. Something looked out of place. My brain took a few moments to understand the sight before me. The cow was lying on its side with its feet kicking out desperately. Its head was almost completely detached from its body and only held on by the back of its neck. The head which looked alien to the body had wide open eyes. The cow's centre of consciousness seemed absent from the head. The cows open neck became the new source of movement and noise. The open neck was twitching and the wind pipe gurgled and sucked air. It was as if this open part of the cow was its new head. It was still very much alive but I couldn't decide where the centre of life was. It was obvious that consciousness was not in its head. Suddenly, I felt at one with the cow in a strange but beautiful way. But that psychotic like feeling was nothing to do with schizophrenia. It wasn't based in fear. It was based in respect, dignity and integrity. It was a moment of Oneness; pure Love.

It took a long time for life to leave the cow. I was surprised with myself standing there, filming the butcher with my smartphone. I felt slightly guilty. But my smartphone was only one among many as all the Moroccans stood there, doing the same. In fact, I had copied them. Even though I behaved like the rest of the crowd, I stood out as the only white man among the hundreds of local people gathered there.

The butcher got to work immediately, once the cow's life left its body. Smartphones disappeared as a new frenzy based on an ancient tradition broke out. Small sections of the white cowhide were handed out among the crowd. I was lucky to get a piece. The guide told me later that it was for good luck. I stuffed it down into my pocket. As I done so, I felt the warmth of its fleshy underside in my hand and then against my thigh. The heat from the fleshy piece of cowhide slowly dissolved into my leg. I felt part of something greater than myself. It was the same hide that was part of a cow who basked carelessly in the warm morning sun that same day.

EMMABODA

Two years into my Degree course and it was time for another trip abroad. I spend the summer holidays in Sweden, volunteering at two different locations. At the first place, I was staying for two weeks with an older Swedish couple and helping as a volunteer. I had my own little wood cabin in their garden. In exchange for a few hours of work each day, I got my accommodation and meals. I mainly helped with gardening, walking their dog, and their summer café business. I had the weekend free. I spent it visiting some nearby town.

The middle aged woman of the house happened to be Irish. I noticed that every evening she would consume a whole bottle of white wine. I guessed that she might have a dependence on alcohol. But who was I to judge because I used to attend Alcoholics Anonymous? She seemed very moody. I avoided her where possible. She mentioned how she missed Ireland and wanted to move back there. I'm not sure how the husband, who was Swedish, felt about that. I could understand her feeling of missing Ireland but I also felt that it was not really about that. It was her own inner struggle and malaise, projected out on to her environment. On return to Ireland, her inner discomfort would probably still be present.

I kept my distance. I felt her negativity sucking me in. I didn't want to get involved. I got the sense that she was the one wearing the boots in the house. I looked forward to finishing the two weeks there. I needed to get my own space again and away from her negative energy.

In another way, I felt sorry for her. But I couldn't do anything.

I didn't feel that I could give her advice or that it would be accepted if I tried. I wanted to help her but I had no idea of how to do that, so I just avoided her. Her bitterness and coldness were also reflections of my own shadow self. It reminded me of the pain than comes with shutting out love. With that, comes fear and mistrust. How many millions of people around the world must feel this way?

All I could do was to be nice and respectful to her and try not to get sucked into her negativity. That's not easy for a highly sensitive person. I could actually feel the vibrations of sadness and fear being emitted from her invisibly. It wasn't in my head. But I was getting stronger and more emotionally intelligent. I could sometimes welcome the uncomfortable presence of someone else, as a challenge. For this, I needed to be alert, fully in the present and self-aware. It could be an opportunity for my own growth being around people's dark spiritual energy. But it was an option too. I didn't have to put up with it either. I didn't need to save anyone. I wasn't Jesus bloody Christ. Self-preservation rather than self-sacrifice is the best way.

Sometimes the real challenge was to stop challenging myself. Self-love is the highest form of love. And that's got nothing to do with selfishness. Self-love is respect for oneself and respect for others. Selfishness is false gain from intentionally denying others. In Selfishness, we need to use others so we can deny them. Avoiding people is different than denying people. If we are going to interact with others, either we do so with respect or we don't initiate any contact at all.

When I finished work each afternoon, I would borrow one of their bicycles and cycle around the nearby forests and lakes. One day I arrived at a nice secluded lake. It was one of my days off.

I leaned my bicycle up against a tree and went to find a place to sit near the lakes edge. I sat on the grass looking out towards the middle of the lake. I noticed a rock that stuck up out of the water. Triangular in shape, it must have been about three hundred metres from the shore. Its sides were gently sloped. I imagined that climbing out of the water onto it would be easy. A gentle wind blew from behind me. The surface water rippled across the lake as if the water and wind were one. It was a sunny warm Saturday afternoon. I was surprised that I was the only person around. I had brought my swimming togs for a swim. I had only intended to have a small dip at the shore.

Mentally, I began challenging myself to swim out to that rock in the middle of the lake. The peace and serenity was broken by my demanding mind. Having escaped that annoying Irish woman where I was staying, I now became annoyed with myself. I just wanted to chill out and relax. But my head kept insisting on it. Maybe I was just the same as her and that's why she annoyed me. My mind kept poking at me. Eventually, I made a deal with myself:

In return for swimming out to that rock, I would never again have to give in to my mind.

This deal would make me master over my mind instead of a slave to it. If I done this one last challenge, no more would I have to force myself to do something which I do not want to do. It seemed like a silly little dialogue that I created to kill any boredom of being alone. But that deal was deadly serious. It was a pact, a deal between the two MEs in my head. More importantly, it was also the start of learning and practising self-compassion. I stood up, knowing that this had to be settled once and for all. I would have shaken the other ME's hand, if he was standing there next to me. The deal was done. I clapped my hands twice. I was anxious as I stripped and got into my swimming togs.

I never considered myself a great swimmer but I was confident enough that I wouldn't get into trouble out on the lake. I walked slowly into the cold water. I was feeling determined as my heart rate accelerated. It wasn't terribly cold but my body was hot from the sun. This made the water feel colder. I swam smoothly and slowly out towards the rock. It seemed to get bigger and bigger as I approached it.

I arrived at that curiously shaped rock. I touched its dry summit which stuck out of the lake. It was about the size of a white cow. Then I looked down into the blackness of the lake. I saw the giant rock expand and disappear downwards into the water. My feet touched its sloping and slimy surface, below the water's edge. I imagined it and its entire shape like a pyramid, resting on the bottom of the lake far below. Only the little summit of the pyramid was exposed in the golden sunshine above the surface of the water. It was like an iceberg that would never melt.

I pulled myself up onto the dry surface. I lay back on one of its sloping three sides. The Midday sun beat down almost vertically from above. There was a feeling of great relief and satisfaction as my body sucked up the rocks heat. I took a moment to enjoy that feeling. I looked up at the clear blue summer sky stretching in all directions. I savoured that moment for a little while.

I sat up and shivered. A cool breeze blew past me gently. Looking all around and towards the banks of the lake in the distance, I felt very much alone but in a good way. I felt connected, I felt alive. I sat there for some time knowing that this was something special, knowing that it was a worthwhile deal I had just made with myself. It was a deal to be at peace with myself. It was an unconditional acceptance.

My gaze fell down upon a tattoo I had on my leg. It once meant something to me. The tattoo was composed of a small triangle inscribed within a circle; the symbol used by Alcoholics Anonymous. I had gotten it done some years back in Bulgaria. I had held the firm belief then that I was an Alcoholic.

Afterwards, when I saw that same symbol in the church in Kosharitsa, I once again felt that I was God. I wasn't ready for that revelation. My mind created a psychosis to deal with it. I didn't know that God was beyond the human mind.

It had now been two years since I was allowing myself to drink again. I was able to moderate my drinking, something I once thought impossible. I was careful about holding any black and white beliefs anymore. The tattoo had now lost its initial meaning of being in a fellowship of incurable alcoholics.

In a flash, its meaning had been reborn. Sitting there in the middle of the lake, the tattoo now made perfect sense. The circle symbolised the lake and the triangle was the pyramid shaped rock which I was sitting upon. I took a moment to mentally sign off on the pact. The deal was done. The stamp of approval was in permanent ink on my leg. I swam back towards land and towards an unknown future, but a future I felt positive about.

The next day was the Summer Solstice. We celebrated the traditional Midsommer party in Sweden with vodka and herrings. I secretly celebrated the deal I made with myself. That Irish lady seemed more bearable after a few drinks. I left their home soon after.

The rest of my holiday in Sweden was great. I stayed in a few different hostels and I done another volunteer stay with other Swedish people. It involved two weeks helping to brew and bottle homemade beer. There were another two volunteers from Japan with me. It was a great time there. We were fed really well and looked after by the hosts. The Brewer even told us to help ourselves to a few beers every evening. On my days off, I got to hike a small section of the St. Olav's way or the King's Road.

Sweden is a beautiful country. I found inner peace there.

BRUGES

I finished my degree. I began working in my new career as a Social Care worker. There were so many people struggling and suffering in their lives for all kinds of different reasons. They had lost hope and lost power. Each person has a different story. But I just wondered what if they really knew that they were the Godhead and that they were the ultimate power unto themselves. Would it change anything? I wasn't sure. I kept my mouth shut and just tried to be as nice as I could while doing my job.

What was I supposed to say? Hey buddy, do you know that you are actually God. It doesn't come out so easy. That realisation must come from the inside out. I can't tell anyone that they are God. It would be like telling a dog that it's a K9. Well not really. I admit it, I don't have a comparison. And really, it wasn't that I just wanted people to realise that they were God. What is necessary before that realisation is coming to accept that the identity we cling to is actually a hoax. That knowing must come first. That is the only way that we can know that we are God without inflation of the ego. God doesn't have an ego.

During the next summer I took three weeks holidays. I travelled to Belgium. While spending time alone, I learned to distinguish between what I called good self-discipline and not conforming to societal norms for the sake of it. What do I mean by good self-discipline? It involves adopting healthy daily routines for the respect of oneself. It was as simple as taking a shower once a day, sticking to three meals each day and getting some form of exercise in. Seems obvious, but it's not always so. I reminded myself to be present in life and enjoy the simple things.

I slowly became aware of the extent to which I denied and fought against the natural flow of life. If I remained very present with a still mind and an accepting attitude, the Kingdom of heaven which psychosis can dramatically reveal, could be experienced in everyday life through gentle glimpses. The mind had to be quietened for this to occur. My will had to be replaced with divine will, even in the smallest of everyday tasks. In doing so, indecision melts away. Trust and confidence replaces it. Trust in life is trust in our true self.

I took time to reflect on another important aspect of life which I gave much attention to; the idea of comfort. My internal discomfort was not dependent on a physically comfortable living situation. I could feel anxious and uneasy but still be surrounded by great comforts. The opposite was also true. Denying anxiety went hand in hand with shying away from taking risks. I had to get back out into the world and meet it head on. And I was doing just this. But, in order to maintain a healthy self-confidence, I had to tune into my feelings and emotions too. In other words, I didn't have to put up with shit if I didn't need to. There was no point letting my spiritual buzz lead me into the delusional state of becoming a pushover at the hands of others. I could still be loving and assertive at the same time.

There was a lot of sadness that had been blocked in my life. The soldier in me didn't allow me to feel it. There was still fear holding me back. For that reason, it was difficult for me to feel happy and allow myself to have fun. I learned that both my sadness and happiness were connected. It sounds simple of course but the illusion that they were separate was part of the problem. That had become part of my living reality on which my actions were founded. Unlocking my feelings involved being true to myself. It meant being true to my present experience and being true to my heart.

Is there some fear in living too comfortable? I would ask myself this question. I answered yes. I felt that this involved limiting my potential. This meant living a life devoid of meaning and feeling dead inside most of the time. A diagnosis of schizophrenia was the root of this fear but the human condition of denying our true self was the seed of schizophrenia. In fact my question about comfort was irrelevant. I needed both comfort and discomfort, internal and external forms of both. Comfort itself was relative. But again, it was just another endless cycle of mind made duality; a necessary blindfold.

I realised that I longed for and needed good healthy mature relationships as well as intimacy. I needed relationships based on respect. I needed people in my life that were reliable. I took some time to reflect and look at my circle of friends. Surprisingly, I learnt that I was often unable to say whether I was comfortable or not in their presence. I had learned to tolerate people I did not like or even detested, for most of my life. Most of the time, I believed I didn't have a choice. The delusion of being some perfect holy Jesus Christ, sweet and tender, tolerating every person everywhere, did nothing to help.

Now with the possibility of choice, there was an irrational fear of welcoming good people into my life. This fear had to be watered down and swallowed like a bad tasting medicine. I deserved good people in my life. We all do.

After all was said and done, being kind to oneself involves expecting a standard of physical comfort. I thought back about my time in rough living conditions in Portugal. It was acceptable for a short period of time to have that experience. I had developed a very strong sexual attraction under such uncomfortable conditions. I tried to rationalise some sort of connection between increased sexual desire and being uncomfortable. It reminded me of times when my living conditions were extremely uncomfortable in the Legion, and my sexual needs seemed to increase as a result. Maybe there was a link. It made sense as a way of distraction from my uncomfortable living situation. It made sense from a biologically rooted survival mechanism perspective. But it was hard to accept. It felt animalistic in nature and uncivilised. It was important that I did not deny this part of myself even though I felt uncomfortable with it. What I ended up concluding was that apart from depending on external levels of comfort, the strong sexual attractions were in their own right, uncomfortable. This was the essence of it.

I had lived with a sense of guilt and shame because of that. I needed to break this negative mind set. I needed to allow myself this liberation. I needed to unlearn this maladaptive response. I felt that it was probably linked to my childhood. Sex and love were always taboo in my childhood. I never felt comfortable with the idea of having a girlfriend or even being attracted to someone, girl or boy. Somewhere along the line there was a negative association built up. This had to be taken down. The first step was this realisation. The second was putting it into practice. I learned about these aspects of myself in Belgium.

I began this trip as a volunteer on a small Organic Farm. I had completed many various volunteering placements by this point in my life. This time, the owners, a middle aged couple, reminded me of my parent's authority. Immediately on meeting them, I got a bad vibe. I soon felt my lack of interest in them as people. The fact that the volunteers were being fed tasteless left over scraps from their B & B accommodation didn't help the situation. I saw immediately that I wouldn't fit in there. And there was no point fooling myself otherwise. I was no longer conditioned or obliged to tolerate or put up with bullshit and bad treatment. If I was to remain respectful to myself, I had to leave.

A remark which the owner had said sent my head into a flurry of thoughts. It caught me off guard. Four days later, I still felt anger towards his comment. Maybe it was because there was some truth to it. But more likely it was the fact that he had no idea about the private hell of Legion Life and the struggles I had been through since then. I was never going to share it with him. I had mentioned briefly before I came that I was in the army when I was younger.

"Have you gone soft after the army?" he sniggered on the first day that I arrived. I had taken a nap for an hour that evening before dinner. He pulled the right trigger too because my head went into overdrive. Past memories were dug up of volunteering at similar places that I didn't like. I used to put up with a lot of shit even in civilian life because I felt that getting through the Legion meant that I can tolerate anything. I could put up with shit but so what? I didn't need to. I had made a deal with myself too, that pact in the middle of a Swedish lake. That deal was one of self-respect and it was unbreakable.

My anger raised a shield of protection because of his comment. That first evening there at the volunteering place, my mind was made up. I'm outa here. I allowed my mind to go wild in its flurry of thoughts. I drank a cold beer that evening and planned to leave the next morning. I gave my head free reign to go off on a silent frustrated rant, digging up past insecurities. I watched my innocent and vulnerable mind:

"Maybe I was always a big softie, Maybe I was just a big sissy deep down, So be it, I'm not staying another day in this shithole of theirs, I had a siesta on the first day after work cause there's fuck all else to do, I was tired, so what, I've been through a lot in the last four years, recovering from schizophrenia is tiring work. Old dirty sponges at the sink, I hate this filth, a new pack of sponges would cost nothing to buy, These people are more hippie idiots than real farmers, blown in from a rich

German background, not even real Belgians, Living in their own shitty jungle seems stupid, thinking they are tough, thinking they can give us volunteers a tough taste of life, plants and animals can have some order without neglecting beauty, their place is a big dirty mess, I don't buy their philosophy, Their idea of hard physical work and very little salt intake, how stupid. Memories of bedbugs before in Portugal, probably same shit here, those filthy yellow pillows have never been washed, a very damp and dirty bedroom, loads of mosquitoes, No thanks. A previous experiences of uncomfortable living standards in Australia, I put them all under the same category; Eco fanatical hypocrites I named them, All living in their own shit, It could be actually done well if they had some cop on, More memories, In Australia, another weird German lady, she was a right bitch, a bully and a skin doctor, weird combination, showing off her homemade yogurt, tasted crap, and I like good yogurt, divorced and now with a Maori gardener chap, he was a rude asshole too, don't like them, why did I pretend too, Shit food, moving patio rocks, senseless jobs, no composure, stupid work. What about that other rich hippie, Austrian this time and German speaking, a religious nut, Lots of money but living in the shit, fridge freezer full of old pieces of meat, disorganized chaos, rotten food. Back to the Portugal experience, they think it's cool to isolate and its brave to begin resenting the world which they are not separate from, don't kill the beg bugs, that's murder, the final straw, don't kill the mushrooms, immature people, but sexy she was, No more of this crap if I don't need to, I've nothing to prove anymore, I done my five in the Legion, Eat that bitches. I'm outa here, God, I need a good shag!"

The sleeping conditions with those WOOFING hosts in Belgium were dirty. There was no need and no way that I was going to expose myself to undesirable conditions. I left the next morning, leaving the hosts very displeased. I left without saying goodbye. I was asserting myself. Another volunteer dropped me to the bus stop in the village. She was a young French volunteer. I felt sorry for her as she seemed trapped there. She didn't seem to mind. She was blind to the filth and bad conditions which reflects disrespect on behalf of the hosts. But maybe my action to leave was enough to make her think.

What did I get from that experience? A solid reinforcement about the balance between my actions and the universe unfolding, between trusting in my decisions as part of the flow of life and the way things go anyway, believing in my path and being confident to take action. As a result of leaving that shithole, a spontaneous holiday and unplanned three weeks in Bruges unfolded. I had delicious sex with a gorgeous local girl. Divine will can be great if we tune ourselves into it. Thank you God!

I walked through the medieval streets of Bruges after booking into a nice hostel. I imagined about how life must of been centuries ago. I was still pondering the theme of comfort but this time it was 'comfort throughout the ages.' Life was harder, surely. But there was still comfort and cleanliness all those centuries ago. There always has been. We have been sold a lie that comfort and hygiene comes with wealth and more civilised societies. That's simply not true.

We have a choice. Some people are just dirty and have been throughout the ages. You can still live a tough physical life without living in shit conditions. I saw this in the Legion. Some of the lads were just dirty fuckers and some were not. I saw that in the most poor of countries, local people can be very clean and organised. They are forced to be that way. My anger was fading. It was time to just enjoy myself for the remainder of the holiday.

This mental analysing of the world and the frustration it brought with it vanished completely when I met Marina.

Or maybe it just went into the background. Or maybe it just transformed into sexual energy. Energy was energy after all, whatever form it took and life was just life.

I fell deeply in love with this Belgian girl who had Croatian roots. Despite the uncomfortable feeling of a previous breakup with Charlene, I allowed myself to fall in love again. Marina was stunning, clever and kind. I was blind in love. I couldn't see any faults in her. The comfort of being with her turned into an almost unbearable feeling of being uncomfortable when it didn't work out. This was after I made her into my drug and my ecstasy. The passion was too quick, too fast but never too good.

What did I learn? That sexual attraction is probably the closest thing I can use to describe absolute truth because it's beyond control. It is beyond logic or rationality, beyond the mind. And I learnt that I was still a sucker for love. There was no point rationalising it. There was no point running away from it either. I was willing to feel the pain in order to indulge in the immense pleasure. The golden lesson this encounter with Marina taught me was an age old one "Beauty is in the eye of the beholder." Enjoy it while it lasts. Accept it. Own it. Move on.

Some logical reasoning led me to understand, that whether I had a sexual relationship or not, with the woman of my dreams, in this case Marina, the feeling of desire wouldn't change. I desire even more what I can't have. If I forbid myself from having God, I then desire God with all my being. The closer I get to understanding sexual desire, the closer I get to understanding God. This was the unlocking of my guilty and uncomfortable feeling towards sexual attraction, regardless of whether my focus was a woman or a man; Ariana Grande or Justin Bieber!

And so I realised that I will never fully understand God because God's true nature in human form is beautiful insanity.

Is that disappointing? Yes it is. The mind sits frustrated with folded arms, a stubborn child within its own prison. The mind is unable to understand a puzzle that itself created. It is possible, on the other hand, to feel God and to experience God. How? Go find out for yourself! I don't know how! Only God knows!

THE PHOENIX PARK

The Phoenix Park is a huge park in Dublin city. It is said to be the largest city park in Europe. There is a monument with a phoenix, a mythological bird, in the centre of the park. However, the name of the park comes from the Irish words Fiann Uisce meaning Clear Water. Said in English, it sounds like "Feenishk." I became familiar with the Phoenix Park. I spent many hours running, walking and wandering through its many trails and tracks. It was great to be living on its doorstep. It became my back garden.

I focused on my new life. I didn't look back. I looked towards the blank canvas of the future. The endless possibilities kept me feeling alive. I had completed my Honours Degree in Social Care with relative ease. I had travelled every summer and Christmas holidays. I had dated some girls with increased awareness around my vulnerability to become lost in them. I took risks. I allowed myself to get hurt once or twice. But that was ok. And maybe I even hurt others by rejecting them. It was no longer an issue to fall in love. I even welcomed it. Bring it on!

I had most of all proven to myself that I had truly recovered from schizophrenia. Being my own free agent, I felt it was no longer necessary to convince others. But I also recognised that I did have a strong message of recovery that could help others through the fog of mental insecurity. This was part of my motivation to write about my experiences. But there was something more, something really important that began to shine through my new recovered self, something very clear.

I began to understand that there was more to schizophrenia than I thought. My message of recovery would be incomplete if I just said that people can recover from a mental illness and stopped there. There was more.

From a professional perspective as a qualified Social Care worker, I was unsure and concerned about how potential employers would view my history of mental health issues. Would it be seen as a strength which I could use in my profession or would it be seen as a liability? I wasn't sure. But really, I didn't want either of those. Slowly, something more was being revealed to me and it was nothing to do about "Recovery from a Mental illness." More important was the nature of the experience itself and what can be learnt from it. I began asking myself what lessons I could bring back from psychosis, from the Otherworld. This was the new direction I felt myself going. And it wasn't towards madness, it was towards truth.

Unfortunately, a few scenarios unfolded that confirmed for me that there was still a large amount of fear and misunderstanding in Irish society towards Mental Health. And it wasn't just in Irish society. It was a worldwide rational and mechanical view that was dominating the field of 'Mental Health Services.' The spiritual nature of schizophrenia and other disorders was being completely ignored. They could have done with a major rebranding and upgrading of 'Mental Health Services' to 'Spiritual Health Services.' But there would be a problem with that. It would automatically disqualify probably ninety percent of all the clinicians working in the services. As medical practitioners, they would need to look elsewhere for employment.

We had centuries of disconnect and ignorance behind us in Ireland. It was a tremendous weight that was a collective blackness in the Irish psyche. Irish people were now torn between a disappointing Catholic dominance and an increasing secular, rational and modern world. Of course there was an in between. Some modern Irish soul singers were coming to the fore. They could sense it. The Soul of Eire was crying out for what she had lost. The eternal light was still shining just about, through a modern revival and renewed interest in our roots, our connection to nature. Halloween was gaining momentum and there were smaller festivals during the times of solstice and equinox. The Macnas performance company from Galway was keeping some ancient wisdom alive through the Arts. All these traditions and much more were previously demonised by Religion.

A former employer of mine in Dublin had breached confidentiality. They disclosed my past medical diagnosis of schizophrenia to a future employer without my consent. When it surfaced during my new employment that I had a history of schizophrenia, I was constantly put under pressure by management to prove how I was managing my illness. The fact that I believed and felt that my former issues were no longer relevant or posed any risk wasn't good enough for them. I even told them that I had five years of complete recovery behind me but that still wasn't enough for them. The S word created much fear and scepticism.

Once again, I found myself being manipulated and treated unfairly. They wanted something on paper to say that I was "Sane." But that was impossible to get in an insane world. But I still tried.

Saying I had recovered from schizophrenia felt like I was lying to myself. Because it wasn't just that I had recovered. That was missing the point. I had finally come to terms with what psychosis really is.

In my heart I wanted to explain it to them but I knew anything I said would be interpreted as madness. They weren't ready. They wouldn't get it.

For example, I could say that I had been to Tír na nÓg. While there, I learnt about our divine nature and eternal youth. I could also have said that I met with my ancestors and got guidance from them. I would surely be let go from my job on the spot. I may even be reported to the Mental Health Services as having signs of a relapse. They just didn't get it. If I tried to explain myself, I might not even be able to register in my profession as a Social Care worker. The rationalists would think I was a liability and unfit to work in my field. There would be a huge number behind them to support that too.

Homelessness, mental illness and crime were growing steadily in Ireland. A new Spiritual and National rebirth was needed. But we were still traumatized from centuries of betrayal. The nation was in a state of PTSD. Ireland was having an identity crisis. And I wasn't separate from this. It was in my blood.

I even went along within the rational world view, in an attempt to become credibly sane. After all, I still had to survive in this world. So I made an attempt to free myself from stigma by starting a clean sheet. To achieve this, I attempted to get assistance from psychiatrists both from the public and private health services. These were the 'Authorities' who could approve my 'Authority to speak.'

My own General practitioner (GP doctor) refused to certify that I was well. He said that it was "not his area of expertise." I then approached the top private mental health service providers in Ireland. I discovered that when I tried to get written confirmation from them, declaring that I had recovered and was mentally well, nobody was willing to put this on paper. They refused to engage with me. I only got a verbal response from them when they said basically, "We only deal with sick people."

For my future professional career, I was hoping that someone would certify that I was of sound mental health. But I discovered an insidious fact that lies at the core of the whole problem with the mental health services. The obstacle I kept hitting was that mental health clinicians do not certify mental fitness. They only acknowledge mental illness. This was the crux of it.

In other terms, they can't or won't undo a diagnosis which has gone before. But they can always give us an extra one. They only add more labels on to the clear surface of our being. Our health, vitality and hope, is covered up in labels. The saddest thing is when we even start to play out these roles.

Nobody I met had the courage to support me, and my claim of being of sound mind. I kept hitting the same wall. The attitude I kept facing in Ireland was that I have been, and I will always be, more vulnerable than the general public with regards to mental health. I was just a statistic. I was just a number. I had schizophrenia but I no longer had it. In their manuals and textbooks, it is a chronic, incurable condition, medical in nature. It may respond to treatment but only treatment that includes medication. All of that was a complete contradiction. My case proved their manuals wrong. But my view didn't exist in their world nor did the idea of a spiritual struggle towards a higher consciousness.

When I asked them how come I had recovered from schizophrenia and I no longer had it, I was met with all sorts of inconsistent answers and attempts to avoid that question. I was wasting my time. The other option was keeping my mouth shut about it, letting it be water under the bridge. But my full recovery was the motivating factor for a career in Social Care so this would be counterproductive. It would never sit easy with me.

If I did choose not to conceal it, I would be viewed as mentally unsound and vulnerable. It would affect my life in a range of ways; refusal of visas and foreign residency, employment barriers, relationship difficulties, dehumanizing of my integrity, less credibility, deficit of character, the list goes on.

I felt stuck. On one hand, I wanted to get on with my life after schizophrenia. On the other hand, I knew in my heart that I could not run away from the spiritual calling in my life. I knew that spirituality and schizophrenia were part of the same thing. My mind did not like this. But somehow I knew it was true. I also knew that it wasn't a choice.

I strongly believed that people who have recovered from schizophrenia like me were not mentally ill to begin with. The false self and the ego was the mental illness, not the person. We were simply shedding our old skin. We, those who have struggled through psychosis, can actually be very advanced in our consciousness. But it depends on each one of us, how we compare ourselves to others and how much fear is still left inside of us.

I have had a complete inflation and collapse of the ego. I broke down mentally and spiritually. In some sense of the word, I actually died. After that, I accepted the ego once again, and I embraced a healthier self. I have really understood what it means to take responsibility for my life. I dare to say that I am likely more mentally stable than the average person who claims no history of mental health issues. It's not about competition. It's about fact. But in a world of statistics and probabilities, it has proved impossible therefore to get support of this claim. So the obvious solution for me was to deny any history of mental health issues. That is sad.

This decision didn't sit well with me. I would disappear from statistics and my recovery would be in vain. And I was passionate about working in the area of peer support work or at least getting my message out there to others. I felt that I could guide others through their psychosis, to be the peer I never had. I was an expert by experience. I had an Honours degree in education but a PHD in experience.

At this point in my story, I need to make a very important point. I could have denied ever having schizophrenia if even for my own peace of mind. But there was something larger at play here, much larger.

The fact was that I did have and meet all the criteria for a correct diagnosis of schizophrenia over a two year period. I am not saying the psychiatrists got it wrong. In fact, they had done a great job. They made a correct and accurate diagnosis. During one hospital admission, the head psychiatrist once commented, "Kevin is showing all the classic signs of schizophrenia, he is a textbook case. No doubt about it."

As I recovered and withdrew from the services, I knew that there would be an attempt by psychiatrists to explain those two years of madness and numerous involuntary admissions as something else. In order for them to maintain the credibility of their "Illness of Schizophrenia," what I had been through would now be explained as a transient psychotic disorder, a period of mania due to bipolar disorder or schizoaffective disorder. This was the message I got, having years of recovery behind me, when I approached the mental health services for assistance to certify my mental fitness. Can you see my point here? My case questions the very validity of the "Illness of Schizophrenia."

As a result of recovering completely, my lived experience goes against that firmly held and protected belief; that schizophrenia is a long term illness without a cure. It was important that I held onto this diagnosis in order to dismantle it.

My argument and the point I am trying to make is that schizophrenia can be an illness within a specific timeframe and therefore it can be limited to that period. But there is more. It is also only an illness within a specific culture and society. That is the social nature of it. It is a mental illness, in a mentally ill society.

It was in the interests of Psychiatry to say that I never had schizophrenia. Why? Because my recovery without medication was damaging to their faulty and failing model of treatment. I was discrediting the medical illness model of Psychosis. In its place, I was offering Grace, Cosmic mind initiation, or spiritual mastery. The naming of my alternative was really not that important. In fact, it was better not to name it at all.

Because they couldn't accept my complete recovery from Schizophrenia outside of their model of "treatment," they began using other labels such as Transient psychotic disorder, Schizoaffective disorder or Bipolar disorder to try and persuade me to agree with them and comply. They tried hard to stick those labels on. I will admit that it was a clever attempt on their behalf. They were very persuasive but only because they really believed their "work."

The old me would have bought it and accepted a downgraded label, thinking I had got off lucky. And even thanked them for loosening the chains. With a new, less stigmatic label, I could now get my life back on track and stuck into the rat racing materialistic samsara once again. Sorry guys, not for me, but maybe try the next poor soul!

The old me had died. A new me was born. I've seen through this Maya of our world. I will never forget what's on the other side because the other side came back with me. We are now getting to know each other and becoming best friends. We know that we are one but we like the play of being two. Sometimes we become one. Love split us apart. Love brought us together again.

My story acts as evidence that schizophrenia is not always long term. But more importantly, it shows that it is not always an illness. It is a work or a challenge that one goes through. It is a spiritual quest. There is much to be learned from it. Not everyone gets this opportunity. Some may find spiritual gold. Some may find nothing. Some may find more puzzles. That's up to the individual. Or maybe it's not. I really don't know.

Psychosis can be a truly terrifying and bad experience. That is only the consequence of fear belonging to the individual and to the society than formed them. Psychosis is an opportunity to work through these supressed fears and traumas that manifest in the living world of nightmares. Denying this experience and seeing it as nothing more than rubbish, produces a very different outcome. Many will do this. That is their choice. It is a dangerous choice. It is a risky choice.

Some will deny it so much that their fear takes over and drives them to commit terrible crimes, unspeakable evil. But these crimes are not committed as a result of mental illness or as a result of psychosis. They are committed by fear. They are committed by a responsible and socially conditioned self.

The responsibility always remains with the false self who is responsible for the denial of grace, denial of the inner deity. This denial commits horrendous crimes. The person is guilty. Sanity or insanity is not even a question. It's not about that. The nature of such terrible crimes is always insanity, with or without a psychosis. This is why we must nurture, support and encourage people who are offered a truly divine and important gift. This is why psychosis must be acknowledged as a sacred and spiritual experience. In denying that, we disrespect the divine and we disrespect ourselves. In doing so, we harm ourselves and harm the greater good.

The experience of the Otherworld can also be a positive and beautiful experience for some people who are ready. In many ways, psychosis is an evolutionary attempt to evolve. It is the natural healing capacity within us calling us to love ourselves and reconnect with our true nature; Nature itself. Is the great power of the human spirit that rises up to protect them and show them who they really are. It is the Great spirits work.

Since the beginning of our human existence, many have

used various plants to get a glimpse into this otherworld. These plants were used with a sincere respect. They were used to gain wisdom. They were used as a sacrament. Even to a lesser degree, alcohol was used in a respectful way to get a glimpse of the spirit world. To think that we are separate from these "Drugs" is the primary illusion itself.

But it requires courage to bring back the wisdom and apply it in our everyday life. The knowing of God must be followed by the doing of God. Schizophrenics don't even need the use of these 'drugs.' In fact they are not drugs. Drugs are man-made synthetic pills created in a lab. Schizophrenics are experienced without any aids. A recovered and integrated schizophrenic can use these sacred tools (natural) with already a heightened sense of balance and ability to navigate the otherworld. We say that schizophrenics are 'unbalanced' and they sometimes are unbalanced in our everyday world, the illusion we find ourselves in. But in the otherworld, they are more balanced than the average person. Again, it's a question of integration.

Mental illness lies in the failure of integration. Addiction lies in the denial of the possibility of integration. Both are forms of fear. The schizophrenic can learn that they are not schizophrenic by experiencing the otherworld offered by these sacred medicines. The addict can cure his/her addiction when they come to accept their own divinity. Denial will only kill them.

The most mentally ill person is the person who has no mental illness or no underlying vulnerability to mental illness. They are the ones we need to watch out for, not the schizophrenics!

In the midst of psychosis, Love becomes alive. It becomes a living pure divine flow. At the same time there is fear. The fear comes from our damaged self. This fear is the collection of traumas we have been through. It carries generations of hurt from our ancestors. It also becomes alive. When we learn to be kind to this damaged part of ourselves and love it, our divine essence shines true. We heal deeply.

The darkness of Fear is crying out for the light of Love. Psychosis, similar to a high dose of THC from Marijuana shows us this love. Bob Marley sung about it. U2 sung about it too. This Love is still sung about and will always be sung about. It is outside of time. It is Divine Love. It is who we really are. Our false self is afraid of it. Our false self is the one who is mentally ill.

If we can come through and except our psychosis as something sacred, we get better and recover. In the words of Psychiatrist Karl Menninger (1893-1990) we can become "Weller than Well." In other words, we have lived and known the reality of Self-Transcendence. Putting this into practice allows for self-transformation. We have embraced and forgiven our fearful shadow. Our identity is no longer trapped in a limited, conditioned and mechanical self. We can see God hiding in everyone else. We can laugh at ourselves and the trickster who is ever present. After our experiences, we are not the same person than before. That person has died.

If you have been through this, it will make complete sense to you already. If not, perhaps you have not spiritually died and been reborn just yet. Don't worry, it's coming for you. Or more accurately...You are coming! You can decide what you want to call your new found consciousness went it arrives, your new found self. But be careful what name you chose. Naming it, may split you in half once again.

As I was gaining integration of the two worlds, I was not only pointing to the cracks in Psychiatry, I was pointing to the cracks in much larger belief systems. But my fight against greater and greater institutions, societal structures and a whole global materialistic way of life always came back to a fight against myself. I was part of the problem because the part of me that cared so much was not really me. That's ok too.

Let me ask you this: Through whose eyes is an enlightened being enlightened? Through the cracks in our belief systems, what do you see?

As I previously mentioned, under the freedom of information legislation, I requested my complete medical file from that two year period when I was "treated" and "diagnosed" without my consent. Initially there was an attempt not to release my file as I was suspected of not being of sound mind. But I eventually got access to it. I now had written evidence from at least eight separate psychiatrists in three different countries showing an undoubtable collective opinion that pointed to Schizophrenia. I had further evidence showing that I had 'treatment resistant Schizophrenia' and medicated with the last resort antipsychotic drug Clozapine, at a high dosage. That treatment had not worked.

The new dilemma I was faced with was being able to share my experiences in order to help break down stigma while safeguarding my professional credentials. The other dilemma was integrating the spiritual with the materialistic way of life. But these were both the same dilemma really.

I was beginning to feel that Ireland was not ready to have experts leading the mental health field who have lived experience and recovery from mental disorders. And it was certainly not ready for experts who have recovered without medication. There were many positions and career opportunities available for psychiatric nurses and psychiatrists working from a medical disease model. There were very few and low paid positions for peer support workers with lived experience. And usually that work was under the direction and careful surveillance of the medical model and its clinicians. I would be seen as irresponsible for coming off meds. I would also be seen as a bad influence as I held a different view than that of illness.

Ireland and its people were tired of confronting decades of abuse towards children and young women in institutions. But no one was ready to consider decades of abuse at the hands of mental health institutions that was continuing to the present day. It was looking more likely that I would need to pursue my career abroad. Or perhaps, maybe I would even discover a different path to follow.

On my road to recovery, I have met many people who have been diagnosed with schizophrenia. Unfortunately, I am yet to meet someone like myself who has recovered without the use of medication. With the use of the internet however I see that there are others out there like me. As our numbers grow, so too will our voice.

I cannot recall any of the many people I have met with schizophrenia who did not have some form of significant trauma in their past. Not once was I asked from psychiatrists in that two year struggle, about my experiences in the French Foreign Legion. It was as if I had an extreme form of diabetes that required hospital admissions and a padded cell. And all of that "purely medical behaviour" I was exhibiting had nothing got to do with past trauma and unresolved personal issues! I don't think so.

My view may seem hypocritical. I do believe that during a psychotic break, there is excessive electrical activity and dopamine being released in the brain. I accept that. I do believe that there are areas of the brain that would light up during a possible scan, explaining the completely subjective and real experience of hallucinations. But the important difference is that I believe the environment, of which we are not separate from, causes these physical differences to occur. Nobody has a genetic makeup that makes them immune from schizophrenia. There is not one person on this planet that wouldn't have abnormal brain chemistry and electrical activity when exposed to certain environmental conditions such as extreme sleep deprivation. But it doesn't actually matter.

I realised that all of this has no relevance, nor does the term 'chemical imbalance.' The use of all these scientific terms for chemicals in the brain is not helpful. Serotonin, dopamine, DMT, the list goes on and on. They are all part of the mechanical model and a distraction from the bigger picture. They are only part of a very limited cycle of rational thinking that becomes more and more distant from the irrationality of spirit. The use of chemistry as superior knowledge is blurring our vision, ignorant of the bigger picture.

Some of the wisest people on this earth are often illiterate. They use nature to describe our true reality. The use of these scientific terms is meaningless to them and rightly so. Don't take this for ignorance, its actually true understanding! Drugs are something produced by scientists in a lab. The brain doesn't produce drugs! If we are to believe that drugs come from nature, then our bodies are just an amalgamation of living drugs walking around on a giant ball of drugs, floating in space. In this regard, chemistry means nothing. What is more important is accepting that there are four seasons, four elements: Earth, water, air and fire, there is night and day, the changing of the tides, stars to guide us, and that we are part of all this.

For the sake of it, I can still agree to a certain extent with the physical reality of mental illness. However, it is the external that affects the internal until the internal reflects the external. Often, with an abundance of creative potential the unconscious brain, as a sort of defence mechanism for trauma, creates an elaborate fantasy of delusions and hallucinations.

In my case, I unconsciously chose to become God to avoid dealing with the amount of psychological pain underneath. But this God was still trapped in my limited identity. I did not understand that I was being showed my true self which is not encapsulated within my body. Forget about the word 'God,' I was being shown who I truly was. There are too many built up associations with that word. Instead of being light as a feather, the word God is weighed down with millennia of manmade ideas. God doesn't call itself god. God doesn't call anything any Thing.

I am pretty certain even with my very basic knowledge of neuroscience, that during the seven years since my last acute psychosis, there could be no possible scan or physical test done to prove that I had a mental illness. The irony lies here because this might not be the case if I was still on medication - pharmaceutical drugs. If I was still on medication and took a brain scan, they may well be able to point to my brain and say "Look you have abnormal brain activity, just as we expect in people with schizophrenia."

I was confident enough to say that I had cured myself. How? You may ask.

I may answer: Self compassion, Self-discovery and Self-empowerment, and all this without being selfish. Then you may ask: How is that to be achieved? My answer would likely be: Go find out for yourself. Then your final question might be: Is that not a selfish way? My answer could be something like: Yes it is, if you think so.

Another element of my recovery, as I previously mentioned, required becoming estranged from my parents. The decision to cut my parents and older brother out of my life was very difficult. The decision was uncomfortable. I could feel it deep in my chest as raw emotion, when I doubted it. I would sometimes imagine my mother's suffering caused by my estrangement. I imagined her weeping. This was both sad and necessary for me. It somehow helped me heal the dysfunction I had before I left for the Legion. She was not present when I was a child. Her mind always seemed elsewhere when I sought her attention.

Estrangement was an essential decision to make along my spiritual path of self-healing. But it was a decision that was renewed in the present time because no eventuality could ever be ruled out about the future. There was always the possibility of reconnecting at some future point with them. The mind battled for certainty which it could never have.

I couldn't be myself or find myself while surrounded by other people telling me who I was. I had to go off into the wilderness. I could not be in their presence with open wounds, wounds that were inflicted in childhood and others while away in the Legion. I needed to lick my own wounds. I knew that the reason for my estrangement would become clearer in the future. Sometimes there are greater forces at play than our little selves.

Having taken the power back into my own hands, I cut my parents and older brother out of my life. This allowed me to imagine them giving attention to the fact that they were now powerless over the situation. I liked that idea. Maybe the hope was that they would not take our family relationship for granted, if given a second chance. But maybe they would even mirror and exaggerate my decision and not want to see me again. Could I deal with that? - Their estrangement from me, a piece of my own medicine? I was sure I could but it would be sad. My deepest instincts told me that estrangement was not good.

I couldn't know why but something told me that it was a necessary step despite it going against a deeply rooted and biological human instinct for family loyalty. But it was for the greater good, in some unconscious way. The future would reveal why this was necessary further down the path or it may not.

No longer would my expected loyalty to them taken for granted. With a feeling of inner guilt, I imagined how their attention to my estrangement would turn to despair when I no longer performed their expectations as a son. I kind of liked that too. But even though, I really did not want them to suffer, I knew that if they did suffer, that it was a necessary suffering too. This was without any blaming or hatred. If they did suffer by my estrangement there would be positive growth for them afterwards.

I had to trust in my decision for estrangement. It did not come from my intellect alone. But what I did figure out was that I became more sane and more at peace within myself while they were out of my life. This was a hard truth to swallow. The deep rooted feeling of duty and love for family was slowly being eroded by the disturbing and shocking realisation that I never really liked them. That idea was completely unacceptable. It disgusted me to my core. But there was something true in it. And that was hard to swallow. But at the same time, the fact that I did think about them often meant that they were important to me. There was no quick answer and no quick fix.

The more I separated myself from them, the more it became a search for my own deeper identity. I felt that it would be too painful to separate from my younger brother and my sister so I have kept them in my life. But there was also no reason to separate from them. We had a good bond. I realised the obvious that had once remained fogged. I liked my younger brother and sister, as people in their own right, regardless of our biological obligations. I trusted them. They were my friends. This helped me further develop a better sense of myself in terms of what kind of people I do want in my life.

Allowing good people into my life was central to Self-compassion. No child will ever say that they come from a bad family. That is too upsetting to admit.

Of course, loneliness and hopelessness have crept in during this process of breaking away from part of my biological family. There were times when the emotion in my chest built up as if from nowhere. Instead of running to distractions, I welcomed it.

I cried alone. Each time I cried, I released pain. I felt something deep down was healing inside of me. I was healing myself and I was becoming myself at the same time.

Many years after my hospital admissions, I wondered why I was fortunate to survive and recover from schizophrenia. Some people might say that I became estranged from my parents because I had schizophrenia. But actually, I became estranged from them in order to cure my schizophrenia! There is a huge difference between the two.

My mental breakdown or as I prefer to call it, my mental breakthrough, had allowed me to embark on my own inner journey. Staying well was a long process of being brutally honest with myself. There was no hiding. This honesty required me to look inside. This is what I would say to somebody else faced with this same challenge:

It can be more helpful to you if you view this process as an adventure. Viewing schizophrenia or other forms of mental illness as a burden that must be carried through life is unhelpful. I know. I've come through it. It's worth the challenge, trust me. If you embark on and embrace this adventure of yours, you will make a new friend too. You will find yourself who you lost a long time ago.

From what I have experienced, psychosis is the minds way of dealing with psychological stress, past trauma and physical exhaustion. In some way, developing schizophrenia was an opportunity for me to take a break from life, to face myself and ultimately to get to know myself better. It was the mud from which the lotus flower could grow. But it was also the same mud that could dry up and nothing could grow. Some people get stuck in the mud and don't seem to be able to move on. They can remain forever star struck by their encounter with God.

For me, this whole saga was an opportunity to take a new and healthier approach to life. I had no choice but to begin the journey of living true to myself. If not, I would face further relapses, further denial.

Psychosis is an experience which is impossible to put correctly into words. There is an important reason for this; psychosis points to the illusion of this reality. If it was easy to describe then it would also confirm the realness of our everyday experience. This book is my best attempt at describing the Mystical experience of psychosis. But my description of it fails in offering a direct experience of God to you. It always will fail.

If you use this book like the Bible you will not experience your own divinity as you will be using me as the intermediary. Just like those who read the Bible and expect Jesus to provide them with a place in heaven and a meeting with God, those who read the Quran leave it to Muhammad to lead them to their God. Be your own prophet!

The very best I could hope for, with this book, is to ignite the spark of divinity in you. But that eternal light has been burning already. You wouldn't be here without it. Psychosis is a wordless experience just like God is undefinable. The knowing comes in the unknowable. After all is said and done, sometimes less is more, like when we say, "God is love" or when we speak of "Allah the Compassionate."

Music and Art can often be better indicators of divine union. For many people they can be better tools than words to arouse the sense of the mystical. Perhaps, I will resort to these at a further point. But I don't find myself particularly talented in Music or Art despite my immense appreciation of them.

Psychosis is a life changing experience. For me, it was a direct experience of God without any intermediary. I began to understand that I was not uncomfortable with the man called Jesus Christ. I was uncomfortable with the people who expected me to use him as an intermediary. In fact, I understood Jesus very well. The bliss and awe of God overcomes any fear and paranoia, but only once we realise that there is no intermediary.

The more I came to understand psychosis as a mystical experience, the less I feared it. My 'fluid days' as I call them were days when I was mildly psychotic. There was a wonderful flow to these days during which my 'will' would dissolve almost completely. I had overcome the fear implanted in my conditioned mind that they were signs of a relapse. Instead, I used those days to my advantage. They were like training in a way. I could function with one foot in the otherworld with the presence of God, and the other foot grounded in this reality we take for granted. I told nobody of these training days; my fluid days. I didn't have anyone around who could understand it.

I was becoming a master at integration and even without the use of any psychoactive substances. These states were completely natural to me.

Are there any alternatives other than becoming Mad, in order to experience God? Yes, but they are second class experiences. Orgasm, through sexual means or masturbation, is the next closest and easiest thing we can get to Divine Union, but even that falls short of the mark. When sex addiction or porn addiction becomes a problem for some, it points to the desperateness with which God is being sought.

Sex is a superb manifestation of the eternal search we are all born with. But actually, you could also say that it is God who is seeking to be acknowledged within the individual. That is closer to the truth. Addiction to drugs of any kind including addiction to gambling, overeating and masturbation, is the denial of the God within.

During my recovery, I got involved in new sports. I travelled to new places whenever I could. I set small goals to keep myself motivated. I learnt that it was counterproductive when I pushed myself too hard in sporting pursuits. My peace of mind could not rely solely on my physical condition. A deeper immaterial spiritual basis was essential, however elusive it may remain. My own personal enjoyment in exercise and sports must be the motivating factor, rather than seeking to impress others. Being physically active and productive was important but I knew it must be done in a manner which was kind to the body and to the mind. I no longer found any truth in the motto which I once lived by; No Pain No Gain. At least on the physical level, I didn't.

I was born, raised and spent most of my life living in Dublin city. I learnt that living in Dublin city or any city for that matter, can cause a disconnection from nature, or the illusion that we are something other than nature. The search for meaning in life can become more and more elusive in the frustrating but addictive hustle and bustle of city life. Sometimes, I didn't want to go into nature because I would have to face myself. This was a sign of disconnection. The lie that my disconnected mind made up was that "nature is boring."

Exposure to nature reminded me that meaning can be found in just living. But "just living" was a slower pace of life, a natural pace, not a rushed city life. In order to get out of my head and into my body, I needed to go on trips into nature. To remind me of this, I felt the need to step out of my comfort zone and to let my body feel cold, hunger, thirst, fatigue and discomfort. This allowed me to appreciate the comforts of everyday life. A simple task such as collecting wood in the outdoors and making a fire can be so healing. Even going for a walk in the rain shuts up the disconnected mind. I even allowed myself to feel deeply lonely so that I would appreciate and value the connection with people when it came.

To sit and watch a campfire, in a state of thoughtless awareness, can be a soothing way to become centred and present. Bathing in a cold stream of water snaps the sense of "I" from the mind and flushes it into every extremity of the body.

In some instances of awe, the sense of "I" can be set loose, even out beyond the body.

I regained a healthy new interest in the outdoors. I managed to break a negative association in my mind between the outdoors and my suffering in the French Foreign Legion.

A huge part of getting well for me included an important period of labelling and de-labelling myself. What do I mean? Here, I talk not only of mental disorders but of other identifying factors such as addiction issues, religion and sexuality, and eventually ending up at more complex ideas such as race, nationality, group affiliation and identity. Coming to understand this process of identifying, re-identifying and ultimately not defining myself, has contributed to so much of my recovery. Let us look at them.

Personally, I am not religious. I feel that I must distance myself from Christianity even though I really feel complete understanding of what Jesus went through. At the end of the day, Jesus was not a Christian. And I feel that he is largely misunderstood and misquoted in most, if not all, Christian doctrines. Initially, I felt that religion could be a trigger for my grandiose delusions. That fear dissipated over time as my confidence grew. But eventually, I simply realised that most Christian people didn't really want to hear my story. They were pretty rigid in their faith. Any discussion with them was usually one way.

How could I present my view without insulting their religion? And my view may seem as a contradiction to many people; I believe that Jesus was God and Jesus was Mad. They were inseparable. And Jesus also had his shadow side, like all of us; the Devil within. In that regard, the trilemma of C.S. Lewis, for me, offers three choices, all of which are correct, and all of which are necessary.

Regarding who was Jesus Christ, it is my opinion that he was experiencing grandiose delusions. If alive today in our society, he would be labelled with Bipolar disorder or Schizophrenia. This is not to say that he wasn't a compassionate spiritual man, with a highly creative streak, just like many carpenters tend to be. Over the time of his life, he was both a Mystic and a Schizophrenic. He was both enlightened and psychotic. Some of his teachings such as denying thyself have similarities with Buddhism. But if he was truly enlightened, he would not have ended up nailed to a cross. He would not have been such an active revolutionary. The fact that global religions are based around his life, I find really amazing, along with the immense corruption of power that goes with that.

For me, the most important thing is that the story of this man's life highlights how innocent and naïve the human race is. It points out our denial to follow our own hearts and find the deity present inside each one of us. Accepting Jesus as our brother rather than our saviour comes with taking personal responsibility and accepting our own authority. In religion, we give this away and we limit ourselves in the process.

Religion is not all bad. It can be a good starting point. But from there, you got to paddle across to the other side by yourself. You can't rely on hope that Jesus will walk on water for you or that Moses will part the sea for you. You got to learn how to swim out of your own depths.

There is a fine line between spiritual enlightenment and a psychotic break. A psychotic break is a glimpse of God by a fearful conditioned mind, by the false self. Love and compassion can turn to anger and confusion in an instant just like Jesus going berserk in the temple. Because that Love and compassion is ego generated.

Enlightenment is complete acceptance and integration of our divinity into our material self, allowing God to look through our eyes, pump blood from our hearts, and inhale oxygen into our lungs, while we ourselves dissolve along with thought. It is beyond love or hate. God just watches. God does not need to proclaim his presence. He is already in all. The false self tries to own God and then becomes a false messiah. The true messiah is God and that messiah is within us all. Very few will let it come forth, many wont.

But times are changing and more and more people are shedding their illusion to create a space for the divine. There was an attempt in the 1960s by God to break free in the minds of many people across the globe. It now seems that another period of mass enlightenment is brewing across the world. The powers of control and Authority will do everything possible to stop God awakening in a critical mass of people. But I feel that it is an inevitable stage in human evolution. There's no going back. The truth of nature as ultimate authority is a timeless one. The only thing left for the universe to imagine is to make it a living reality on earth.

Once you have felt the presence of God, the cracks have already appeared in you. If you continue to deny who you who really are, you will continue living a frustrated human existence. You may even develop or relapse into psychosis and chronic Schizophrenia. But most of all, and in the end, you will regret not listening to your heart, your higher self and not fulfilling your destiny while you lie on your death bed. As your time of death approaches, you may even whisper to yourself in fear, regret and disappointment "Why have you forsaken me?"

In the course of my short life so far, I have gone from considering myself as Christian, to Atheist, to Agnostic to Buddhist to realising that to define myself in this regard would create a limited self and distance myself from others. I have come to believe therefore that our essential self is actually indefinable.

Spiritual growth was an ongoing part of my recovery and

wellbeing. Thinking less about myself, but not of myself, was important to staying well. I had been to support groups for both alcohol addiction and sex and love addiction. AA and SLAA support groups where both founded on the same twelve step programme of surrendering oneself to God or to a higher power. All my forms of addiction seemed to have come from the same insecure lost sense of who I was.

I do believe that addictions can be overcome. I believe that abstinence is not the only way but it may be necessary for a period of time. Carrying an internal label of being an incurable addict can be more self-defeating in the long term. Having said that, by accepting that I had an addiction, it helped me to admit to myself that I had an issue to be addressed. I could then seek help and support for the first time.

From a young age, my drinking took the form of binges, a habit which I took to be normal among young Irish people. Alcohol was a way to relieve misunderstood stress. It produced a sense of pleasure, free of anxiety. It induced a disinhibited sense of self in me. In some ways you could say that like a mild psychosis, it gave me a small glimpse at God. I binged drank during my teenage years and this continued during my time in the Foreign Legion where drinking was very much part of the lifestyle there.

Later I concluded that my heavy drinking, which took the form of binges, was really a form of temporary escape or dampening of my mind which had been overactive and usually negative in nature. This constant erosion of my self-esteem from a self-destructing mind was happening unconsciously. There was unresolved trauma to deal with.

Fortunately, I learned to have more understanding and insights into my feelings and behaviours. As I began the search to get in touch with my true self, I became more in touch with my moods and emotional needs. I then began to gain more control over my drinking. I learned to practice being present in everyday life with the aim of simply less thinking until that slowly became, more and more, my normal state of being.

At the very least, I could begin to feel the separation of thoughts from the thinker. My mind began welcoming the sense of unknowingness which it once detested. Some people call this meditation. I call it accessing our own inner peace.

Recovering from schizophrenia allowed me to become aware of other spiritual maladies. Tackling these helped prevent me from becoming a victim of further episodes of negative psychosis. Sex and love addiction contributed to my development of schizophrenia. This was not an easy thing to accept. Nobody wanted to talk about it. It terrified me.

Facing Sex and Love addiction, involved stripping back my malformed sense of self to the very core of my being. This included surrender to life and a surrender to my manhood. I began identifying a pattern in my life of attempting to complete myself by becoming addicted and "falling in love" with someone who could never fill the void of my aching soul. My aching soul was a denial of my true Self. This could always manifest into many forms of suffering.

I felt that I had been living a lie for so many years. It had taken a diagnosis of schizophrenia and some painful addictions to women and alcohol to wake me up. For a two year period when I gave up alcohol, I realised the extent to which I wasn't being true to myself.

I attended another recovery group called Sex and Love Addicts Anonymous (SLAA). Similar to Alcoholics Anonymous (AA), it uses the twelve step principles. However, as sexual drive is a completely natural phenomenon, everyone in the group had to decide on their own bottom lines. Unlike alcohol abstinence in the AA programme, Sex was not required to be ruled out completely in the SLAA programme. But abstinence from all sexual acts, including masturbation, was encouraged for a period of time to get in touch with, acknowledge and accept supressed emotions.

The support of the group was invaluable. I got some insights into my tendency to suppress emotional issues with sexual impulses and visits to prostitutes. I was careful however of not falling into black and white thinking. The unknown element of life must remain. When I no longer found the group meetings beneficial, I moved on, with increased self-awareness and higher emotional intelligence.

Love addiction on its own is a complex issue little discussed. It was certainly connected to my childhood and relationship with my mother. It was connected with fear of rejection and the need of outside approval. I remember being rejected by friends in my teenage years and being isolated in school. I deserved good people in my life. The possibility that my parents might not have been so good was very hard to face.

I felt that I could never bear to be close emotionally or physically with my parents. At a very young age, maybe four years old, my mother stopped me when I attempted to kiss her. She pushed me away from her bedside, leaving me confused. The same thing happened again, around the same period, when I attempted to kiss a cousin of mine. We were playing in my grandparent's garden when it happened. I was told off by all the family. I was left distraught, embarrassed and ashamed in front of all those adults.

My Irish childhood was a cold one. From then on, I had struggled with healthy intimacy. Any "love" I later experienced was defined on this blueprint. In my dictionary, Love was painful. It manifested in a needy and wanting form of desire that lead ultimately to rejection, jealousy and hate. My fear of rejection and being alone only fed this love addiction. When I had to let go of each obsessive relationship, it felt like returning to a place where I was completely lost and isolated, in complete darkness, much like a baby uncomfortable in the womb.

This reoccurring pattern of Sex and Love addiction led me to accept that I had a serious issue to face. It was ok to temporarily surrender this burden onto an imagined separate God or a higher self but a time would need to come when I would realise that the burden only existed because of my false self, to begin with. Sex addiction was just another way that denial of my divine self was manifesting.

Saying goodbye to my private ego identified self whom I thought I knew so well, was met with the acceptance of the true self. Just like letting any obsession go, I was left empty. The false self we create for ourselves is the biggest obsession of all time. Letting it go creates a frightening emptiness. My mind tried everything to hold on, to keep Schizophrenia in the category of 'illness.' But really, I was whole. Madness had revealed this to me.

This emptiness I speak of was sacred. Initially it was very upsetting. But accepting it has allowed for some real healing to occur. I could sense Gods presence in the midst of my worst heartaches.

Mental pain and suffering has been the necessary catalyst for positive change. True love must begin by loving and accepting oneself. Such a cliché, it is easier said than done. Only then can healthy intimacy be found with others. This must be experienced to understand it. This is what it means to love God more than yourself, because your true essence is God.

Who am I? This question has been a terrifying question to answer but one I needed to address. It's too easy to say "I am God." But where is the value in that? Slowly such questions lose their grip as the answers are not so important. The fear of being wrong diffuses with the desire of being right. I could say everything is God or everything is not God. So what!

Sometimes I still want a pizza and a beer! And a good shag! We gotta stay real about the whole thing.

I had found some peace in the idea that the Self is an illusion and the cause of much mental suffering. For my own sanity in the early days of recovery, I needed to ensure the practicalities of everyday life such as eating, sleeping, cleaning and exercising were in order before dealing with such soul searching questions. I began to understand that my ego had been very strong and damaging due to a defensive superiority complex. Alcohol, Sex and "Love" and even psychotic delusions had been ways of escaping because I had lost contact with my true self, whatever the hell that was. So who was I? Once that question remained I knew I would remain trapped. And answering it would only tighten the chains.

I also went through a period of labelling and de-labelling myself as Bisexual. This was a deep ravine in the cracking of my identity. I believe that another trigger to developing schizophrenia was my supressing of teenage homosexual fantasies. During my teenage years in school, I was predominantly attracted to girls in my class. But I also felt attracted to some boys in my class too. I suppressed these attractions to other boys. I felt ashamed and wrong about these feelings. I had a nightmare once, when I was twelve years of age, in which I told my parents about these homosexual feelings. I awoke the next morning, feeling extremely anxious, unsure if I had let out this deep secret. But I told nobody until many years later and only after full blown psychotic episodes.

Maybe if I had just been homosexual it would have been easier to be open about that. Being bisexual allowed me to suppress these feelings and focus my attraction solely on girls. These supressed feelings surfaced later during my psychotic episodes. They manifested in my obsession towards pop star Justin Bieber. Not fully understanding or being educated on the existence or possibility of bisexuality, I had a black and white view that I must be either heterosexual or homosexual. I grew more accepting of myself although I found that bisexuality was less understood in general. The whole idea of it turns our world upside down.

We like to define the world in dualistic terms for simplicity and practicality. The psychologist Alfred Kinsey proposed the continuum of sexuality. Should I need to explain myself, I simply direct people to his work; The Kinsey Scale.

Most importantly, I knew for myself that I was predominantly attracted to women. I no longer needed to label myself as bisexual once I had explored my supressed homosexual fantasies. I was then comfortable once again being heterosexual. But I realised that any term I settled for was just another veil that fogged the truth. Finding my own peace of mind with my sexuality has been very important. I reached a conclusion; perhaps any prefix we place before the word "sexual" is once again defining the self which is ultimately indefinable. It's just another layer on the onion of our identity. Labels and categories can only bring a shallow sense of temporary relief. They keep us blinded, spiritually.

If I wanted to label and limit myself, there would be no end. I could say I had schizophrenia or bipolar disorder type one, or even schizoaffective disorder. I could say that I had major depressive disorder but it wasn't quite this because my depression was more like a state of dysphoria in which I continued to function, having joy locked away by fear. I could agree with the term anhedonia, but this was only another manifestation of unease from the denial to face myself.

Perhaps I could say that I had post-traumatic stress disorder from my time in the Legion and being viciously attacked by my comrades. I had a good argument for that one. I could also say that I had obsessive thinking patterns and anxiety. I could say that I was an alcoholic and a sex and love addict. I could say that I was a chronic stutterer and a bisexual. I could even take a religious perspective and blame it on the devil and the fact that I had not enough devotion to our perfectly clean, Lord Jesus Christ, who never had to clean his rotting teeth, shitty arse or cheesy nob. He was divine so he constantly smelt like roses and lavender.

I could say that just maybe, I had borderline personality disorder and therefore, I am forever doomed.

I could say that, in truth, I had a touch of all these things and that there was no cure for me. On doing so, I would definitely be in a state of anhedonia. I would tick all the boxes for the negative symptoms of schizophrenia.

I could have easily become hopeless and reverted to childhood dependency, living with my mum. In a strange but dangerous way, I could find a sense of comfort in these labels. They made me feel different or even special.

In the long term, though, I realised they would be my downfall. All those labels had to become unstuck, every single one of them. I took responsibility for my own recovery.

What helped me make that life changing course of action? The answer to that crucial question makes me laugh. I realised that, whether I was those things or not was really not that important anymore. Labels, whether good or bad, do not change who I am nor define me. After all, I am far more than these things.

I, the frustrated legionnaire, the rebellious teenager, the schizophrenic bisexual, came from imperfect parents. I was imperfect myself. But we can be perfect in our imperfections. We can forgive ourselves, others and our collective illusion, knowing that all of these things were just trying to protect us until the time was right to embrace who we really are.

There will surely be obstacles to overcome in the future and further manifestations of denial. I will be ready to surrender to them in order to overcome them. Each obstacle continues to help in shedding a layer of the onion, a layer of the lie. Life can tough sometimes, even for God.

Recovery was all about the stance that I took. Mental illness does not have to be a life sentence. In some way, we always have a choice. I have chosen to leave it behind me. In doing so, the labels fell off by themselves.

By learning to accept myself, not compare myself with others and not rely on outside approval, I could live a humble, satisfying and meaningful life which could be both exciting and rewarding. But only being aware of this was not enough. I needed to put it into action.

As I have slowly reconnected with my lost self, I found more inner peace. I have gained mental stability while keeping the wonder of this life alive. If I can achieve this then so can anyone. The cure, I believe is in recovery and the source of this cure is found deep within us all.

I have felt and recognised the human condition of feeling incomplete. For some reason this is a necessary and powerful illusion. Most likely, it exists to protect us. The absolute truth of who we are can be really overwhelming. It is said that most people cower in the presence of God. When you see it, you will be either scared to death or blown away by beauty. Either way, you will be in tears. Eventually, the more you witness it and trust it, you will know that love is triumphant over our fearful mind. Then you will try to comprehend love and you will likely get lost again. But trust in life will remain. This is the same trust that saw you draw your first breath of air. This trust is akin to faith, faith in God, faith in yourself, faith in the Universe.

We are all complete behind the "madness" of modern times, because there is nothing to complete. Your body lives and dies and the greatest actor of all time, who is you, helps complete this process. The search for God is also the denial of God, for once you meet God; you also meet yourself. When this happens, time and space will dissolve, you realise the Eternal. Words lose their grip.

Our unconscious mind can hold many secrets that allow us to reconnect with what we feel separated from. One time and for no apparent reason, I awoke in the middle of the night and wrote this poem from my dreams:

Mother Earth's Sour Fruit

They were desperate and searching,
And using her name.
So she found them,
Digging up her garden.
She explained through the wind,
How her produce was not yet ripe,
But they could not wait,
And they could not hear.
They were starving despite their fat bellies,
Like pregnant whores,
Men and women alike.
They scrambled feverishly,
Their eyes orgasmic,
At the sight of unknown roots.
But these endless roots,
Reached the bottom of their own desire,
Where a dragon slept,
In timeless peace.
Greedily,
They pulled at their roots,
At the anchor of their Soul,
An anchor which never rusts.
They cursed each other,

When their taut lines went slack,
Disgusted with yet,
Another failed attempt at salvation.
Their bellies burst open,
Revealing silver mummies,
Like flies kept in a spider's web,
For a future feast.
Then like spoilt children,
They unwrapped these sticky gifts,
To find loving giant leeches,
Who embraced them forever,
To the symphony of their muffled cries.

SANDYCOVE

I began to really consider that there was no absolute truth in this life, in this Maya. But I thought that perhaps I could attempt to be more true to myself. If not, at least it was worth a try. I felt that we must not and cannot hand over power and responsibility if we are to accept the path of self-discovery and healing.

If we remain unwilling to carry our load, we will not find what we are all looking for. When we hand over our load to a separate God, we don't accept our path. When we accept it, we can rise above it. Our load is our denial. When we truly carry it, it carry's us.

Our path towards divine union requires us to leave uncertainty as it is. It is also a path that sometimes calls for leaving God alone. In Australian slang "God Botherers" is used as a term for religious folk. The more certain we are of God, the more we delude ourselves. The more we concern ourselves with figuring it out, the more burdened we become. We then turn God into a burden. God becomes the cross, not the person carrying it.

This is all uneasy for the modern mind. We grow frustrated when we can't grasp it. It's like using the mind to escape the mind; a futility.

The way out is a way of life that has been called the middle way. It's a path involving no association with religion, but the ability to smile at religions metaphorical attempts towards a known God, while still accepting God as both known and unknown.

I like to describe life, and its path, as a series of waves to be surfed. It is certain that the waves will keep coming but uncertain is the way in which we will handle them or even notice them. I'm no surfer, but I do enjoy watching them from the beach.

After the roller coaster of recovery, my self-esteem had built back up. I started working in the field of Social Care, working with young people living in Care homes. But how I could help these vulnerable and lost young people if I'm not certain about the bigger questions and meaning for my own existence? Perhaps in order to really help these vulnerable people, my approach must be founded in humanity. What I mean here is that my own doubts and uncertainty should be allowed to shine through. Yes, a solid reliable confident role model is required but the importance of remaining humble, modest and calm was important. The use of "I don't know" can be helpful and "Sorry I really don't know," even more, but only if it is genuine.

I was six years free of medication, out of the mental health system, had completed my degree and was back working again, when it was time to start putting this book together. I knew that completing my story and getting in down on paper would further strengthen my recovery and allow me to move forward with my life. The spiritual searching that was once parked aside was allowed to have more of my attention once again. I was faced with a new dilemma, one founded in fear.

On one hand there were the positive symptoms of religiosity and spiritual delusions that are associated with psychosis and mental illness. My previous psychotic states involved paranoia and the belief that I was God made man. But on the other hand, there were recognised modern spiritual speakers such as Eckhart Tolle, Adyashanti, Sri Prem Baba, Deepak Chopra and many others who hinted at our divine essence, ever so carefully.

Our deepest essence and true self was God. I agree. But once we accept this, how do we integrate this into ourselves? That remained my biggest question. My previous psychosis within schizophrenia was the ultimate inflation of the ego. In believing that my worldly identity was God, I denied past trauma. That belief is a mad belief, but a somewhat rational belief to traumatic events. My mind was the prison that attempted to lock God up.

If we agree for a moment that you are God, I am God, and we all are God, yet not what is commonly thought of as God, this is a paradoxical situation. The knowing of God remains in the unknowing so the self must remain unknown. But at the same time, something that remains unknown to the mind is something which is fixed in time, constant and unable to change. It is like a stagnant pond of water. We have blocked its flow when we were certain that it cannot be known. This is God's paradox.

Slowly, God and the mystery of God can reveal itself to us if we allow it. First, we begin to realise that the word God itself is a falsehood. Every other word is, from then on, a falsehood. We then realise that we have been lost in a false reality which we called normality. In this 'normality' words became words of one big lie in hundreds of languages, on one planet, in trillions of planets. People can argue over what Paprika is and nobody will ever agree. It becomes pointless.

Even as I near the completion of my story, a huge wave of doubt washes over me. What's the point in trying to explain the biggest dilemma of all time; that absolute truth can only be found in madness? Well it doesn't matter. Whether this book exists or not really doesn't matter. Knowing this makes it easier to finish the damn thing. So let's keep going a little more with the pain in the arse job of trying to explain the big G word.

The living God that we are is that which is beyond our names, our sex, our race, and every other category and role we take on. It is the centre of the onion that you never get to, because it was present in the skin to begin with. The living experience of God reveals the dependency of all things in our environment. This experience is without the need of any scientific or academic credentials. It is the foundation of all knowledge, the fountain of wisdom.

The problem I was faced with and even sometimes afraid of, was that I could no longer park spirituality to one side and continue living a materialistic life, full of rationality. Well I could but something would annoy me from the corner of my mind. It kept pushing its head up. It was as if I had no choice of avoiding the pink elephant in the room. So I thought, what is stopping me living both a materialistic and spiritual life both as one?

I felt that I had recovered enough stability, that it was time to allow back those spiritual questions into my life. It was fear that was keeping them parked away for years. That fear did have a place. It helped me gain stability. But it didn't provide fulfilment, meaning or purpose.

And sometimes, I just needed to stop thinking. Often I would take the train to Sandycove. I would jump into the cold sea water at the Fortyfoot bathing area in South Dublin to clear my mind.

FITZWILLIAM SQUARE

I was worried that others may see my renewed interest in spiritual seeking as signs of relapse and a sign of schizophrenia, the chronic lifelong disorder slowly sneaking back in, like an illness that never goes away but just goes to sleep for a little while. But I felt strong enough to face these negative thoughts and question these widely held expert beliefs.

My confidence was back. But it was a different confidence than the one I had before my breakdown. It wasn't founded in belief. It was founded in direct experience, direct feeling and direct knowing. It was founded deep down in some place where no fear exists. I couldn't see it, hold it or even show it to you. I had risen above the limits of rational thinking and the depression that the mind causes.

The old confidence was based on my identity, my roles, and my possessions. Every achievement built up this confidence. Whether it was running a marathon or being a Legionnaire, having a beautiful girlfriend or a great job, there was no depth to it.

Of course sport was great and helped me a lot with my mental fitness, stamina and health. But it was dangerous to rely on sport alone. That would be one dimensional. When I was at the peak of my physical fitness, I ran the Dublin City Marathon in three and a half hours. That is a good time when you weigh ninety kilograms. The buzz on Fitzwilliam square was memorable. Yet, despite being very active in sports, I would still get mentally ill only a year later.

My new found confidence was no longer based solely on my

material and physical condition. It took on a different form. In fact, it was more likely formless. It even allowed for insecurity, having developed the beginnings of self-compassion. It was not completely founded on my identity. My mental breakdown and delusions which could easily be dismissed as illness and irrationality did actually point towards a truth. My heart had always told me that. But I wasn't equipped to deal with this truth before. One person can be labelled schizophrenic but not a global community.

There were others out there, recognising and being recognised for their attempts to put into words this same truth. Some of us are ready to accept this truth and others, not just yet.

Perhaps from the gradual emergence of the conscious self from our ancestors over millions of years, many have attempted to put forward this truth. What seems to emerge is that this truth and the word truth are not the same thing. The same can be said, that God and the word God are not the same thing.

Carl Jung coined the term Synchronicity. What I understand here is that there is a connection between two events. One event is external and the other is internal. When we witness a coincidence of this nature it disturbs us. It disturbs us because it breaks down our firmly held belief of being an individual and separate from the world out there. It also suggests that our conscious or unconscious self is somehow in sync with external events.

I may claim that we are all connected and we are all one. However, this claim is not always my subjective experience. The majority of the time, I am a separate individual and living my life as such. But every so often there are days were everything seems to flow into each other. When I calm my mind and become present, I can begin to see the true reality which we are constantly running away from.

In this hidden reality, everything appears to be unfolding

as if I had no free will. From waiting for a bus, to ordering a coffee, noticing people and their actions, my individuality which is usually preoccupied with a slight anxiety and mental noise, dissolves away. I become the river of life.

Initially, I was afraid of this feeling, thinking that it was schizophrenia coming back again, but slowly I realised that it was something beautiful, something sacred and not an illness. When I saw through the veil of God, I saw myself. I saw both everything that I loved and everything I feared. The mystical wisdom comes from nourishing fear with love.

I have experienced many synchronistic events but I was always left unsatisfied. Each time, I wanted them to provide an answer. I wanted them to prove themselves, to prove beyond doubt that their existence was the true reality. But the desire I was holding that I could use these subjective experiences to prove to other people something about the singularity and the connectedness of all life, was pointless. I was the only one that needed convincing, for the doubt was in me.

If it was true and these synchronicities were pointing to the illusion of separateness, what was the alternative? The alternative is wholeness, one being, one essence, one love, one God. But was I playing with fire and inviting back in delusional thinking that would lead to an egotistical understanding that I am God, and sure everyone else is too? If I really take this to be the truth, then everyone else cannot be seen as everyone else for there is no other.

What if doubt was necessary, as without doubt there is no certainty? Can we then say that without unity there is no duality, that wholeness implies separateness? The veil of God was there for a reason. Without that veil, we would all be long gone from this Earth. We would all be eaten by predators or nailed to a cross. But still, the wisdom is transferable; it can be brought back from the otherworld and applied to our lives.

MANCHESTER

Before I first got 'ill with schizophrenia', I had what I describe as a fluid day on one fourth of April in Australia. On such days, everything seems to flow. I don't like to ruin the credibility of the story but I was also experiencing a hangover from a good drinking session the day before. I'm reluctant to admit this as it lessens the validity and credibility of the experience. But maybe we drink spirits, to raise our spirits. From that day on I chose 404 as a number with significance to me personally. I knew that I had an epiphany. I didn't understand it at the time. But 404 was reminder of it and its realness.

Years later and recovered, that number remains with me. I went for a weekend away and stayed at a hostel in Manchester. I was visiting a good Irish friend of mine whom I had served with in the Foreign Legion.

Arriving at the reception of the hostel, I paid for my two nights stay. The girl behind the desk prepared a key card for my bedroom. As I waited, I noticed the digital clock on the wall displaying the time 4:04pm. Then she smiled, wished me a pleasant stay and handed me my card key. I smiled to myself when I looked at the card in my hand. My room number was 404.

Once I read an interpretation of the Indian greeting Namaste as meaning "The divine in me respects the divine in you." I regularly ate from an Indian takeaway called Namaste. I found out one day, that the address of this takeaway was a certain road number 404.

Synchronicity no longer disturbed me. I no longer doubted

their existence. I no longer needed to interpret them because they were beyond the rational mind's grasp. They are just a beautiful reminder that all is unfolding as it should be.

VILLARS LES DOMBES

I have continued travelling. It has always helped me very much with my recovery and confidence. One of my trips involved volunteering at a monastery for three weeks in France. I felt this would challenge me, being around religious beliefs. I was slightly nervous that I may become delusional at some stage. However it was worth facing this limiting fear. My time there went very well. When asked was I a believer, I replied that I once was but that I no longer held any religious beliefs.

The first day I arrived, I went to mass in the monastery, just for the sake of it. During the mass, the priest announced that it was the feast day of St. Vincent de Paul. He then spoke a little about the Saints life.

There were many bedrooms in the monastery, over two hundred. Every bedroom had a different Saints name on the door. My bedroom had St. Vincent de Paul carved on the door. I noticed the coincidence. That same day my volunteering job was in the cheese factory. I spent the day working alongside an employee named Vincent. We got on well and chatted all day while making cheese.

After work, in the late afternoon, I cycled to the small village nearby and to its only café. I sat there alone, enjoying my Café au Lait. I admired a copy of a painting by Vincent Van Gogh hanging on the wall. My mind wandered back to the time I spent at the Saint Vincent de Paul homeless shelter in Christchurch Dublin. I had come a long way since then. But I was back in France where my story began and in the land of that same Saint.

There was an Indian man at the same monastery. He was of a similar age to me. He was a brother in the Catholic Order. We had agreed several times that we would find time to have a talk. As the weeks passed I thought we would never have that chat but I didn't want to be the instigator. Then on my last day, I saw he was cutting someone's hair. I asked if he would cut mine too before I left the next morning. We agreed to meet that evening after dinner. He would cut my hair and we could then have tea and a chat.

An important aspect about my recovery was to keep my past mental illness to myself. I no longer felt a need to tell everyone about my experiences. For me, I never had an illness and I was only starting to understand how to explain it as a mystical union with the divine. Very few people would actually understand anyway. So I didn't bring it up.

But during our chat, he spoke of his own encounter with what he called "The Love of God," as he described what sounded to me like a hallucination. I was grateful for his willingness to share this personal story of his. But I felt that he probably had a mini psychotic break, not that there is any difference with an experience of the "love of god."

The fact that he interpreted his experience as a Christian one was the work of his mind. Mystical experiences can be backed up and supported if we associate ourselves with a belief system. But for the person who is outside religious collectivism and protection, their experience of the Divine can be labelled as mental illness. They are on their own.

I proceeded to give my own views on religion in a respectful manner. I also told him that I had similar experiences of "The Love of God" too but I didn't go into detail.

I then explained carefully, in a manner assuring my sincerity, what I thought about Jesus Christ. I told him how I felt strongly that Jesus went through a manic phase and a possible psychosis when he was in his thirty's. I explained how the stories in the gospels clearly pointed to exactly the type of behaviour of someone in mania and in a deluded state. I gave the example of how Jesus sent his disciples to fetch a mule for him when they approached Jerusalem.

I could just imagine exactly how that scenario must have been; a grandiose Jesus, who already knew of the Jewish prophecy from the book of Zechariah foretelling that a messiah would arrive on a donkey, riding into the town high as a kite. He loved the fame. Then his mania took over and he trashed the temple. He needed a good shag so he went out to Bethany that night, to get laid in a brothel. He knew that sooner or later he was going to get his ass kicked. But he was too far gone into his psychosis. I didn't say all this to the Indian brother.

I mentioned to the Indian brother Jesus's erratic moods and aggressive behaviour in the temple and his confusing parables which obviously reflected his own struggle and doubts in realising his divinity. I talked about how Jesus's mind was uneasy, switching between the father and the son and back to the father.

I finished by admitting, without revealing my own story that I truly believed if Jesus was alive today he would be labelled with a mental illness called schizophrenia. I said all that in as much as a respectful manner as I could. But before I ended, I stressed that I was sure that Jesus was still connected to God and that he had a very real awakening experience. He was the Son of God, just as we all are.

After Jesus's own experience of "The Love of God," his whole life focus became an attempt to try and explain, just as many spiritual writers try explaining to this day, that our true essence is God. But because not enough people were able or wanted to hear it, he slowly took the position or was given the position of God the Son, the incarnate Father. This occurred through religion, over time. But this was a diversion of his original teaching.

It felt good to be able to share my point of view with the Indian brother, while remaining sincere and respectful. At the end of our chat, we shook hands, and sharing a kind gaze, we bid each other farewell with a gentle "Namaste."

Not long after leaving the monastery, I searched the internet hoping to find someone else who genuinely shared my point of view, the view which proposed the possibility that Jesus Christ experienced mental illness. And there was a book written by an English Professor of the University of Cambridge, The Madness of King Jesus, by Justin J. Meggitt (2014). Because of his status, this view would surely be more credible than mine.

But my view was not exactly the same. I knew in my heart that everyone's true essence was divine, just as Jesus knew. This realisation pushed him over the edge, into mental illness, and it lead to his death.

CARCASSONE

During that same trip to France, I revisited many places that I was familiar with. It had been ten years since I left the Legion.

I spent some time visiting my extended family in the Corrèze region of France. They had been so helpful during my time in France and in the Legion. Now they truly felt like family to me. When I was leaving, I bid them farewell once again but I promised to always keep in touch. I was heading south to Toulouse.

Instead of taking the train, I used a website for carpooling. My lift was with a French married couple who were driving towards the Pyrenees. The guy was going to run an ultramarathon. They picked me up in a village near my cousin's house. During the two hour drive to Toulouse, we chatted away. It was good for me to practice my French again.

They asked me how my French was so good. I told them that I had once lived in France, as a soldier. It was a huge surprise to the three of us, when it turned out that the guy, the driver and husband, was also an ex-Legionnaire who had served five years in the 1REC. We laughed at the coincidence of our meeting. Arriving in Toulouse, I wished him and his wife all the very best. I felt that it was an important encounter. We both had a sense that nothing happens by chance.

After a couple of nights in Toulouse, I took a train towards Montpellier. I wanted to catch a glimpse of the 4RE in Castelnaudary along the way.

On the train, I was wearing a t-shirt with "Chaos and Disorder Worldwide" printed across the front. There was a group of retirees on holiday sitting in the same area as me. I was minding my own business and keeping to myself. Then just before we were arriving at the town of Castlenaudary, the old man sitting across from me smiled and he said "Chaos and Disorder" as if he liked my t-shirt. He was from Chile.

I smiled back at him and I cracked open a can of beer. I replied without thinking "Yeah that's what they say nowadays, that all the electrons are just randomly flying around, a world of complete chaos and disorder." Just as I said that, the train whizzed past the 4RE. I turned my head and peered out the window. I got a good glance at the regiment. It had the same dull appearance which I recalled. Instantly, I remembered back to that small Chilean Caporal who had given us a hard time during basic training. My mind dug up a random memory of when he was inspecting our weapons after a day spent firing and then cleaning them. He poked his fingers around the guns. He took his two black oily fingers from a Gun barrel and wiped them across two Chinese lads' cheeks.

I came back from my little daydream. We had left the 4RE left behind. The old Chilean man replied to my comment. "I know I'm a professor of physics" he said. I went quiet as if to say, ok you're the boss here. It turned out that he spent many years teaching at Trinity College Dublin. While there, he married a woman from Waterford. Now he was retired. Then he said something strange and out of the blue. He said that he could never quiet be sure about the nature of God.

I kept my mouth shut about God and I just replied "me too," while taking a large sip of beer. It's a small world, but that cliché had stopped surprising me. It's not just a small world; the world is huge but interconnected in ways that would blow our mind. It's just that we don't open our eyes to it.

Soon after our little chat, I wished them all a nice holiday as they descended the train at Carcassone. I enjoyed the rest of my train journey towards Montpellier on my own. I let myself daydream some more.

I stayed in Montpellier for a few days and returned to the Irish bar which I had known so well as a Legionnaire. When I walked in, there were two guys with short hair drinking at the bar. It was very likely that they were Legionnaires. But I decided to keep to myself. I sipped quietly on my beer at the other end of the bar. It was a nostalgic trip back to France for me. I didn't felt the need to strike up a conversation with them. I felt the same way at the train station in Marseille. I saw legionnaires patrolling around the station doing Vigipirate duty just as I had once done.

LYON

Towards the end of that nostalgic trip through France, I spent a few days in Lyon. I had another of my so called fluid days in Lyon. Ordinary events and happenings all seemed to unfold without decision or choice. On getting up in the morning, I decided that I was just going to plan nothing for the day and walk around, letting the day unfold. I slowly began feeling things flowing and happening as if there was no other way. I understood that I could induce this state of fluidity. The plan for the day was no plans.

I visited some large painted murals. I had lunch somewhere. I then decided to get a small tattoo to mark the end of that trip and to help me accept the five years in the Legion as part of my life journey.

I just walked into a tattoo artist's studio taking the chance that there would be time to do it. It turned out there was a free slot in one hour's time just before they closed for the day. I had an hour to kill before getting my tattoo and what better time to go for a beer.

I walked around the old town of Lyon. I stumbled across a bar that was down in a basement. It was like an old cellar or dungeon. I had a glass of dark ale and I noticed the peculiar atmosphere. There were eerie paintings on the walls of demons and drink. There were screens playing silent images of war. On speakers, the music blasting out was heavy metal German music. It sounded as if it was mixed with commands from the NAZI regime. The place was run by big bearded men dressed like bikers. I finished my second dark beer and I went back to get my tattoo done.

The tattoo artists name was Leo. We got chatting when I explained the reason behind then small tattoo I wanted done. It turned out that he was from Nîmes. He knew of the Legion and the 2REI from having lived there for most of his life, before moving to the city of his namesake, Lyon.

There was once a time where these fluid days would spiral out of control into delusions and hallucinations but not anymore. I didn't interpret them or take them personally. I just noticed what I noticed and continued on. I could actually enjoy myself and manoeuvre in this hidden realm without the fear and paranoia associated with schizophrenia.

I stopped at a grocery store on my way back to my accommodation. I saw €6.66 at the cash register for the total of my few snacks. I had rented a bedroom through the website Air-B&B. It was a shared house and the host was out working that night so I could relax and watch a movie on the TV.

The owner had a pet cat. It left when I opened the apartment door. I tried to get it back in but it scratched the back of my hand, piercing the skin. I cleaned the scratch with alcohol and sat down to watch TV for the evening. That night, I watched the film The Deer Hunter. There is a lot of serious PTSD in that film. I watched it in French. The title was changed to Voyage Au Beu De L'enfer, meaning; Journey to the bottom of hell. That film was directed by Michael Cimino, with whom I shared the same birthday, February 3rd.

I went to bed at the end of that fluid day. I remembered that I once created the abbreviation G.O.D. which stood for Grandiose Obsessive Delusions. Previously, I would have tried desperately to interpret synchronicity. But now I knew that it was beyond the conscious mind. I had learnt to ignore the obsessions of my ego. I slept soundly that night.

THE PLACE WITH NO NAME

As a child, I used to be able to manipulate my dreams. I knew, even from inside my dream, I was dreaming. I could create scenarios within the dream as I wished and I could stop things happening that I feared. I could even force myself to wake up from a dream. But as I grew older, I became more rational and logical within a materialistic society and I forgot about this ability. I also had the habit of talking in my sleep for as long as I can remember.

During my recovery, I recorded my dreams for a period of time. I wanted to look at the dream world of my unconscious. I would say that the vast majority of my dreams were nightmares. I laid a pencil and a small notepad at my bedside.

I made the habit of scribbling down a few words when I would wake from a dream during the night. The next morning those few words would help me write more about the dream, otherwise they would vanish from my memory quickly. Is there any sense in them? I asked myself and then, I just let the dreams be. I felt them disturbing but important too. Here is a sample of some of my mixed up dreams which I noted down…

Green cactus monster, I fly as a rocket from the forest, Smoke heroin in a homeless hostel, A Guy with a stroke, half of face badly sagging, Lots of money in a mattress, Cops tie people's hands and my hands in white towels, The place will blow up, Hurry everyone runs out, another place, Some muslim extremists are doing a ritual with incense before burning me to death, I'm kneeling together with a former legionnaire, another place, a rich PR man sabotages the party, so close to getting laid with beautiful women, Small black mamba lessons, Pick it up by the head, I feel it crawling between my legs, Runaway, run boy run, another place, A bear attacks a small Bulgarian village, I cook its huge head alive in a large pot, Female hyenas are talking together in a car, One of them eats my hand as I'm driving, another place, A large grey seal is cracking a boy's head open in its jaw on a spiral yellow water slide going downwards, It's not slimy and slippy enough, Waiting for the noise, I really don't want to hear that, Yellow against black, like a wasp, waking up now. I scribble something on the notepad and I fall sleep again, back to the underworld, back to healing.

Dreams helped me realise that there was a lot more remaining for me to discover about myself, possibly an infinite amount. Those dreams also explained an anxiety I felt on waking up every morning. It was an anxiety that could easily be ignored by reaching for my smartphone or any other distraction. But it was just energy, that anxiety, and there was wisdom in it trying to get my attention. I learned to let that energy be, to feel it, to accept it, to be kind to it and let it transform into positive productive energy.

I realised that I was just a ball of energy. You can call that energy whatever you want, good, bad, sexual, supressed, reactive, etc. But it turns out to be all the same energy and capable of transformation. It is capable of assisting our transcendence. It's the same energy that comes from the sun, the same that buzzes through our planet, and through our body.

My Journey through madness helped me to like myself more, to accept myself, to love myself even. Most certainly, loving myself was the hardest part because it was infinite and unconditional. How could I truly love myself when they say God is Love? How could I possess this love without possessing God? To be separate from God would always leave a gap; incompleteness; the human condition, the spark to all wars.

For a human being to feel complete, he/she must therefore become God and accept their divinity in their humanity. But to be God is to be schizophrenic in the world's eye. There was one annoying exception to this, according to many. Jesus Christ was allowed this, but only after all his suffering and tragic death, a death that did not save us but made sure that we could never become God.

We put him on a pedestal and ignored his original message which only sounded like a psychosis. By doing so, we ensured that we remain in our human state of frustration, fear and desire, living a lie and chasing the carrot. Fuck that. Let each one of us be God, a crownless King or Queen, even a schizophrenic if needs be, because after all is said and done, it's the only thing that really truly matters in our short pathetic existence. It's the one thing we will surely regret on our death bed, not being all that we could have been.

It seemed that living the unknown path was a journey that gave my life meaning. Perhaps it did but so what? It also created a whole lot of doubt and anxiety. My conditioned humanity feared the unknown. It craved certainty, wanted separateness, and used depression to distract me. It fought to hang on to the label schizophrenia. It clung on for dear life like a drowning boy. My mind desperately fought to hang onto any form of identity.

After all, my mind was made for naming and categorising. It was as if the battle between my shadow self and my conscious self only took place because of my mind made identity, which separates known rationality from irrationality and the unknown. How could their possibly be a union of these two opposing forces?

The Ying and Yang opposites, however, were created within the same Oneness. Whatever term you want to call that Oneness is entirely up to you and whether you decide it is a conscious Oneness or not is also up to you. But once you create ONE, you also create half and you create the split.

Eckhart Tolle, the Spiritual writer, explains how the power of our mind and the reality in which we live is based on words. This only limits us and keeps us blind;

"Words reduce reality to something the human mind can grasp, which isn't very much." - Eckhart Tolle, (A New Earth, 2005)

The medical experts were using the words Avolition and Anhedonia to explain abnormal behaviour in people with schizophrenia. But really these words only describe the effects on the person of denying and supressing their true self in a society which remains terrified that its participants might one day realise their inner deity.

Schizophrenia is a purely social phenomenon created by our conditioned mind in a rational shallow society which attempted to bury the truth. Even my stammer, which prevented me from talking much in social situations, was ignored and Alogia took its place, explaining my poverty of speech as yet another symptom of schizoprenia. But despite all of that, it's very strange how my incurable stammer disappeared in the heights of psychosis.

All these terms used by psychiatrists pointed towards part of the prodromal phase of a lifelong medical illness that had only gone into remission. Bullshit! But the reality is that many have bought into this crap.

I took back the steering wheel of my life. We schizophrenics, stigmatised with more holes than Jesus Christ, were on to something bigger, much much bigger. Every Schizo is Jesus and every Jesus is Schizo, but...

Not every Schizo is mad.

Some may not like my use of the word schizophrenic and prefer to say that a person has schizophrenia. But this only emphasises the illusion of illness. In fact, both terms are wrong.

You see, some of us have broken through the veil of God which we were never born with. Schizophrenia is pure fear, completely irrational yet curiously necessary at the same time.

Yes, okay, I admit, for most of us, it's been too overwhelming. But I know there are others out there who are strong and ready to be true to themselves despite the lack of support available. I have already met one of them. On meeting him, I have met myself. The fact that we can both laugh at our divinity and individuality is the only proof that I have needed. So I know for certain that there are others out there.

The important thing to remember is that the illness of Schizophrenia begins in a futile attempt to understand our divinity. The mind fails to understand its place in a synchronised oneness. It then self-destructs. You only have to go into any mental hospital. Half of the patients think they are Jesus, Mohammed, The Buddha, Shiva, or an alien. It just depends on their culture. This is no coincidence. They have been blasted and drowned by the illuminating presence of God. Their struggle is the same; it is one of integration.

As the years passed, the memory of psychosis and the sensation it produced began to fade in my memory. The only thing that was similar to it was the experience during my fluid days which happened every so often. But by synchronistic life events and by keeping an open mind, I had heard of a sacred drink created by two plants from the amazon.

BRAZIL

Ayahuasca was a traditional medicine used as a respected sacrament among Amazonian tribes. It was made from a brew of two different plants; Banisteriopsis Caapi, using its vine and Psychotria viridis, using its leaves. When I first saw the strength of that vine, I knew it pointed to both the strength of our mind made prisons and the strength required to step out of that prison into the only true freedom we can ever know and become one with God and with the Universe. To be able to do this requires strength, strength to realise that the mental physical and spiritual parts of us are all one part really.

Something deep inside me was pulling me towards taking that sacramental drink. I didn't know why. Its use was for spiritual healing, a natural medicine. My limited conditioned mind told me that it was only a drug and nothing more. But this was the same intellectual mind that once told me I had schizophrenia. I didn't know why but I had to take it to see for myself. So I did. Answers came to questions I didn't know I held.

Ayahuasca, proved to me beyond any doubt that my psychosis and schizophrenia many years back were in fact a spiritual connection to my inner deity, my inner fountain of collective unconscious wisdom. Deep into this healing experience which lasted a good few hours, any residual fear disappeared and I was in a state of pure joy in the knowingness of my true essence.

I was initially very surprised that this experience was not new for me. How could that be? I never took any psychoactive substances in my life. I was right back in the same realm that I was in many years ago without using any sacred plants. This was amazing. It confirmed for me the writing of this book and it confirmed to me that the way of nature, the wisdom of the earth, the plants, and the power of life that pulsates through every living being, motivated the writing of this book. The Truth of who we are motivated this book into being.

I wrote down what the ayahuasca experience showed me even though I already knew that words were a poor substitute for direct experience. I was beyond words and beyond myself but I could still use them, just without the desperateness associated with schizophrenia.

I learnt from reopening up my third eye through Ayahuasca, in a safe environment with caring supportive people, that schizophrenia was a spiritual experience beyond any doubt. That was the one primary and central answer which I had been searching for over the many years of my recovery. My psychosis was in fact what Abraham Maslow called "A peak experience" or "Self Transcendence."

All that I was missing eight years previously was a guide, a peer who had been through it themselves. I never had that and becomes of my surroundings, I was classed as a "Sick Schizophrenic."

It took many years to understand that I could enter altered states without the use of sacred plants. I didn't need sacred plants to have a mystical experience. But in the end, it was the plants that answered this question for me. Just as they have generated oxygen, shade, food, clothing and made human life possible, the wisdom of the plants showed me by direct experience what the reality of symbiosis is. To simplify it all; we are the plants.

Schizophrenia and The French Foreign Legion were part of my initiation onto the spiritual path and not a mental illness. But because there was nobody around to guide me through my psychosis, my mind made fear tried to rationalise and interpret my divinity. In other words, schizophrenia can be a bad trip without guidance. This is why some people believe that there is no cure. And yes, they are right! There is no cure if one keeps denying their divinity.

Some people say that psychoactive plants and drugs are risky for people with Schizophrenia. I believe the opposite to be true. They are risky for people with no experience of psychosis. The recovered schizophrenic, who has understood integration, has the strongest spiritual immunity to a bad trip.

The mystic knows that we are all children of God, God is in us. We are God. It doesn't matter how you want to express it. God is beyond words, beyond description. So are we. It is only in this approach that we can truly see ourselves in other people, and in everything else. We can then truly feel compassion for all living things. We can be gentle when the ignorance of fear rises up, it just wants to learn.

Recovery is wrongly seen as a lifelong process because we can never run far enough from ourselves. There is nowhere to hide. The unconscious will always be there and our other half will always remain hidden in the dark. Trying to find it creates fear, because our other half is the dark.

Schizophrenia is of the mind and not of the heart, but it can be a doorway to Heaven for those strong enough to step through. This is the same door that leads to hell and we can go there if we chose to. Hell is our creation, rooted in fear, fear of our divinity. In that dark place there are many demons of that I have no doubt. But these demons are of our own making just as we create angels to comfort us. Both creations are only attempts to shift responsibility.

So I say to you, step up to the mark! Take your cross if you so wish. Whatever you decide to do, everything remains in balance and has always been. You don't exist but God in you does. Don't even bother define that truth! Light and darkness is the same thing. When you can love Love and hate Hate, then you are ready to love Hate and hate Love. Then you are truly ready to laugh, cry and reach divine union with your lost self. And it is that same Self that existed before your parents had sex, remember that. It was the twinkle in their eyes when they first met. That's who you are.

Taking Ayahuasca many years later, I was right back in the middle of that exact same experience of schizophrenia which I had begun to forget. Immediately, I remembered the beauty of it. The only difference now was that it was induced by the medicine Ayahuasca. I knew how to manoeuvre within that infinite realm while dis-identifying with the mind. I spent a lot of time smiling and laughing. It was a great and happy realisation; that I never had an illness to begin with. The futility of the logical mind was humorous. Something beyond my rational mind had called me to take Ayahuasca. My Soul had called me. The plant had called me. I had called myself.

Normal and rational everyday life feels like a prison limited by our mind. But this is a healthy and necessary illusion because realising our inner divinity can be overwhelming. This prison of everyday rationality is only unhealthy when we live as though that's all there is to life. So we must realise that we are in our own little prison or shell but that we also have the keys to leave anytime we want. The keys to Heaven are not only with Saint Peter.

The only true reality in our lives is a subjective one. For instance, imagine yourself as a soccer player in the final of the World Cup. You may feel like the whole world is looking at you. But in fact there is only each person with their own inner reality looking at you. By realising our own subjective relativity, we can say that the only true authority and omnipotence lies within each one of us. This is when we truly take responsibility and understand the power of Love and the path of the heart.

Once terrified of my inner deity, I was now ready to accept

it. It was the assurance I needed to send my book to print. Jesus had the same experience of divine union, probably without the use of Ayahuasca. Maybe he was extremely sleep deprived. But who knows whether he became psychotic by taking Cannabis, by Schizophrenia or by magic mushrooms. It doesn't really matter. Was he mentally ill or the son of God? That doesn't matter too because they are really just the same thing.

On taking the plant medicine, Ayahuasca, I got a powerful insight that "Any people in this world whom I don't like are the ones that keep me from God." It's not them but my own disliking of them that keeps me from God. In avoiding them, I am avoiding myself. But that's ok too because I can now integrate myself into the material world, my divinity into my humanity. I don't need the continuous experience of God. Wisdom is enough. Once touched by Grace, it never leaves. And most importantly, I don't need to prove this to others either. This is a huge relief. It is the cross off my back.

Jesus Christ avoided rich and higher status people and he spent his life among the poor and outcasts of society. He could have integrated more his divinity if he also mixed with people of higher status than himself. It is too easy to only deal with those who appear inferior to us, there's no challenge in that. When faced with someone who threatens us and makes us feel inferior; that is the real opportunity to know more about God.

The only way to connect with people is through joy. This connection with people through joy is the way to connect with God. Someone once said "Hell is other people." In fact, the opposite is true.

We are all sons of God. We are all God. But this is not for me to say. Only you can say that you are a son of God when you are ready to say that you are and when you truly know that you are. Until that day comes, you will continue to run away from yourself and put others above yourself. In doing so, you automatically place others below you. If the day comes when you are ready to be true to yourself, it's enough to keep it to yourself, unless you are willing to be persecuted and mocked just like Jesus was. God does not need to proclaim its presence. I am what I am. You are what you are.

Our normal existence is a reality of introversion vs extroversion, our outer world a mirror of our inner. The phenomenon of thinking in the evolution of human beings from our more primitive roots and the mind made ego that slowly developed over time, is actually the real schizophrenia. But we don't want to admit this. We continue to raise children in this way. It has led us to believe that we have conquered the earth. We were raised to act on our thoughts. This way of living is clearly mad. How far must we go into a world of increasing technology and disconnection from nature before we realise this global delusion?

During my Ayahuasca spiritual work, I could slip deeper into my own inner introverted world but beyond the shallow realm of egotistical thoughts. Like an amplified daydream, my sense of I dissolved into an ocean of being beyond the physical body. This is where the answers came. This was the healing power of the medicine. Only when the shallow mind is split open can our true nature be revealed to us. Only then can the light of consciousness shine in the darkness.

There is a wisdom that illuminates our shadow side. It is the wisdom of the earth and of our ancestors. Such wisdom can make you feel that you are God; infinite knowledge. Yes, you are God but only when you don't limit that idea. The ego may want to hold onto that idea but it is too immense to fit back into the mind and the physical body. Like a visit from a beautiful bird landing onto our open palms, it must be let go again. Like looking at the sun, you must not stare. He or She, who becomes God, in their mind made way, is immediately blinded.

Feeling that you are God has nothing to do with your identity. You become a vessel, a carcass for divine life. Your words and actions will flow through you, but without you. You will no longer hesitate or stutter. Your life path until know makes sense as if it was an unconscious search for this realisation. You can relate to others who also know this truth and have felt it themselves. From one God to another, all you need to do is wink, a simple nonverbal "Namaste."

The medicine of Ayahuasca produces a completely subjective experience. Simply put, I would say that the medicine of Ayahuasca has rekindled my belief in God through the reality of experience. It has confirmed to me once again the limits of words and the limits of the everyday mind. I have no doubt that we are infinite beings.

The reconnection I made with God, through Ayahuasca, gave me the confidence to finish my book. It banished any hypocrisy that I was feeling and it gave me courage to accept any further doubts that will surely creep back in as time goes on. They will be welcomed.

Doubts and a critical outlook keep me closer to the truth; they allow me to take decisive positive action in my life. My autonomy and confidence is founded in my humanity. Taking Ayahuasca was the experience that I needed to support these intellectual claims. It was the experience of God that I needed to validate my belief in God and my belief in myself. It renewed my hope. It enabled me to say with confidence that I know God in its unknowingness. It was a deeply spiritual experience. It was Soul revival.

I must admit that there was a desire in me to get others to experience it. But at the same time, I understood why people must only go of their own accord. Not everyone is ready. Not everyone can handle Gnosis. Not everyone wants it. And not everyone will have the same experience. This was the same desire that lead Jesus to preach to the people.

Instead, I chose to remain hidden and not interfere in people's lives. I will let the words on these pages do all the preaching. And what could I possibly say that hasn't been said before anyway? Everybody's own God can only wake up from within themselves. That's not new news. And despite how much I would really like to make that happen, I cannot. But maybe, I can just hold their hand, and that's enough. Maybe I can be the peer to others, the peer that I never had. And maybe I won't.

While I was in Brazil, I went back to the church of Santo Daime, for another ritual or "work" as they call it. Again, I took the medicine or "Daime." But this time I wanted to allow myself to go deep into the journey, deep into the depths of myself. I needed to visit the dark. I wanted to see if there was a bottom. We took three doses that night and the effects lasted for about six hours or more.

I closed my eyes. I kept an open chest with deep breathing. The singing of hymns and strict routine kept us all focused. Now and then I opened my eyes to get my bearings and joined in with the signing.

My eyes flickered like in REM sleep as I broke down the divide between my inside and outside worlds. I wanted to know if Hell exists. It does. That was shown to me. I wanted to integrate my shadow self into my conscious self.

"Daime," the medicinal plant teacher showed me that; I see what I don't want to see and I don't see what I want to see. I entered the spirit world. Faceless spirits patted me on the shoulder. They put out their hands to shake my hand and to lead me away with them. Initially, I refused. Then, I let a black woman lead me into the Sun. She had a straw dress.

I saw the Pope being crucified, in his ultimate ecstasy. I saw the sign of God in a black sky. It was Gold and it was stretched in the sky like a kite. It was a golden Star of David, mounted on a metal plaque. But it was made of plasma like the Sun. Gold bullets shot through the Plaque, sending drops of golden blood in both directions. I let a giant cobra wrap around my body. I became the Jagube vine wrapped around a large, stone, Celtic cross.

I felt the fear and I embraced it. I opened my eyes for a moment. But I preferred the dark, so I went back down.

I moved in the shape of an S like waves on the sea. My face became narrow like a snake and broad like a lion. The teaching came and I welcomed it; Schizophrenia was in the world but not in the underworld. Heaven is other people. We choose either darkness or light, but there is no separation between the two. We create our own hell and our own heaven. In fact they are the same realm and they come from a disconnection of our true divine nature. God is Love, Yes, but Love Yourself first. I went deeper.

I inhaled deeply in my inner darkness and I exhaled into the light, as I opened my eyes. Looking at the wooden Caravaca cross in the centre of the wooden, star shaped table, it moved slightly. In the corner of my eye, I saw one guy bless himself. Then the girl near the table burst into tears as she showed her heart expanding out of her chest. She was hallucinating. The leading guy of the church stood up near the cross to give an Alleluia. But he was pulled back to his chair by a tremendous invisible force. They brought him candles. I closed my eyes again leaving that madness behind me. I went back to the comforts of my darkness, my own hell. To understand the light, I must keep walking in the darkness.

I was ready to face Satan. I wanted to face him. I had faced the Red dragon in Australia many years back and that was a piece of cake. Instantly, it made sense to me why the Caravaca cross had two horizontal beams; one for Jesus and one for us. The plant showed us the second coming. The closer we get to being God, the closer we get to the crucifixion. Lucifer ascended Gods throne and then he fell to his own hell.

Before I came out of the darkness, I saw a white dove carrying a fern leaf in its mouth, the fern of New Zealand. Then wings grew out of my back. They wrapped around my body in silver feathers. Demons came towards me. They put their hands on my belly and took my baby away, No problem. I smiled and came back into the light.

Four hours into that deep healing work and with the singing of hymns to keep us focused and grounded, I never purged. I only went to the toilet and took a long piss. Some people there did throw up. It is expected and normal for people to purge during their first experiences. It's not a bad thing either. I expected that I would. But on the contrary, I was really hungry so I went and took a peanut bar from my bag. But before it met my mouth, I was asked to wait as the ceremony was just coming to an end. No problem. I hid the bar away. I joined in, singing the last few hymns.

By the end of the ceremony, my body was exhausted so I sat down. That long "Work" ended. We all embraced each other like brothers and sisters. We all mingled and chatted for some time after. I ate my peanut bar and I looked for milk to drink but there was none. So I ate some stew in the communal kitchen and drank a black coffee. I could see other people attempting in vain to share their wisdom and insights. I didn't feel any need to say much. I just listened to others.

I told one guy that I had a stammer when I was young. I asked him what a person with a stammer was called in Brazil. I wasn't sure what he replied, something like Dodo, the extinct bird. I drank some water and ate an apple.

I told another guy, who was a friend by now, that he was an angel. He smiled and he was pleased. Then I told him that he could be more than an angel, if he wanted to be. But he told me that he didn't want to visit another planet. True. I understood. Then I told him how I learnt Morse code in the army; binary code in sound; a combination of short and long beeps, used to create the whole Latin alphabet.

It was nice to stay for a while and talk with the others. But I had little energy left for people after that long healing work and my Portuguese was limited. My body was spent and drained. I longed for my bed. A friend of mine, Francesco, dropped me home. It had lasted six hours. I felt that I had lost a kilo of energy.

I took "Daime" for a third time with the Santo Daime church before leaving Brazil. I realised and accepted both the light and darkness inside of me. I chose to stay with the light but not to deny the darkness for my last healing work. I got the perfect balance that I needed. I left with my inner child feeling even more healed. A good old friend of mine from Dublin used to say to me; know the truth and the truth will set you free. I couldn't agree more. Be true to yourself, my friend, and your Kingdom will come.

WESTPORT

It had become routine for me to travel on my own. The west of Ireland is a beautiful place. I could never get to the root of my Irishness, even in the simplicity of its cold beauty. But I knew deep down that the lie of race would keep me trapped forever. My great grandfather had fled Italy at the beginning of the twentieth century to live in Ireland. Could I love my country without loving my childhood? Can I love myself without loving my country? Why is it mine anyway?

Sometimes I wished I was born on no man's land. Tired of rules and regulations of a blind society in a blind world, I felt myself constantly pulled towards the spiritual path, a fruitless path. I had been to the top and rolled down. What did I see at the top? I saw nothing but inhibition; a baby without a self. How could my mind ever accept insecurity or doubt? What was the point in being God and knowing nothing?

Maybe after all, I am nothing but a schizophrenic. I can live with that, if needs be. I can die without it too. Maybe I can even bring it along for the next game, get an upgrade to the latest version of Bipolar.

It was hard to admit to myself that I had a human to need to socialise. I isolated myself during recovery but that was necessary. I felt the need to be alone as if I needed to slowly figure things out. It is true that I have learned things by being both alone and in others company. "I" facing "me" along with the feeling of loneliness has been a journey. I was sure that it would be a lifelong one. Relationships are equally important. They help me grow as a person.

I always disliked the word "Boring" but it was a word on which I would often dwell. Once, a kid called me boring when I was an older kid. This crushed me. I wanted to be exciting. Maybe this comment transformed my life. I tried anything to escape boredom, anything to escape myself; The Foreign Legion? Bring it on. It was as if I wanted to get to the root of that word. What is the relationship between boredom and depression? Have people always been bored? What if there is no such thing as boredom? What if we had never created that word? Could boredom simply be the inability to relax?

I slowly learned that if I allow myself to be bored, it reaches a plateau. Its illusion is then revealed and it dissolves. I learned that there was an experience of believing the lie of boredom. That lie took many forms of thought. Indecision was a friend of boredom. Fear, denial and indecision had met at the crossroads with boredom and they caused a psychosis.

There was another certain feeling and experience that existed which aroused my curiosity. I could say it involved the sense of being blind in the present moment. Not blind in sight but blind in my feelings, mood and thoughts. Whether I feel good or bad depends on the present moment, a moment which is really not a moment at all but a shapeless flux. The idea that the present is a moment is itself the problem because of attempts to define it and stop time.

This blind, elusive feeling that gives birth to boredom also depends on how my mind classes good and bad. This was initially all deeper stuff and less conscious. I knew I wasn't conscious off it because it made no sense. Uneasiness, anxiety, discomfort and the feeling of boredom were usually classed as bad in my mind. This created depression. But by leaving boredom alone to be itself, it could stimulate creativity and positivity.

These things I learned by being alone with myself for large periods of time. I learned that I could always count on a gentle reminder. It was a personal reminder forged in past suffering. I gifted it to myself. When boredom rolled in and depression crept in along with loneliness, this reminder was ever present. It confidently reminded me that all is well and simply unfolding. It was a reminder to accept the void. For only in emptiness can God dwell.

It is the idea of permanence which feeds negativity. Loneliness is a big thing but it doesn't have to be. It occurred to me that a lot of my interactions and relationships with others were a distraction from loneliness instead of real connection with people. The interactions were often disappointing. They even fed the loneliness when I returned from their fleeting company to it, and to myself. My own sense of boredom made other people seem boring to me, not unlike a mirror. The more I faced loneliness, the more I understood the positive nature of solitude.

During a trip to the West of Ireland alone, I looked at the great view from the summit of Croagh Patrick. It was a spring morning. I was alone on my hike but not lonely because I could see the sky. I had climbed through four seasons on the way up.

At the top, I felt I should be enjoying the view more as the clouds were drawing in. This was a silly thought, trying to force myself to enjoy it. I laughed silently at the stupidity of it. Then my body reminded me that I was very cold. It was time to go down again.

KINGDOM COME

For me, the future remains both unknown and unwritten. That simple truth keeps life interesting. There is even the possibility of reconnecting with my estranged family members now that I have healed myself. Anything is possible in the future. I no longer look for myself in them. I can accept and integrate my ancestral roots along with my true essence into my everyday self. But nothing is ever set in stone.

I continue to allow myself everyday normal material goals, for the material and the spiritual are one. The experience of the Kingdom of heaven will come and go just as it has for many throughout the ages. It is always there, a parallel reality, hidden by our busy and culturally conditioned minds.

I would like to begin a family of my own one day, if it happens. But whatever the future brings, I will accept it, even if denial comes first. I would hope to share my version of the truth with my future children. But ultimately my wish is that they discover their own truth, a truth more evolved than mine.

I carry with me everywhere I go, a little reminder, as a flashlight for dark times ahead. It's a gentle reminder that everything will work out in the end even if it doesn't. My five years spent as a soldier in the French Foreign Legion left me with an emotional scar. It contributed to a period of acute mental illness. Paradoxically, it has also given me the strength to overcome mental Illness and to overcome myself. The cockroaches in my head were golden. For that reason, I will now eat my words and accepting my once adoptive family, admit:
LEGIO PATRIA NOSTRA.

Legionnaires walk a slow pace of 88 steps per minute with their hands bearing open palms. Those open palms always remind me of the same opened hands of somebody, rigid in the depths of a psychosis and the spine tingling orgasmic high of God's presence.

"Loss is like a shrapnel wound, where the piece of metal's got stuck in a place where the surgeons daren't go so they decide to leave it. It's painful at first, horribly painful, so that you wonder whether you can live with it. But then the body grows around it, until it doesn't hurt anymore, not like it used to, but every now and then there are these twinges when you're not ready for them and you realize it's still there. And it's always going to be there. It becomes part of you now, a still hard part inside."

- A Small Death in Lisbon (1999) by Robert Wilson.

I had lost many things along my journey. My spirit left me through the wound of schizophrenia and the beating I got in the Legion by my fellow soldiers. My integrity, my credibility and even my self-respect crumbled. The loss of my self was the biggest loss and finding it again has been my life journey, often an unconscious one. It has been a journey taken as much on the external as the internal. It's this same journey that ends in a pathetic ending, death, but an ending that keeps me living all the same.

It is said that the chemical Dimethyltryptamine (DMT) is released by the pineal gland in the brain just before death producing the same effect as a psychosis. Schizophrenia has been described as a splitting of the mind. In all of our last moments, the illusion of self and our limited "reality" is split open. We get a glimpse of our true self; Infinite wisdom; God. Depending on our own inner judgements and depending on the extent of how we have lived true to ourselves, we enter a Heaven or Hell. We judge ourselves. We are the gatekeepers of the Eternal. We are not separate from the power of life.

The future, a blank canvas is always welcoming our next move. We are the artists and the Godhead, that which is untouchable and sometimes utterly terrifying. We are unstoppable because we are not what we think we are.

So, let us be sad when we are sad, happy when we are happy and horny when we are horny. Let's drink when we are thirsty and eat when we are hungry. Let us sleep when we are tired. Let us die when we are afraid as only in death can there be a rebirth. Let whatever love we know break down our identities in this crazy world. Let us tune ourselves back in to the power of life. Let words lose you and let them bring you back. But above all, let us be patient and great things will come. We are waking up from a nightmare only to fall asleep into a dream. What is not lost cannot be found.

Now, look here Kiddo…
Stop looking! Stop kidding yourself…
As they say in the French Foreign Legion…

Réveille-toi là!

REFERENCES

A New Earth (2005). Eckhart Tolle. Penguin.

A Small Death in Lisbon (1999). Robert Wilson. Harper Collins.

Adieu Vielle Europe (1931). Chant de la Legion Etranger. Rene Mercier, Henri Forlerne, lyrics - Simon Deylon.

Angels and Demons (2000). Dan Brown. Pocket Books (US).

Good Feeling (2011) Music video. Flo Rida. Atlantic records.

I'm Not There (2007) Film. Dir; Todd Haynes. Endgame Entertainment.

Invictus (1888) Poem. William Ernest Henley. Book of Verses. England.

Kingston Town (1990) Music record. UB40. Label: Virgin.

Motivation and Personality (1954). Abraham Maslow. Harper & Brothers.

Sexual Behaviour in the Human male (1948). Alfred Kinsey.

Sun of gOd: Discover the Self-Organizing Consciousness That Underlies Everything (2009). Gregory Sams.

Synchronicity – An Acausal Connecting Principle (1972). Carl Jung. Routledge.

The Black Swan (2010) Film. Dir; Darren Aronofsky.

The Book of Restorative Verse (1910). William Stanley Braithwaite, Ed. Quote from My Own Epitaph by John Gay (1685-1732).

The Da Vinci Code (2003). Dan Brown. Transworld and Bantam Books (UK).

The Deer Hunter (1978) Film. Dir; Michael Cimino. Universal pictures.

The King's Speech (2010) Film. Dir; Tom Hooper. Momentum Pictures.

The Madness of King Jesus: The Real Reasons for his Execution (2010). Justin J. Meggitt. I.B. Tauris Ltd.

42010726R00239

Printed in Poland
by Amazon Fulfillment
Poland Sp. z o.o., Wrocław